DOES MORALITY CHANGE?

DOES MORALITY CHANGE?

Seán Fagan, S.M.

Gill & Macmillan

Gill & Macmillan Ltd
Goldenbridge
Dublin 8
with associated companies throughout the world

0 7171 25920

Index compiled by Helen Litton
Print origination by Kenneth Burnley, Wirral, Cheshire
Printed by ColourBooks Ltd, Dublin

A catalogue record is available for this book from the British Library.

1 3 5 4 2

Dedication

To two of the
most outstanding and inspirational
moralists of our time

Bernard Häring, C.Ss.R.
and
Richard A. McCormick, S.J.

CONTENTS

1

Confused by Change

Twenty-five years ago Alvin Toffler wrote a disturbing and challenging book about a phenomenon for which he coined the term *Future Shock*. This is the name he gave to the disease of 'change.' It is not a disease in the medical sense, but it does cause dis-ease in a great many people, and it can produce disorientation and stress in individuals who are subjected to too much change in too short a time. Change has been a constant feature of human life on earth, but recent decades have seen vast changes in almost every sphere of life: technology, education, social organisation, physical and mental health, communication, life-style, religion. What is peculiar to our time is the accelerated rate of change. The vast majority of all the material goods we use in daily life were developed within our own lifetime, and our world has changed more in the past fifty years than in all of previously recorded history. Another element of the problem is that whereas in former times people had time to adjust to change, since it was localised and gradual, nowadays they are overwhelmed by major changes every few years. Young people seem to have fewer problems adjusting to rapid change since it is part of their culture, but for serious, reflective adults it is more difficult to cope, especially when the changes have repercussions in such basic areas of life as morality and religion.

It would be a worthwhile exercise to reflect on the changes that have so radically altered our world and see how they affect our understanding of morality. It is taken for granted that morality does not change: what is right must always be right, what is wrong is always wrong. But this is only partly true: it is an over-simplification. Murder is always wrong, but what kinds of killing qualify as murder? Modern technology has increased our capacity to interfere with nature, but it does not explain that merely because we *can* do certain things means that we *may* do them. Where do we draw the lines when it comes to choosing and deciding?

Morality is based on reality, but reality itself changes, and our under-standing of reality likewise changes, so inevitably there will be cases where what we discern as morally right may be judged differently as we change. Besides, the 'moral norms' formulated by tradition are based on 'reality' as experienced, understood and interpreted by peo-ple, in the light of their culture. But there have been vast cultural changes in the last few decades, so that the so-called 'crisis of morality' or 'moral crisis' today is linked to a cultural crisis. Furthermore, there have been radical changes in the Catholic Church's understanding of itself and of the world, and within moral theology there have been new methods and approaches in discussing moral issues. An awareness of all these changes and their effects may help people to get a clearer understanding of morality, encourage them to trust their God-given conscience, and to grow in the freedom and fidelity to which God calls them.

Church in shock
Of all the institutions in the western world, until recently the Catholic Church stood out as the personification of unchanging permanence, a kind of Rock of Ages washed by the changing waves of history, but itself ever remaining the same. This image was badly shaken when the shock waves from Vatican Council II began to spread around the world. The documents of this Council are now the official teaching of the Church, and in many cases they overturn completely 'truths' that have been taught for centuries. So radical were the changes that the former mono-lithic pillar of truth, renowned for its order, efficiency and control, could aptly be described as *The Runaway Church* by the late Peter Hebbleth-waite in the title of his book on the Council and its aftermath. Cardinal Siri of Genoa declared that the Council was the greatest mistake in the last few centuries of the Church's history, and the famous Archbishop Lefebvre rejected it totally.

The human being is the most adaptable animal on earth and can even-tually adjust to almost any circumstance. But to adjust successfully it is necessary to understand what is happening, and the saddest part of the Church's post-conciliar history is that so little was done to explain in rea-sonable, adult fashion what was actually happening. In fact, the Council did not 'decree' any new truths, but merely gave official approval to the faith-insights that had been quietly developing and maturing among the faithful in the previous decades. But most people, including some office-holders in the Church, did not understand or accept the changing reality.

In fact in recent times there has been a distinct effort to ignore or even oppose the Vatican II vision.

This negative reaction is understandable insofar as the Church's traditional stance itself had inoculated people against change. In popular presentations, and indeed in catechisms and official documents, Catholic teaching was clear and unambiguous. Morality was largely a precise list of do's and don'ts, and for every moral problem there was a clear solution or at least fixed principles to be applied in the rare cases of doubt. In general, teaching was simply 'handed down' and people were conditioned to acceptance and acquiescence. They were given answers before they had even formulated the question. They were not curious. They believed and accepted that 'the Church' knew best. They attributed an unlimited authority to the Church and its clerical leaders. Too often the Church became a prisoner of the image it made for itself at a particular period in history. For centuries Church authorities believed that the main function of theologians was to explain and defend the official position of the Church, like public relations spokespeople for popes, bishops and Vatican congregations. To question beyond a certain point brought warnings and condemnation, and it was taken for granted that the logical step for a dissenter was to leave the Church.

Exaggerated 'continuity'

Traditional teaching on the Catholic Church as the 'one true Church,' with its divinely-revealed 'deposit of faith,' had emphasised continuity to such an extent that changes in doctrine or discipline throughout its history tended to be presented as minor modifications. Because of this emphasis, few people were aware of the substantial changes that had actually occurred over the years. Positions once vehemently defended were quietly and conveniently dropped, in a process criticised by Irish theologian Gabriel Daly as 'reform by amnesia.' In spite of preaching humility for almost two thousand years, the Church has never liked to admit its mistakes and hardly ever does so explicitly. Pope John's *Confiteor* at the opening of the Council, when he asked pardon for the sins of the Church through the centuries, shocked and angered more than one member of the assembly. Pope John Paul II has suggested that the Millennium would be a suitable occasion for repentance for past wrongs committed in the name of the Catholic Church. In his 1995 letter on ecumenism he mentioned that the papacy is a difficulty for most other Christians, 'whose memory is marked by certain painful recollections,' and added: 'To the extent that we are responsible for these, I join my

Predecessor, Paul VI, in asking forgiveness.' These few tiny expressions of regret in two thousand years of history are not exactly shining examples of humility. Moreover, almost five centuries of rigid censorship of theological writings reinforced the picture of an unchanging Church.

But thinking Christians could not stand aside from a world of constantly accelerating change, nor could their faith be sheltered from the new questions for which there were no ready-made answers. Church leaders, concerned to safeguard the 'deposit of faith' and protect the 'simple faithful' from danger, often tried to control the new movements of thought and experiment. At times they behaved like angry parents in despair over the problems of their teenage children. They blamed the child for growing up and its teachers for giving it ideas. But Pope John's Council provided a forum in which the Church openly, honestly and officially faced up to the new problems. The documents from the Council mark substantial changes in the Church's self-understanding and teaching. In not a few cases they teach the direct opposite of what had been taught for centuries. The changes affected fundamental areas: the nature of the Church itself, divine revelation, liturgy, ecumenism, the secular, social, political and economic evolution of mankind, the role of the laity, religious freedom. Unfortunately the new insights were not systematically explained with their historical and theological background, and most people heard only bits and pieces out of context. The confusion has been further complicated by debates since the Council about the meaning of its texts. They are far from being the last word on any subject, and they do not have the precision of a legal text. In many instances they reflect different theological positions set down side by side with little attempt to harmonise them. This gives rise to conflicting interpretations. The lack of agreement can be confusing for people who do not realise that it is often the ambiguity of the texts themselves that is responsible. There were questions the Council did not treat fully, others were not sufficiently prepared, and some were simply shelved for lack of time. The Vatican II documents are not simply an updated catechism, and were never meant to be.

Theologians not to blame
It is unfair to criticise theologians as though they were responsible for all the confusion. Most of them do not merit Cardinal Heenan's criticism: 'It is a form of pastoral sadism to disturb simple faith. Those close to God are untroubled by the winds of academic controversy ... A man with the soul of a pastor never indulges in the pastime of shocking the pious.'

Serious theologians do not deliberately set out to disturb people, but it is a fact of life that their discussions can at times prove disturbing. However, there is such a thing as a healthy disturbance, a creative tension, enabling people to develop a more critical understanding of their faith. There is no question of pushing people who wish to keep to their own slow pace in accepting change. But it is no service to such people to leave them totally on their own, or worse still, to reassure them that nothing has changed, that it will all pass over, or that a new catechism will provide the definitive answer to all their questions. A false security can be far more harmful than the discussions of theologians.

There are many people in the Church who still lust after certainty, who imagine that religious truth and moral life should be totally clear, with no grey areas or hazy boundaries. To cope with insecurity and tension they look to authority for dictated solutions, and fail to realise that reality is too complicated for that. It has been said that the major political, social and religious divisions are not between people who are liberals and those who are conservatives, but between people who think that the world is simple and those who know that it is not. It would be a genuine service to people to admit the confusion in today's world and Church, to recognise that it is natural and understandable, not necessarily a matter for fear and condemnation. Many of the reasons for it can be identified, and an understanding of them may lessen the confusion or at least enable people to live with it without undue stress. The underlying reason is simply the extent and the speed of the changes and the fact that the majority of Catholics thought of the Church as an unchanging monolith, all of whose teaching enjoyed the same degree of absolute certainty. The rigid personalities who clung to one set of certainties in the past find it hard to let go until they can be provided with another set to be held with equal certainty. They find it difficult to accept that although the basic truths of faith remain, we are a pilgrim, searching Church, being gradually led into the truth, and that there are many grey areas in our understanding of that truth.

Confusion in morals
Perhaps the area of most confusion and distress is Christian morality, because people feel that here their personal lives and indeed their eternal salvation are involved. The *Humanae Vitae* encyclical raised serious problems of conscience for people in the most intimate and sensitive area of their lives, and the ensuing debate added to the confusion. Certainties that had never before been questioned even in private were now openly

discussed in the media. Not only the specific issue of birth control, but authority and obedience, the very nature and function of Church teaching, and the role of personal conscience suddenly became matters for debate. In a few short years people became aware of the over-simplifications they had been accepting as absolute truth, and soon realised that some of the answers being preached by the Church were simply out of touch with the facts of their daily lives and the experience of their God-given conscience.

The moral teaching most people were brought up on was largely a matter of law and obligation, authority and obedience. Life was pictured as a journey, for which law provided the map. Only by following the map could one reach one's eternal salvation. Like the map, the law was the objective norm to which individual acts had to conform. In this perspective, the main function of conscience was to discover what the law said and judge how it was to be applied. Formation of conscience was mostly a matter of learning the law handed down by the Church in God's name. But with Vatican II's more positive emphasis on conscience, people were suddenly confused. For so long their conscience had been in the keeping of clergy, and now abruptly in the midst of conflicting views about what was morally right or wrong, they were handed it back without warning or preparation and simply told to 'follow their conscience.' Many conscientious Catholics are still struggling with that burden, but sadly large numbers of younger people have no qualms about insisting that they are following conscience when they simply do what they feel like doing.

Pope Pius IX proclaimed as a 'madness injurious to the Catholic Church and the salvation of souls the opinion that "freedom of conscience and worship is the proper right of each person, and that this should be asserted in every rightly constituted society".' In fact Vatican Council II solemnly declared the opposite, namely that the rights of conscience have their foundation in the very dignity of the human person. A further source of confusion is that although the bishops of the world accepted *Humanae Vitae*, they soon began to interpret it in such a way that many of them, indeed whole hierarchies, modified its teaching substantially. The 'teaching of the Church' includes both pope and bishops, and people are unsure which to choose when the two no longer coincide. There are significant differences between hierarchies on the interpretation of the encyclical, and people wonder whether they are free to follow their own bishop or choose those of another country. Can their eternal salvation depend on what part of the world they live in?

Pluralism and publicity

Theological pluralism in today's Church is another source of confusion. There were always differences among theologians, and the casuists had a busy time weighing opinions to distinguish what was certain from what was merely probable, to discover which opinion was safe to follow. But the differences were seldom substantial and there was often a decree from Rome to limit the choice. However, theologians today are divided quite radically even on major issues, and while they are respectful of papal encyclicals, they do not fear to go beyond them and even contradict them. *Humane Vitae* is an obvious example, but there are many others. Publicity adds to the confusion. Theological discussion was formerly restricted to professional journals, but reporters now bring the latest theories into the limelight almost as soon as they are expressed, and they are often presented sensationally. People seldom have the opportunity to hear these views discussed seriously, but they often hear them condemned from the pulpit before they have even been understood by the preachers themselves. But publicity is a fact of life in today's world. In 1954 Pius XII declared that 'it is just and right that adults should not be ruled like children,' but too often in the past the teaching of morality was confused with methods of authority. Children can be given orders without explanation, but adults need to be persuaded and convinced. Their God-given reason must be appealed to and respected, not merely their loyalty or obedience. Indeed one of the saddest aspects of the *Humanae Vitae* controversy is that it is seldom discussed as a moral problem, but is immediately treated as a question of authority and obedience. Moral teaching cannot be 'decreed': it must be reasonably argued and explained. To speak of 'obedience' in the context of teaching is a category mistake. As Aristotle pointed out, no teaching takes place until the learner begins to learn. The good teacher strives for acceptance and conviction on the part of students, and this can only come from the truth itself, clearly presented and explained.

Confused guidance

Differences among bishops are another source of confusion, although such differences, when seriously studied, can help to relativise people's false absolutes. In June 1977 a committee of the Catholic Theological Society of America published a study of human sexuality. The Bishop of Steubenville wrote a pastoral letter in which he called the authors 'prideful people . . . free-wheeling people who in intellectual conceit strive to twist the word of God . . . destroyers . . . self-excommunicates who uphold false doctrines they contrive out of their efforts to gain worldly renown.' Cardinal Medeiros of Boston called it an 'irresponsible attack on the Church's teaching authority . . . weakening the allegiance in faith owed by Catholics to the holy Father.' On the other hand, Archbishop Hurley of South Africa welcomed the report and commended the authors for their effort. Referring to the 'dialogue, heat and controversy' which the report generated, he said that it was 'all to the good, even if it does cause us bishops to squirm a bit.' Moral guidance from bishops in the area of politics can be equally conflicting. When Spain was voting on its new constitution in 1978 the bishops held a meeting to advise people on how to vote. Fifty out of seventy five declared that people were free to vote according to their conscience, fifteen dissented, and a group of eight, led by the Cardinal Primate, published a pastoral letter which virtually instructed people to vote against it. When Switzerland held a referendum on a new abortion law in 1978, the bishops urged Catholics to 'examine all the advantages and disadvantages of the new law and vote according to their convictions.'

Prior to a national referendum in Ireland in 1995 on removing the constitutional ban on divorce, the hierarchy as a body encouraged people to vote according to their conscience, but individual bishops insisted that it was a moral duty to vote against the proposal. No wonder people are confused. Before a previous referendum on the same subject the bishops' conference did not take sides, but the papal nuncio later said in a press interview that he had been very busy during the campaign, lobbying the heads of religious congregations, telling them that 'in supporting divorce they would be going against the Holy Father, that they were in danger of falling into mortal sin, and were not only acting against the Holy Father, but against God himself.' It is no wonder that people are confused when they know they have a moral obligation to follow conscience, but in practice many Church leaders make them feel that they cannot be following their conscience in good faith if their decision does not coincide with what those leaders dictate for them. Confusion can turn to wonder and indeed anger when solemn Church statements dealing with intimate details of family life are proclaimed without any consultation with married couples, and in complete ignorance of the Christian experience of the laity, especially women, who make up the bulk of Church membership.

People who felt this kind of anger would be considerably heartened by the lecture given at Campion Hall, Oxford, in June 1996 by John R. Quinn, former archbishop of San Francisco. Responding to the Holy

Father's request for suggestions on how the papacy might be improved to meet the challenges of today's world and be less of an obstacle to ecumenism, he listed areas of the Church's life and structure crying out for reform: the *curia* in Rome, the system of papal nuncios, a too narrow view of collegiality and subsidiarity, and more openness and dialogue in discerning God's will. That an archbishop of unquestioned loyalty and obvious love of the Church could be so outspoken is a consolation to mature Catholics who are made to feel guilty when they are sincerely trying to follow their well-formed conscience.

Disunited leaders

A further consolation is the brave statement issued in August 1996 by Cardinal Bernardin of Chicago, together with twenty-three other prominent Catholics, lay, clergy and religious, including seven bishops, entitled *Called to be Catholic: Church in a time of Peril.* It was a plea for the American Church to face up to the disquieting realities that threaten to tear it apart, especially the polarisation of its leaders, and to work together to rediscover and affirm the vital Catholic legacy its members have in common. The Cardinal was deeply concerned at the state of the Church, confused, divided, at war with itself. His call was an echo of the gospel: 'Let us leave behind whatever brings discord; let us recommit ourselves to our great heritage of faith.' His analysis of division in the Church was proved accurate by the reaction of some of his fellow cardinals. Cardinals Law of Boston, Hickey of Washington, Bevilacqua of Philadelphia, and Maida of Detroit took issue with Cardinal Bernardin's initiative. They roundly criticised it as unnecessary and likely to do more harm than good. Cardinal Maida condemned it for causing confusion among the faithful and he stressed the need for Church leaders like himself to clarify matters. Catholics today are much more confused, and saddened, by the spectacle of Church leaders whose primary role of bridge-builders and peace-makers is blurred by their over-riding concern for authority and obedience, law and order.

These are just a few examples of the tendency, which seems to have increased in recent years, to go back on the Vatican II vision of the Church as sacrament of Christ, people of God, mystical communion for mission, herald of the gospel, servant of the world. The irony is that those who accuse others of infidelity to the Church's teaching like this seem to ignore the fact that the Vatican II documents are the Church's most solemn and authentic teaching. Ten years after the Council, the late Bishop Butler of Westminster said quite bluntly that when authority speaks with one voice in the Council and with another voice in its day-to-day performances after the Council, the faithful cannot easily determine where their duty of consent lies. Shortly before his death, Cardinal Suenens, who, with Bishop Butler, was one of the most influential contributors to the work of the Council, expressed his deep sadness that the vision and insights of Vatican II had been so neglected, if not opposed, during the past thirty years.

Over-simplifications
A healthy development in recent times is the fact that moral questions are more openly and publicly debated. But unfortunately such discussions, and indeed even ecclesiastical pronouncements on moral matters, are often marred by over-simplifications. Many terms and phrases are used as though they were crystal clear in meaning and so self-evident as to be beyond question, but they are ambiguous, to say the least, and they show up badly under today's more searching criticism. Among the concepts that are less simple and more confusing than was once thought are: God's will, divine law, natural law, intrinsically evil actions, objective morality, specifically Christian morality, 'the constant teaching of the Church,' absolute moral norms, phrases like 'error has no rights,' and quotations from scripture taken out of context, like 'He who hears you, hears me' applied to any and every Church pronouncement. Because of the uncritical use of such terminology, people often find it confusing and difficult to reconcile what is sometimes presented as the 'official teaching of the Church' with their God-given reason and their personal experience of daily life. Those who voice their difficulties should not be silenced by an appeal to authority, as though morality were simply a matter of command and obedience.

It is true that many people have solved the problem of conscience by making up their own minds about contraception and abortion, and they are not particularly worried about Church pronouncements. Some better-informed Christians may indeed be happy about their freedom of conscience, even at the risk of some superficiality and perhaps even bad faith being swept under the carpet of the subconscious. But there are very many less fortunate people who are genuinely confused and live in a strait-jacket of fear and guilt, unable to make an autonomous decision of conscience because they are oppressed by a burden which in many cases has been placed upon them by the Church itself. Too often the authority of scripture, Church teaching or natural law are used as substitutes for moral thinking rather than as pointers and helps in moral discernment.

An example of the heavy price the Church is paying for its autocratic approach in the past can be seen in Ireland. In 1990 the European Values Survey found that 85 per cent of Catholics nationwide went to Mass at least once a week, which was close to a world record. This had fallen to 66 per cent in 1996, but the most striking statistic from the 1996 *Irish Times/MRBI* survey is that only 21 per cent said that they followed Church teaching in serious moral decisions, whereas 78 per cent said that they follow their own conscience. Some clerical commentators pointed out that the teaching of the Church is that people should follow their conscience, but it seems likely that many who claim to follow conscience are not doing it out of loyalty to the Church, but rather out of a new sense of freedom which sadly pays little attention to specific Church teaching on moral matters.

Challenge to the Church
If Christian pastors are to escape Jesus' condemnation of the Pharisees, who heaped burdens on people's shoulders and never raised a finger to lift them, more pastoral activity ought to be directed towards liberating those fear-full and guilt-ridden people who are crippled in their response by an infantile notion of conscience and the confusion caused by the many changes in today's Church and world. Such people will not be helped by paternalistic preaching exhorting them to 'accept the teaching of the Church' in simplistic formulas and pre-packaged solutions to problems that are far from simple. The 'teaching of the Church' today is that they should be helped to grow towards moral maturity by being trusted, being listened to, being invited to dialogue about their experience. The pastoral challenge is to raise the level of their moral reasoning, to help them fully understand conscience and the decision-making process, the role of community, scripture, Church teaching, and the meaning of freedom and responsibility, moral values, principles, conflict situations, responsible and loyal dissent. It would be a genuine service to people to tease out these topics in ordinary language, without the over-simplifications that cause so much confusion, to present the reality of conscience in the context of Vatican II and the insights of modern theology.

It is not a question of producing a new catechism to be memorised by the simple faithful, though such a text could indeed be helpful in their study and reflection. It is rather a practical exercise of 'sharing' among the people of God. It is what Bishop Butler had in mind when he explained that, despite an unfortunate modern use of the word *magisterium* to designate the bishops and the pope, magisterial authority in the

Church is not limited to this official magisterial authority. The Church is not made up of two separate sections, one teaching and the other learning. In fact, the whole Church is a learning Church (including pope and bishops), a community of believers in which we must listen to each other and learn from each other. At the same time the whole Church is a teaching Church insofar as every mature Christian has, at some time or another, to play the role of teacher, *magister*.

For this emphasis to become a reality, there must be a new emphasis in Christian preaching. Rather than being told what to think, people must be helped to think for themselves, and morality must be presented without moralising. The official leadership in the Church cannot have the concrete answers to all moral problems in advance. The Vatican Council said as much: 'Let lay people not imagine that their pastors are always experts, that to every problem which arises, however complicated, they can readily give a concrete solution, or even that such is their mission' (*Church in the Modern World*, n. 43). Authentic morality can flourish only when people are helped to grow in maturity, when consciences are formed not primarily by way of a casuistic instruction going into more and more details, but by being roused and trained for autonomous and responsible decisions in the concrete, complex situations of human life. Some of these problems are no longer completely soluble down to the last detail, in fields never considered by the older morality, precisely because they were unknown.

Despite a certain trend towards conservativism in today's Church, more and more Catholics have the courage to live by their own conscience, making their own choices in personal responsibility, even in pain and difficulty, and they contribute to the welfare of the Church by their discernment and experience. This is in line with the Vatican II ideal of people 'who will be lovers of true freedom, who form their judgment in the light of truth, direct their activities with a sense of responsibility, and strive for what is true and just in willing co-operation with others' (*Religious Freedom*, n. 9). It is also an echo of St Paul's exhortation to his converts to become 'mature people, reaching to the very height of Christ's full stature' (Eph. 4:13). To the Corinthians he wrote: 'Do not be like children in your thinking, my brothers; be children so far as evil is concerned, but be grown-up in your thinking' (1 Cor. 14:20). If conscience is the ability to make rational judgments based on proper evidence and coherent argument, people need to be tough-minded as well as soft-hearted. They must be encouraged and trusted to think for themselves, critically and realistically, if they are to grow in moral maturity.

The power of example

Vatican Council II acknowledges that freedom of conscience and of honest conviction is one of the most basic human rights, rooted in the very dignity of the human person, a right to be respected by all, but more conscientiously by Christians (*Religious Freedom*, n. 9). The Church loses credibility when it acknowledges this on the level of principle, but seems to forget it in practice, when it sets up too many fences and controls, and relies on a system of sanctions and rewards to have its teachings accepted. Church leaders need to trust the faithful, and the only way to trust them is actually to trust them. This calls for a radical conversion among leaders in the institutional Church, an invitation to take Jesus at his word when he said that the truth will set us free.

The concept of freedom is at the very heart of the gospel, and it is a fact that the Christian Church has been a powerful force for liberation down through the centuries. The Holy Spirit incarnate in individuals and in the community brought forgiveness of sin, reconciliation of enemies and a more than human love reaching out to all in need. The gospel preached and lived by Christians dispelled ignorance and superstition, and the Church made an enormous contribution to science and art, to education and social services for the poor. During the centuries-long dark ages when the civil order was in collapse, the Church was the only institution to guarantee stability. In its missionary outreach it brought the riches of its culture to the four corners of the earth. In a very real sense it can boast of a glorious history, not only of fidelity to the gospel and to the call of Jesus to make disciples of all nations, but also to the civilising development of the world. At the same time, however, the darker side of its history cannot be ignored. Through force of circumstances it identified too closely with the Roman empire and its structures, and down through the years allied itself to political regimes that blurred its true nature. The Crusades and the infamous Inquisition are parts of our history we should be ashamed of and repent of. But it is even more sad to realise that in spite of preaching freedom, unity, peace, harmony and inclusiveness for centuries, so much of our history is a series of condemnations, rejections and excommunications. Unfortunately, something of this attitude is still alive and well in today's Church. The fact that many of the theologians who made the most substantial contributions to Vatican Council II were condemned and silenced for decades before it, is still a scandal for which there is no justification. None of them ever received an official apology for the appalling way they were treated and the personal suffering it caused them. Even today, when 'dissenting' theologians are stigmatised and threatened, there is no dialogue or due process of the kind that civilised courts in the modern world now take for granted, even insist on as a human right.

Admitting the past sins of the institutional Church is simply recognising its human and sinful dimension. The authoritarian pattern of Church governance and the repressive obedience so common in the experience of Catholics until quite recently are facts of history. In today's more open and more critical society it is far healthier for the Church that they be acknowledged. But a critical stance towards the institutional Church should not mean that 'institutional Church' becomes almost a term of abuse, justifying a flight into individualism. The Christian community has a corporate faith and identity and while it began as a movement, it must function as an institution in order to survive beyond a generation or two. It is thanks to the institution of the Church that we have officially recognised and guaranteed scriptures, the special presence of Christ, continuity with the apostles and their faith, the sacramental channels of grace, and especially reconciliation and Eucharist. The Church is a corporate body as well as the body of Christ, and any separation of body and spirit means death rather than reform. The challenge to its members to grow in freedom and responsibility, therefore, is not an invitation to individualism, but a call to build up the body of Christ. We can be fully free only in the context of fidelity; but we need a critical, responsible and creative fidelity.

An exemplary teacher

A shining example of what a Church teacher ought to be is the life and writings of Bernhard Häring, the German Redemptorist who is one of the most highly regarded moral theologians in the world. He was very harshly and unjustly treated by the Roman ecclesiastical authorities for many years in the 1970s, at a time when he had cancer of the throat, lost his power of speech and painfully had to re-learn to speak. Even before Vatican Council II he had transformed the whole science of moral theology with his three-volume *Law of Christ*. His books were read and studied throughout the world and were a revelation that brought enthusiasm, a new vision and new life to readers worldwide. Before his time moral theology as generally taught in seminaries had degenerated to a level where the primary concern was legal prescription, needing an elaborate casuistry to measure the degrees of sin. In fact sin played a central role. Häring insisted that the law for Christians is the law of Christ, and this is a law of love. He discussed the whole of Christian morality from this point of view.

Twenty-five years later, instead of imitating other authors who re-issued their books with quotes inserted from Vatican II documents, he re-wrote the whole of his moral theology from a totally new perspective in his three-volume *Free and Faithful in Christ*. In the new work the central conviction is that we are created in the image of God, and we are most like God in our freedom. The mission of the Christian Church, continuing the mission of Jesus, who came to set us free, is to enable people to experience that freedom, so that more and more they can grow into the fullness of the maturity of Christ. This ought to be a central concern of all Church teaching. If we are really preaching the truth it ought to set people free. But sadly psychiatrists and counsellors tell us that their Catholic patients have a more than average burden of guilt, engendered by their experience at the hands of parents, teachers and preachers. The therapists claim that although the illness or personality disturbance may not have been caused by the Catholic experience, it was very frequently aggravated by it. Some have even spoken of a 'Catholic neurosis.'

The pastoral aim of this book is to free people, to help them find their way in the confusion, by explaining the phenomenon of change in today's world and Church, by listing the more significant changes in different areas, considering some of the implications and effects of these changes, and in the light of all this, to take a fresh look at some traditional topics in moral theology. Hopefully, reflections along these lines may serve, in the words of St Paul,

> for the building up of the body of Christ, until all of us come to the unity of the faith and of the knowledge of the Son of God, to maturity, to the measure of the full stature of Christ. We must no longer be children . . . , but speaking the truth in love, we must grow up in every way into him who is the head, into Christ, from whom the whole body, joined and knit together by every ligament with which it is equipped, as each part is working properly, promotes the body's growth in building itself up in love. (Ephes. 4:12–16)

2

LIFE IS CHANGE

Perhaps the most basic experience of human life is that it is a constant process of change. Dramatic changes take place in the womb from the moment of conception, but the movement continues from birth to death. The changes are not only physical, but also emotional, intellectual and social. The same process of growth and development, and hence of continuous change, is to be seen in the human family as a whole. It would seem that the first human species evolved about five million years ago. These evolved into modern humans about 100,000 years ago. We find the first evidence of art about 35,000 years ago, the rise of agriculture 10,000 years ago, the origin of writing 4,000 years later, and the development of cities about 1,000 years later again. Some animals can make and use tools, use symbols and recognise themselves in a mirror, but the radical change which is distinctive of humans as we know them is the discovery of language, which seems to have occurred about 35,000 years ago. This brought more complex social organisation and eventually culture, morality and religion. As dimensions of human life, these three realities have been in a continual process of change, growth and development, and changes in each one affected the others.

Material goods change human life
The growth and development of modern humans has been a slow and gradual process over more than thirty millennia, but the speed of change has grown enormously during recent centuries. Indeed it is no exaggeration to say that today's world is as different from the 1920s as the 1920s world was from that of Julius Caesar or Jesus of Nazareth. The vast majority of the goods we use in daily life were developed only within our own lifetime. Plastics came in the 1940s, transistors in the 1950s, computers in the 1960s, microcomputers in the 1970s, biotechnology and genetic engineering in the 1980s, and the present decade has seen the explosion

of information techniques, giving instant access to unlimited sources across the globe. Each new invention seemed to be just an improvement on what went before, but in fact several of the discoveries radically changed human life. When the printing press was first developed, it was seen as a speeding up of the process of copying by hand, but in fact it radically transformed human life insofar as it became possible for vast numbers of people to have access to the printed word, which transformed education. The railroad and the motor car were first seen simply as faster and more comfortable means of transport than the horse, but in fact they introduced a major social change, particularly the car, with the increased mobility that enabled people to work in one place, live in another and take their recreation in a third. The ease of travel enabled people to break out from their immediate social environment of family, village or town. The anonymity of modern cities provides an escape from the pressures to conform that can inhibit personal freedom, but it also removes the support, example and challenge of the smaller community when it comes to preserving traditional values and making difficult moral decisions.

With our God-given creative intelligence we change our material environment, we have new experiences, and we are continually changing ourselves. Moral responsibility remains a constant, but how we exercise it in terms of discernment, decision and action cannot abstract from the fact of change. Pre-modern or traditional society tended to remove the burden of choice from individuals, but large areas of human life, previously determined by fate or community tradition, are now seen as occasions of personal choice for people. Improved health, higher and more general education, rising living standards, and urbanisation are social factors that impinge considerably on morality.

Impact of social changes
Increased population and urbanisation are major changes of the present time. The United Nations Population Fund Report of 1996 states that world population will pass six billion by 1998, and this, together with the growth of cities, will be the single largest influence on development in the 21st century. The report forecasts that the increase during the next twenty years will be nearly equivalent to the present population of Africa. These developments will cause major social changes that are not only moral challenges to the world community, but factors that will also affect individuals and families in their personal morality. Within ten years, more than half the people in the world will be living in cities, and

nearly all the urban population increase will occur in developing countries. At present two out of three urban dwellers live in poor countries. The report forecasts that by 2015 it will be more than three out of four, and by 2025 almost four out of five. Many of the new urban dwellers, particularly women and their children, will be among the poorest in the world. It is estimated that 600 million people in urban areas of the poorest countries at present cannot meet basic needs for shelter, water and health from their own resources. In itself, increasing urbanisation is a neutral fact. It has the potential for improving human life or increasing human misery. The cities can provide opportunities or frustrate their attainment, promote health or cause disease, empower people to realise their needs and desires or impose on them a simple struggle for basic survival. Whatever the outcome, the migration of such vast numbers away from their home territory and their concentration in cities will have an impact on their experience of morality.

On the other hand, yearly birth rates in Europe, North America and Japan are below world average, and Italy has the lowest in the world, followed closely by Spain, which is expected to surpass the Italian record fairly soon. In Italy especially, children are highly valued in the culture, and the ideal of the majority of women is to marry and have children. But they find that they have to limit the number of children largely out of economic necessity, since husband and wife need to work to cover housing and the standard of living they want. A further reason is that women who have been educated and have had the satisfaction of a regular job do not want to forgo this. The fulfilment that comes from professional work is something that is not limited to men. Many women feel that, while they recognise that home-building and child-rearing are worthwhile activities, even emotionally attractive, the economic pressure against them is too great, and they are hesitant to sacrifice their other jobs. They turn a deaf ear to moralists who preach against contraception, because they believe that they have little choice in the matter. Once again, a rising standard of living and consequent social changes influence moral decisions.

Cultural change

Material and social changes are easily identified, but the deeper changes in human history are not always noticed immediately. Human culture is in a continuous process of change, mostly imperceptible, but often quite radical. The fall of the Roman Empire, the discovery of America, the European Renaissance, the Protestant Reformation, the rise of Marxism and communism, the recent advances in information technology were all crucial historical developments. Each of these brought about not only material and social changes, but in many cases altered people's way of thinking and feeling, resulting in cultural changes, which in turn impinged on morality and religion.

Culture is used here not in the popular sense of intellectual or civilised development of an individual who can be described as a person of culture; it refers rather to a wider and deeper reality, so that a person can be said to belong to a particular culture. Culture in this sense refers to a people's whole way of life, their social symbols and rituals, art, language and literature, social relationships and groupings, and especially the particular way of thinking that guides their decision-making in economics, politics and morality, as well as in religion. Culture includes all the meaning systems of a society. It includes religion, although religion seeks the deeper meanings of human life. Culture is a set of meanings, values, models and patterns incorporated in and underlying the actions and communication of the life of a particular human group or society. This ideology is consciously or unconsciously lived by the group as expressing its own human identity and reality. It is learned and passed on from one generation to the next. It grows and develops as it is passed on, insofar as each generation modifies it in the light of its own experience. At the heart of every culture is a world-view, a way of looking at the world and all of reality. All of a people's value-system stems from this way of looking at things. Morality and religion reflect and express a people's culture, and they are always coloured by culture, since the cultural background affects all dimensions of human living.

Secularisation
Secularisation is a good example of a culture change that is generally recognised. For centuries in western culture there was a close alliance between throne and altar, Church and state. Religion permeated most areas of daily life. But gradually scientists, lawyers and politicians gave up looking to religion, let alone the Church, to find a frame of reference for their thinking. This attitude has today become a way of life and thinking that dominates daily life, in the classroom, the media, the hospital and the home. Young people in many countries are more familiar with the Shell or Coca-Cola symbols than with the sign of the cross. God and religion no longer hold a central place; at most they have been moved to the margin of consciousness, and are now seen as a matter of personal option and private concern. This has meant a radical change in people's

way of looking at life. Human persons are seen as the centre of the world, and all the world's goods are at their free disposal. People use only rational means to solve human, social and physical problems, without reference to any religious or other authority. Priority is given to individual persons and their right to take charge of their own destiny. Authority is accepted only to the extent that people consent to it and are convinced by it. All sets of ideological, religious and ethical truths are a matter of personal choice, free expression and public debate. These are aspirations that are increasingly found everywhere, especially where they are most frustrated. The secularising approach is not limited to sophisticated societies, but is making headway in many Third World countries.

Insofar as secularisation wants to acknowledge the lawful autonomy of this world and the dignity of the human person, it is in no way incompatible with faith or religion. It can be said that the process began originally with the Jewish experience of the one God as creator of all reality. This faith 'de-sacralised' all reality by banishing the many gods of nature and outlawing magic and superstition. The world was good in its own right and nature and the things of earth had their own autonomy and worth. Secularisation is a rediscovery of that healthy insight. There is no longer a need to fall back on mythical or religious sources to explain reality. God can be equally present in our rational explanations. We do not have to drag him in to fill the gaps in our knowledge or fall back on him only when all human efforts fail. A deeper and more all-embracing spirituality has no need of magic.

It is true that through modern secularisation there can be an erosion of faith, that religious practice is abandoned, people are more selective about doctrines and moral behaviour, religious institutions are questioned, the Churches have less influence on civil legislation and they lose control of schools and hospitals, but it can also provide the occasion for a more mature faith and morality. It can be a process of purification for the Church and for faith, a communal experience of the dark night of the soul. On the other hand, uncritical acceptance of secularisation can lead to the rejection of transcendental and religious values, and this is often called *secularism*, the negative consequences of which are often more visible than the positive elements of *secularisation*. Preachers do no service to the Church when they confuse the two in their condemnations. The *secularised* world can be a healthy and challenging environment for mature morality and religion, but the positive exclusion of God and of transcendental values that is *secularism* leaves a spiritual vacuum that is often filled by ideologies such as Marxism, astrology, New Age spirituality, extreme ecologism, wicca-religions, fundamentalist sects and movements, or even new forms of statism.

Modernity

Humanity's growth and development has had many high points which brought radical and far-reaching changes, like the development of agriculture, the discovery of writing and later of printing, and the industrial revolution. The most recent peak is the phenomenal increase in the amount and depth of human knowledge spread by efficient means of communication and transferred into technology. This can transform human living through the effects it has on almost everything used in daily life, from computers to medical technology. This process, commonly called 'modernity,' may be called a new culture, changing the way we think and feel, judge and act. Modern technology not only increases the efficiency of human activity, but it affects the very process of human knowing itself. It involves an intellectual, technological and social revolution, transforming our relationships to time, to nature and to other persons. It affects personal identity and moral values, freedom and responsibility. For good or ill, this phenomenon has repercussions on people all over the world, in all areas of human living: in genetics, economics, politics, ecology, culture, morality and religion.

This new culture is morally neutral, neither good nor bad, but it can and does raise moral questions. Morality is about making choices, and modern technology provides almost limitless choice. Power brings a corresponding burden of responsibility in how one uses it, but today's technology puts enormous power in the hands of ordinary people. Modernity as a culture can be cannibalistic, swallowing up all other cultures, leaving no room for the deeper experiences of life in art, philosophy or religion, and reducing morality to a mere question of efficiency, speed and results. As parents watch their children becoming adept in the new culture, totally at home with the internet and web services, they can't help wondering what will become of them in this addictive, mindless, unpredictable mono-culture. The technology has immense potential for good, breaking down barriers, linking individuals and groups across the world, encouraging openness and sharing, but can it be harnessed and cultivated in a way that will not destroy the deeper things of life, truth and beauty, morality and religion?

Historical consciousness

Secularisation and modernity are cultural changes easily recognisable by most people. But not many are aware that the past several decades have witnessed the greatest cultural change in the whole history of humanity, namely the change from *classical* to *historical* consciousness. This change involves a whole new outlook on reality, a move from objectivity to subjectivity, from metaphysical certainty to probability. Until recently it was taken for granted that the world was simply 'out there,' and one had only to look at it and study it to know it. Disinterested observers could walk around it, analyse it and discuss it, whereas today the concerned enquirer is conscious of being part of the reality in question.

The classical approach of most human science was enshrined in traditional Catholic theology. Moral teaching took for granted that one had only to look at 'nature' or reality untouched by human interference to discover God's law, and that from this source it was possible to conclude to detailed moral prescriptions in the various areas of life. It was taken for granted that the world of morality had a clearly recognisable centre from which all deviations could be measured, that any dissent from this meant unfaithfulness, and that any reference to pluralism would lead to anarchy. It was common teaching that there was an identifiable 'deposit of faith,' a package of truths entrusted by God to the Church to be defended from all attack and promoted with the gospel. Gradually the Church came to see itself as a citadel defending God's truth against the onslaughts of a wicked world. From this arises the false dualism between Church and world, Church and society, in which the Church is pictured as an ideal mystical body of absolute truth and enduring, unchanging beauty, while the world is viewed as a demonic region, individualistic, rationalistic, and centred on power and pleasure.

This unreal dualism is a far cry from the positive evaluation of earthly reality portrayed in the Vatican II statement on *The Church in the Modern World*, whose opening words are 'joy and hope,' *Gaudium et Spes*. One would have thought that thirty years after the Council this dualism would be well and truly discredited. Indeed most modern theologians have long since left it behind; but it is still to be found, with no apology, in the thinking of Cardinal Ratzinger in his pessimistic criticism of the current state of theology in the Church. His narrow 'deposit of faith' view of the gospel gives the impression that an objective a-cultural, a-historical body of truths can be dressed up in different sets of clothes to become intelligible to different cultures at different periods in time. The fact is that there can be no truth that is objective in this sense. When a truth has been understood and stated, it can only be in terms of the culture of the individual or group understanding and expressing it. The irony is that the teaching presented by Cardinal Ratzinger and many official documents of the Church is not objective and non-cultural, waiting to be translated into various cultures, but is itself already culturally conditioned by a particular Roman, neo-scholastic theological culture that has only a minority acceptance in today's world.

When one goes beyond the 'deposit of faith' to the gospel itself, it is helpful to remember that God's word is a living word that becomes incarnate in every culture and is alive and new each day. It is not only gift, but challenge. It is alive in itself, but Christians are called to make it come alive in their own culture. This means that while the same Christian faith can be found in all areas of the world, there is room and need for a variety of theologies to express and explain it. All of these theologies will be culturally and historically conditioned. The Church is enriched by the presence of Indian, Asian and African theologies, black theology, feminist theology and liberation theology. The movement from classical to historical consciousness means recognising that our personal identity is conditioned by our culture and history, and learning to read the 'signs of the times' and discover seeds of the gospel in that culture. The gospel is not a frozen package handed down from the past, but a living word that comes alive in each new culture, and a saving word that takes flesh in the complexity and messiness of everyday human life. Our statements of faith and our discernment in morals must reflect this reality, and that will be the measure of their truth. There is no need to criticise the past in the light of recent developments. Former teaching may have been appropriate in its time and place, but uncritical repetition of it is a disservice to the gospel.

Nature is not static

The shift from classical to historical consciousness means a greater awareness of the importance of change in human life. It was taken for granted in traditional theology that reality, and especially human nature, was fixed, static, unchanging. But that tradition had no awareness of history, of the fact that meaning depends on context, and that through time contexts change, perhaps slowly and gradually, but most certainly. Scripture and tradition can help us to discern meaning, but both of them are culturally and historically conditioned, so they cannot provide concrete solutions to today's questions. In fact, given the limited experience of earlier centuries, the question may be asked whether certain statements about human nature failed to distinguish between what was 'natural' to all humans and what was the expression of one particular culture.

Modern thinking is less concerned with human 'nature' and more interested in human history. History is not simply the stage or the background
against which a Christian community plays out its role, but is part and
parcel of that community's self-understanding, morality and religion.
The word 'nature' is still used in moral discussion, but it is a changing,
developing nature. Natural law is still needed in today's world as the
foundation and the touchstone for morality and legal systems, but it is no
longer the simple 'blueprint' from which concrete solutions can be read
off as God's will. Part of the credibility problem of some Church teaching
on moral questions is its lack of clarity on this point.

This recognition of the historical dimension of all reality is a major revolution in human consciousness. The world has undergone such a
profound transition in philosophy, the arts, the sciences, and in general
culture that some speak of it as a new culture, going beyond modernity.
Old ideas and values are more difficult to hold on to in this new way of
thinking. The closed, static world-view that dominated western culture
for thousands of years has given way to a totally new way of thinking.
Theology cannot escape the influence of the new world-view, and its
effects are particularly noticeable in the area of morality. Moral evaluation is historically and culturally conditioned. Moral norms can change
because of a shift in our value-system. There have been radical changes
in our attitudes to conquest and colonialism, to slavery, to sexual dis-
crimination, to the rights of women, to freedom of conscience, to
self-determination, to capital punishment. These changes can be upsetting for people who long for a multiplicity of absolutes to which they can
cling, but truly liberating for those who are more aware of the complexity of human life and wish to take personal responsibility for their lives.
The new consciousness will mean that moral formulations must be less
absolute than in the past. They will have to be more humble and tenta-
tive, continually open to revision in the light of new insights and later
experience. It is in this context that Karl Rahner, one of the foremost
Catholic theologians of this century, has claimed that concrete moral
statements are of their very nature provisional, and could never be
defined as dogmas of the Church.

A changing Church

It was the same Karl Rahner who insisted that history is of the very
essence of the Church. He distinguished three separate periods in
Church history: the short period of Jewish Christianity, the centuries-
long period when the Church was immersed in the culture of Rome,

Greece and western Europe, and the present period just beginning, when the Church is for the first time a Church of the six continents, a *world Church* in the full sense. As a world Church it cannot afford to canonise any one culture to the exclusion of others. Continuing the mission of Jesus and following the example of Pentecost it must reach all peoples and speak to them in their own tongue. Present Church teaching admits this in principle and expresses it in beautiful statements, but it has a long way to go before people can see concrete signs that it is believed in practice.

Rahner teased out some implications of this, raising questions that need attention if the Church is to be true to its vocation as a world Church. Why should the Holy See, in its various civil service departments, continue to think that it always knows best what serves the kingdom of God, without consulting the faithful who are the bulk of Church membership? In its decision-making, why does it naïvely accept the culture of Rome or Italy as a self-evident standard? When will it realise that Latin or European marital customs may not be suitable for many African societies at the present time? Jesus used bread and wine at the Last Supper, but does it follow that a Eucharist in Alaska must have wine made from grapes? If the Eucharist is at the very heart of Christian community, why must millions of Catholics in South America be deprived of it simply because there are no celibate priests there while there is no problem with married Anglican converts ministering as priests? Why are so many excellent Catholics barred from Holy Communion because their marriage situation is not fully in keeping with present canon law, although their family life may be a shining example of God's love? There are no easy answers to such questions, but they are genuine questions that ought to be studied in the light of our better understanding of cultural and historical conditioning. Officially the Church proclaims that the gospel needs to become incarnate in various cultures, but in practice the discussion is limited to accepting local music and language into the Roman rite.

The Church in fact is now a world Church, even though it will take considerable time for it to realise all the implications of this. But on the level of official teaching, however slowly this may filter down to daily practice, today's Church is radically different from what it understood itself to be fifty years ago. When Vatican Council II brought all of the world's bishops together for several intensive sessions between 1962 and 1965, it cannot be doubted that the Holy Spirit was at work. The bishops studied, discussed, shared and prayed in an effort to discern God's will.

In spite of their limitations, the Council's documents are now the official teaching of the Church. They deserve to be preached from the housetops for a more balanced picture of the Church. They show what radical changes have occurred in the Church's self-understanding and in its assessment of the world. No serious discussion of morality can take place unless in the new context of the Church. It may be worthwhile to mention some of these changes.

A new openness

For centuries the Church tended to be identified too easily with the kingdom of God. This position has now been abandoned. The Church is a *sign* or *sacrament* of God's kingdom, but that kingdom is a far larger reality. The Church's mission is to work for the furthering of that kingdom, but it has no monopoly of it. The erroneous interpretation given in the past to the idea that 'outside the Church there is no salvation' has also been abandoned. The Council of Florence declared that all heathens, Jews, heretics and schismatics go to hell unless they convert to the Catholic Church, but Vatican II teaches that those who have never heard of the gospel or of the Church but follow their consciences, can reach eternal salvation. It is accepted that salvation is not the exclusive possession of the Church. The Church now officially recognises the ecclesial character of non-Catholic Christian communities. It also recognises the authentically religious aspects of non-Christian religions, a recognition that found symbolic expression when the religious leaders of the world joined Pope John Paul II in praying for peace at Assisi in 1986. The arrogance of the Church in its treatment of other churches in the past was downright sinful. The Church's new openness now admits that God's saving will can be recognised outside Israel and outside Christianity, so that it cannot strictly be denied that there are elements of divine revelation outside Israel and Christianity.

In the past the primary, indeed almost the only, model of the Church was the institutional one, with its emphasis on organisation, administration and management. Everything to do with the Church was understood in the light of this model: sacraments, grace, preaching, law, etc. To complicate matters, the Church's institutional dimension developed in the context of the Roman Empire, and copied most of its structures from that source. This institutional way of thinking can lead to conformism, rigorism, juridicism, clericalism, triumphalism and, underlying it all, the male domination that came from western culture. For the renewal of the Church, the Council explained that the institutional model needed to be complemented and corrected by other models, namely, the Church as 'sacrament of Christ,' as community and fellowship, as pilgrim people of God, as mystical communion for mission, as herald of the gospel and servant of the world. In the document describing the Church's nature (*Lumen Gentium,* Light of the Nations), the Council emphasises the Church as the people of God before any distinction is made among its various offices, and specifically before the distinction is made between clergy and laity. It is the whole people of God which has been anointed by the Holy Spirit, and it is this whole people which is the bearer of the Good News and of Christian tradition, and which has been commissioned to carry on the mission of Christ. This is the official teaching of the Church, but the laity, particularly women, are still waiting to see this lived out in practice.

The openness so clearly expressed in the Council's declarations is not limited to the world of religion. In its document on the Church in the Modern World (*Gaudium et Spes*), it clearly affirms the saving presence of God in the secular, political, social and economic evolution of humanity. There is no longer a two-tiered world of natural and supernatural, of nature and grace, of world and Church, morality and spirituality. God is at work in all of his creation, and can be found in every experience of human life.

Moral theology

The Council did not 'decree' any new truths, but merely recognised and formulated the faith, the insights and the experience of the whole Church. During the thirty years since the Council, its documents, linked with the 'signs of the times' and various cultural developments, have contributed to major developments in theological thinking. The changes since pre-Council times have probably been most marked in moral theology. For centuries moralists consulted the various manuals of moral theology for the solution of problems, whereas now sacred scripture and the following of Christ are the major sources. Traditional moral theology dealt mostly with law and sin, authority and obedience, and went to great lengths to measure degrees of guilt. The sacrament of reconciliation concentrated on confession and often resembled a criminal court. It was forgotten that moral law is the law of Christ and this is a law of love. A further development is the move away from isolated, individual actions to a consideration of the person as a whole, so that moral theology becomes more person-centred. When the overall good of a person is used in moral discernment as a criterion determining moral good and evil, right and wrong, it is not a simple concept, but a complex notion of the human person in all dimensions. Moral theologian Louis Janssens lists these dimensions: a self-determining subject with conscience and responsible freedom, not a pure spirit, but a spiritual being with a material body, part of the material world, but with a capacity and a hunger for the transcendent in religious experience, with an essential relation to other persons, with a need for supportive social groups, a person related to time in terms of past history, present experience and future potential. An action is morally right if it is beneficial to the human person in this overall sense. Reason and faith are needed for the discernment, but it is the overall good of the person that is the basic criterion.

A major change in moral theology since the Council is its method of theologising. The classical approach was deductive, deducing behavioural norms from scripture texts and general principles of a fixed, static natural law. When Louise Brown, the first test-tube baby, was born, Pope John Paul I, just before his election, said it was a wonderful step forward and he thanked God that science could help so many sterile couples. But within days the Holy See proclaimed it unacceptable and immoral. Since then there have been many condemnations of medical developments on the basis of instant reactions relying on the old deductive method, sure of its rightness because of the logic of its reasoning. But reality is much more complicated, and the first step when faced with a new discovery or problem is to study the facts, and to be helped by the appropriate human sciences of economics, sociology, psychology or medicine. Each new problem needs to be understood in factual detail and in its context, to discover its human meaning, and this cannot be judged *a priori*, from outside. The voice of experience must be heard, so laity must be consulted and listened to. The saddest experience of the Church's failure and hence its loss of credibility on this point is in the area of birth control and sexual morality. A later chapter will explore this more fully.

A further change in moral theology has been the general acceptance of the distinction between *moral* and *pre-moral* or merely physical evil when judging actions formerly resolved by recourse to the principle of double effect. It remains true that the end does not justify the means, but only when the means is a moral evil, and the morality of an action cannot be decided apart from its human meaning as performed by an individual subject in given circumstances. *Pre-moral* evils (e.g. self-mutilation to preserve life or health, killing an attacker in self-defence) become *moral* evils only when performed without proportionate reason. This seemingly reasonable principle began what has been one of the most intense and lively debates in moral theology in the last thirty years. The majority of world-class theologians would see themselves as 'proportionalists,' but their position is roundly, and unfairly, criticised by official documents of the Church. Connected to this debate is the widespread view of moral theologians that labelling certain actions as 'intrinsically evil' is not helpful in moral discernment, because the human meaning and therefore the moral assessment of an action cannot be judged in isolation from motive and circumstances. This leads to a radical questioning of so-called 'moral absolutes.' Tradition formulated certain moral absolutes as conclusions from natural law, based on values rooted in human nature itself, but if human nature can and does change, these formulations must also change, and the question arises: in what sense can they be called absolute?

Underlying all these changes is the basic question of the *meaning of morality* itself, of the model used in trying to understand it. Traditionally it was the model of law and obedience, doing one's duty, the *deontological* approach. Recent developments still make room for law as an important element in the moral life, but the central focus is on the nature of the person and growth as a person through relationships in furtherance of certain basic human values. This takes account of the end or purpose of human life and individual actions, and this emphasis on finality is described as the *teleological* approach. Closely allied to this is another change, the importance attached to the *overall pattern* of activity and what it does to the individual as distinct from isolated actions analysed on their own. These changes are moving in the direction of totality. Moral theology and personal moral discernment pay special attention to the totality of the human person and to the individual's relation to the wider totality of the human family and the still wider totality of the earth and the cosmos entrusted to human care and stewardship. This *holistic approach* is becoming more and more generally accepted.

Continuity and change

The newer moral theology gives more prominence to conscience and personal responsibility. It emphasises the importance of character and virtue. It gives serious attention to experience, and the experience of laity and especially of women is being listened to. An unmistakable sign of the presence of the Holy Spirit in today's Church is the number of world-class women theologians, although sadly in practice the official Church has a long way to go in acknowledging women's full and rightful place in the assembly. Moral theology is also becoming more open to the experience and tradition of other Christian churches.

Today's moral theology is in continuity with the best traditions of the past, and this is all to the good, but its weakness is that even with all the new insights and changes mentioned above, moral theology can remain centred on the individual person making moral decisions about specific problems and situations, with less attention paid to the strictly theological and socio-political dimensions of morality. Too much concern about *continuity* can limit moral concern to an inherited agenda, a traditional list of topics. A wider approach would treat more fully of birth, sexuality, family, death, violence, justice and peace in their full theological meaning and not just as ethical problems requiring a solution. Liberation theology has highlighted some of the socio-political aspects. Genuine contact with the socio-political context would broaden the list of topics that moral theology ought to be concerned with.

Changes in the Church and in moral theology have met with resistance, but this is the fate of most change. Less than a century ago the steam engine was denounced as infernal, and travel by car was considered a sin against nature. Air travel was condemned as an insult to the Creator. Evolution, psycho-analysis and group dynamics were all criticised in their time. Newness is always a threat to a profoundly conservative mentality, and morality and religion have traditionally been conservative, so it is no surprise that the accelerated rate of change in recent decades has caused division among people. Some cling to the familiar tradition, while others want to be adventurous, forward-looking and creative in their response to the rapid change and unprecedented choices placed before us by today's world. Diversity is normal, but polarisation is sad. The call of Christian charity is to be bridge-builders and peace-makers. Both groups need to listen to each other and try to understand each other in their common search for God's will and God's truth. In coping with change we should take courage from the wise words of Cardinal Newman: 'To live is to change, and to be perfect is to have changed often.'

3

WHAT IS MORALITY?

The changes listed in the previous chapter make it clear that human nature is not a fixed, static entity, but a continually changing and developing reality. The vastly accelerating speed of change in recent decades brings this home all the more, and there is every indication that this speed will continue to increase. For some people the prospect is exciting, for others frightening. Those who are frightened feel that it is all too much too quickly, and they wonder what the future will bring. Will life still be human in any recognisable sense? What will become of traditional values, of morality, of religion? These are quite normal questions, but it is not the first time in history that they have been asked. Several times in the past, people felt that the world was in a mess, and that the period in which they lived was the worst ever. It would be easy to quote from the Old Testament, early Christian times, or later centuries, writers who complained about the wickedness of their generation, as though it were a total disaster. Children were refusing to obey their parents, traditional values were neglected, even derided, the age of unreason had arrived, society was breaking down, the future was bleak. When one is living through such an experience there is a strong temptation to be pessimistic. But a closer look at the wider context of human history can restore balance and give hope and courage for the future. In spite of the dramatic changes through the centuries of human development, there is a recognisable core that remains intact. There is a basic pattern that endures. There are human experiences that continue to link us with our remote ancestors. The medieval theologian Thomas Aquinas, one of the most outstanding Christian teachers, spoke of our 'unchanging, changing human nature.' Discontinuities and changes are an essential part of a deeper continuity. Refusal to change can be a refusal to grow and develop. Morality is not primarily about duty and obligation, but about relationships and growth. It may be helpful to see the various ways in which morality can be understood.

Language and culture

The Bible is not a book of history or of science, but a collection of religious writings giving us the deeper meaning of history, of life, death and human destiny. Its description of the origins of the human race is a beautiful story that carries deep meaning, but it is not a factual account of our 'first parents.' Christian faith does not require us to believe that the human race began four thousand years ago with the immediate creation of the first human couple in an earthly paradise. Our beginnings go much further back, as the fossil record makes clear. Anthropologists claim that the common ancestors of humans and African apes possessed a level of self-awareness equivalent to that experienced by modern chimpanzees, but there is no indication that this level developed much for five million years. When significant changes occurred in brain size, social organisation and mode of subsistence, the level of consciousness increased so that a new kind of animal developed, one who set arbitrary standards of behaviour based on what is right and wrong. For a better quality of hunting, sharing and surviving, rules had to be established, with punishments for failure to obey. This was a primitive form of morality, the discovery that organisation and rules are necessary to regulate behaviour in the group in order to ensure a better quality of life.

The clearest indication in the prehistoric record of a higher level of consciousness is the deliberate, ritual burial of the dead. This points to an awareness of death, and therefore a reflective awareness of self, although at a very rudimentary level. However, it continued to develop, and the intelligence required to plan and organise hunting expeditions, the social order within a group, and the migration of groups from place to place led to the development of language for communicating. Language and consciousness of self mutually enriched each other and their growth speeded up. Modern humans became modern, relatively speaking, when they spoke like us and experienced the self as we do. There is clear evidence of this in the art of Europe and Africa, dating from 35,000 years ago, and in the many examples of elaborate ritual that surrounded burial at that time. Language grew from the exchange of mere practical information to the communication of ideas and deeper levels of personal sharing. Gradually there developed a world of shared meaning which we nowadays call culture. More than just a dictionary of words, culture includes a whole way of life, social symbols and rituals, language, art, social relationships, morality and religion.

Morality and religion

Primitive morality began as a practical way of organising the relationships and social life of the group. Experience taught which behaviours improved group living and which became obstacles. Decisions had to be made about the best way to relate in different situations, and gradually a set of rules was established and values were recognised. This became part of the culture which individuals imbibed as they grew up. The three essential elements in communities or social groups are that they share a common language, they accept common patterns of behaviour, and they construct social structures to order and sustain a common life. In this sense morality is part of a culture. But cultures have a further dimension. Part of human consciousness is the inner voice that seeks explanations for everything, the basic search for meaning, for a vision or belief that makes sense of everything. This is the world of religion, the world of recognition, in which people recognise the deeper meaning of human experience. Some writers describe these three levels as the world of *nature*, the world of *responsibility* and *morality*, and the world of *recognition* or *religion*.

Every human society has created an origin-myth to explain how the world, and especially its own particular world, came into being. The creation story in the Bible is the best-known of these myths, but there are many others. This and other stories in the Bible help us to make sense of our human situation, explaining who we are, where we came from and where we are going, and linking us to a deity to be obeyed and worshipped. Language, behaviour and myth are intertwined and inter-dependent. In this way morality and religion are linked, and quite often obedience to the rules of society is seen as obedience to the deity, and divine punishment is expected for misbehaviour. With the passage of time these attitudes became more refined, so that morality can now be understood in its own right apart from any other-worldly enforcer, and the human person is now seen as the primary norm of moral behaviour, though always in a social context of relationships. Morality is that dimension of human conduct whereby behaviour is described as good or bad, right or wrong.

The Bible myth of the creation of a human couple in an earthly paradise and their disobedience resulting in a fall from grace sees morality as our attempt to bring our damaged and imperfect human nature into line with God's will. It is a simple symbolic story, a powerful myth which has an essential role in our religious culture, but is not an historical account of how we humans began. It has the merit of simplicity, but life is not simple, and never less so than today, so any literal interpretation of Genesis cannot solve our complex moral problems. But there is also a secular, philosophical myth which seeks to explain the origin of morality. It is the 'social contract' theory coming from the Greeks and from Hobbes and Rousseau. This considers the pre-ethical human state as one of loneliness, in which individuals had no fixed abode, had no need of each other's help, and the same persons hardly met twice in their lives, and perhaps then without even knowing each other. In this view, the original disaster was that people ever began to meet. When they did meet they clashed, so morality was invented to prevent war and impose an armed peace. Rousseau developed the notion of the 'noble savage,' who lost nobility when forced into a reluctant bargain to avoid conflict. This too was myth, not intended to be taken literally, but, like the Bible story, it tended to be interpreted literally as historical fact. Modern knowledge provides no basis for either of these myths as historical fact.

Morality is a phenomenon that in itself is independent of religion, although for religious people the two are intimately connected. While morality in practice may have begun as a series of rules, it is more and more recognised nowadays that human beings cannot hide behind any such rules. Although morality is essentially social, its central element is personal responsibility and reasonableness. People need to be able to give reasons for their actions, to justify themselves to others. When they cannot do this, they lose that quality which gives them autonomy in relation to others, the ability to show that their actions are justified, make sense, and are in accord with the values agreed to by all in their society. To be unable to do this is to risk being an outcast, a non-person. Failure to give reasons for one's actions is seen as moral failure, an irresponsibility. Because of the peculiar nature of the human person, there is a need not only to prove oneself reasonable in the eyes of others, but also to oneself. This is the experience of conscience, as will be seen in more detail in a later chapter.

Different models
Probably the vast majority of people think of morality as law, but in fact it can be considered in a variety of ways. There are *different models* to choose from in thinking about morality. As mentioned in the last chapter, for centuries the Church was seen primarily as institution. This was the

model most people were familiar with and it coloured their thinking about every element in the Church. But in recent times it was recognised that this was a very narrow view, and it needed to be complemented by other ways of thinking of the Church, such as sacrament of Christ, community and fellowship, pilgrim people of God, mystical communion for mission, herald of the gospel and servant of the world. These various ways of considering the Church are models, images, symbols or metaphors which enable us to understand better the mystery of the Church. They appeal not only to our mind, but to our imagination and our feelings. The various models provide us with different views of the Church, so that we do not become prisoners of any one way of thinking. Different approaches appeal to different people and indeed to the same people at different times. Each one has its advantages and also its inadequacies, so a variety of models can give us a more rounded approach and enrich our understanding of reality. This is true also of morality. There is more to morality than law and obedience. It may be helpful to look at some of the models used by theologians today: the legal model, the love model, the discipleship model, the inner conviction model, the liberation model and the relational or personal growth model.

The legal model

It is understandable that the legal model should be the most widely used, since the early experience of morality and obligation had to do with organisation in the group, establishing commonly accepted rules to ensure peace and harmony among free beings tempted to go their own way. In primitive times these rules could be simple and few, but in more developed communities they became more numerous and complicated. Each one was enacted for the sake of the common good, and individuals felt obliged to obey them, either out of personal conviction or because they feared punishment. This legal system, however, gave rise to a legal mentality, whereby people thought of morality primarily, if not almost exclusively, as law. This centuries-long experience has left its mark on our understanding of the moral life. Everything is seen in legal terms. God is the supreme lawgiver, and we speak of divine law and natural law. There are rewards and punishments, in this life or in the next. Since laws cover almost every aspect of life, the central virtue for a Christian becomes obedience, and dissent can lead to expulsion from the Church community. Concern to know and obey such a large quantity of laws can give rise to scrupulosity and fear on the one hand or, on the other hand, to an attitude of constantly searching for ways around the law. 'How far can I go without committing sin?' was a not uncommon attitude. The administration of the Church's laws tended to imitate the legal system of the state, even in the case of the sacraments. Penance was often experienced and administered as a tribunal, where the judge was concerned to assess the precise degree of guilt and assign the appropriate penance. Emphasis on law called attention to the authority behind the law, creating an impression that morality is something imposed from without, instead of being a matter of personal conviction and responsibility.

Just as people in recent decades have moved away from the narrow institutional view of the Church and are beginning to appreciate and be challenged by its other dimensions, they have also relativised the legal model of morality. The major defects and the seriously misleading implications of that view are more clearly recognised today. Law is no longer seen as the central element of moral life. This can be a liberating experience, freeing people for a more mature approach, one based on conviction and personal responsibility. But real maturity will recognise that while law may not be central, it is still an important element in morality. While a richer understanding of Church emerges when various models are combined, its institutional elements of offices, organisation and law will always be needed for its continued existence. In the same way, to relativise the legal model of morality does not mean to abandon law in the moral life. No community or society can survive long without generally accepted values, and these will be reflected in the laws agreed on by the community for the common good.

Love and discipleship

Part of the renewal of theology in recent times involved a return to the scriptures, looking for inspiration in the word of God. It is clear from the example and teaching of Jesus and from the New Testament as a whole that the primary value in Christian life is not obedience, but love. The law of Christ is a law of love. This love is not just sentimental attraction, but deep personal concern for the welfare of others. This of course should be the inspiration of all moral behaviour, but in itself it is not sufficient as a criterion for deciding the morality of specific actions. The question 'What is the most loving thing to do?' has no easy answer in concrete situations. Would it be a truly loving action for a son to directly and deliberately kill his terminally ill mother because she pleads to be put out of her misery? There is need for serious discernment, which requires other criteria to be applied, and there can be disagreement about what these ought to be. An extreme form of this 'love ethic' in the 1960s became known as 'situation ethics,' and it was generally criticised for leading to conclusions such as that adultery is generally immoral, but there can be special situations in which it might be the most loving thing to do. There was good reason for Church authorities to condemn such ideas, but unfortunately there was a tendency in Church documents to ignore the fact that the emphasis on love as a central thrust in moral decisions was something that most people were longing to hear. There can be no question of returning to the old legal model of morality, although law will always keep its rightful place. Moreover, some of the condemnations did not seem to be aware of the fact that a long tradition of the best Catholic theology was in fact a healthy situation ethic, taking account of all the details of a situation before deciding an issue.

Closely allied to the love model of morality is the discipleship model. This is built around the invitation of Jesus to follow him, to become disciples like his first followers. The morally good life for the Christian is not just imitation of Jesus, but a following of him in an intimate personal relationship, living by the power of his Holy Spirit, and working for the kingdom of God, a kingdom of justice and peace. Although the following is intensely personal, it also involves living in a community of believers, the Church, called to be a sign and sacrament of the kingdom of God, in which people can experience what this kingdom can be. This model has a very strong appeal, with its roots in the New Testament, and like the love model, it can be a healthy counter-balance against the rigidity and narrowness of the legal model. But, like the love model too, it does not provide a fully satisfactory criterion for deciding what is morally right or wrong in the concrete. Discipleship can be a motivation and general thrust in decision-making, but other criteria are needed for the actual decision as to what is right or wrong, so this model in turn needs to be complemented.

The liberation model

Moral theology in the 1960s and 1970s was enriched by South American theologians who had been formed in the academic tradition of Europe, but who discovered a new way of doing theology from their experience of living in a situation of deprivation and oppression, in countries where a tiny minority of rich people owned most of the land, while the vast majority were virtual slaves to the economic system, and continually suffered gross violations of their civil and human rights. This harsh reality brought home to theologians the need to read the gospel through the eyes of the poor, and alerted them to the fact that God was speaking not only in scripture but in the daily suffering of God's holy people. They recalled the anguished cry of Spanish theologian Bartolomé de las Casas at the time of the conquest: 'I see so many Christs continually crucified here.' It was realised that morality was not just a matter of personal piety, but had an essential social dimension. It was gradually recognised that the struggle for justice is an essential part of preaching the gospel. The saving mission of Jesus is not simply to save us from personal sin, but to bring about liberation in social, economic, political and other areas, so that people can be truly and fully free. For the first time, 'social sin' was condemned, and Latin American bishops deplored 'the unjust distribution of the world's resources and the structures through which the rich get richer and the poor get poorer.' This attitude is a major advance and can be a corrective to the over-individualistic traditional approach to morality.

This model is inspiring and can give hope to the millions who experience nothing but oppression in their lives. It broadens the notion of salvation and redemption, even for those not living in the tragic situations of Latin America. It reminds us that the voice of God is to be heard in the experience of people, especially when it proclaims that 'this state of affairs should not be, this economic, political or ideological structure is an affront to the image of God in his people.' It impels to action, to change and reform, so that the gospel is no longer mere words. The fact that some of its activists may concentrate too much on the social and political aspects of life to the neglect of the deeper spiritual dimension should not be an excuse for condemning or ignoring its basic thrust and valuable insights. The challenge is to integrate the liberation model into our understanding of morality and develop it to the point that it becomes relevant in situations beyond those of Latin America.

Inner conviction

For most of human history group consciousness took precedence over personal choice, and in some primitive societies this is still the case. Premodern or traditional society tended to remove the burden of choice from individuals; but recent times have seen a dramatic change. Large areas of human life, previously determined by fate or tradition, are now seen as occasions of personal choice. Instead of conformity to pre-determined rules imposed from without, the emphasis has moved to personal responsibility. This does not mean that we make up our personal moral code as we go along, but that we are personally convinced and freely commit ourselves to what is morally right. We may be helped by directives from the law, but we mature to the stage where we personally accept the values enshrined in the law and these become the ultimate basis for our moral decisions. This is the experience of conscience. In this model of morality we are judged not on the basis of our conformity to tradition or obedience to law, but on our integrity and authenticity, on the degree of fidelity to our inner light and our true selves, on the consistency between our knowing and doing. The Vatican Council speaks of human freedom as an exceptional sign of the image of God in human beings. It goes on to explain that 'people's dignity requires that they act out of conscious and free choice, as moved and drawn in a personal way from within, and not by blind impulses within themselves or by mere external constraint' (*The Church in the Modern World*, n. 16).

Conscience is not just a ready reckoner for deciding what is morally good or evil, right or wrong, but a special level of consciousness involving the whole person. It is not simply a question of 'What shall I do?' but 'How shall I live?' 'What should I become?' It is about a whole manner of life. As a dimension of personality, conscience grows with the person. It has its beginnings in childhood, when we learn correct and acceptable behaviour on the basis of rewards and punishment. It is further formed through obedience to law, when a person realises that law is for the sake of the common good, and that it pays to be good, because well-organised and harmonious society increases one's own well-being. The highest level of conscience is when we act on the basis of personally accepted principles and values even without the guidance or obligation of law. Development of conscience is not just a matter of intelligence and knowledge, but a deeper sensitivity to values that comes from habitual morally good behaviour. The one who habitually tells the truth not only becomes a truth-full person, but also develops a special insight enabling one to recognise what truthfulness and deceit mean in concrete situations. The same is true of all values and virtues, of justice, fairness, courage, temperance, prudence, etc. One becomes just, prudent, temperate and courageous by being just, prudent, temperate and courageous, but in the process one is also becoming a better person in all these areas, and one's sensitivity and moral judgment are becoming more and more refined and authentic. It is for this reason that Aristotle claimed that the basic criterion of morality is the judgment of the morally good or virtuous person, and not simply a code of ethics.

Morality is about relationships and growth

An important question to be asked in moral life is not simply 'What am I doing?' but also 'What is the "doing" doing to me?' What kind of person am I becoming because of the way I behave? Physically I am what I eat, and intellectually I am what I think, but as a person I am what I am through what I feel and think, decide and do. However, I do not live in isolation. Nobody grows alone. People need people, and I am as many persons as the people I meet, because each one brings out a different facet of my personality. I need others for my growth as a person, just as they need me. In this sense, morality consists in a complex network of relationships between persons individually, in community, and between communities. In this context, morally good actions are those that foster good relations, that facilitate relationships which will enable me and others to grow as persons. Morally bad actions are those which damage those relationships and block personal growth.

One of the best presentations of this relationship model of morality is that of Enda McDonagh in his book *Gift and Call.*[1] His basic insight is that morality begins with an encounter with another, that every person who crosses my path is gift to me, and at the same time a call or invitation so to relate to that other person that we both grow in humanity as persons. The meaning of morality is given in the Creator God's reflection that 'it is not good for people to be alone,' and so we are called out of ourselves, out of our aloneness, to join with others so that we can all grow together into the fullness of our human nature, in the image and likeness of Jesus, the perfect human being. Our lives are constituted through relationship and response. We do not grow in selfhood and personality by manipulating or overcoming others, but by being in the right kind of relationship with them. It is in these relationships that we first become conscious of the moral call, of moral obligations. It is the presence, person and needs of other people that give rise to these obligations. McDonagh's central insight is that our primary moral experience is what happens to us when we stand in the presence of other persons. We experience their presence as a call to come out of ourselves, a summons to respond to their presence, and there is something unconditional and absolute about this call, it is something that impinges on us at the deepest level of our being, even before we have discerned any of the specifics of how we ought to respond. This is what being moral is all about. To recognise, respect and respond to those who come our way is our basic moral duty, and we simply cannot refuse to respond and still claim to be moral.

This relational model of morality marks a clear break with the legal model, but it has close links with the love and personal conviction models. Its greatest advantage, however, is that it has solid foundation in the psychological experience of people, who are nowadays more conscious of the importance of relationships for healthy growth. The irony of the modern situation in the developed world is that there is a widespread individualism in all areas of life which is strong enough to be corrosive of any healthy society, and at the same time there is a deeper awareness of the need to be in touch, to be in relationship with others, to be rooted in our world, to be part of a network, if we are to have any true experience of genuine self. While the business world of competition and aggression praises the so-called self-made man, our psychological experience assures us that the self-made person is a contradiction in terms. We cannot be fully human persons unless we have others to whom we respond. Our response to others is an essential element in our own growth as persons. Nobody grows alone, people need people. We are what our relationships enable us to be. It would be worth reflecting a little on what this means.

Experiencing others

Physically I am the centre of my world, and the horizon of that world is the boundary of what I can see, touch, hear and smell. But I am also the centre of my psychological, emotional, intellectual and spiritual world. As centre, I experience everything else in relation to myself. In the case of most of the objects in my different worlds, I can change them, reorganise them, dispose of them. But I find some that are different. They are persons like me, centres of their own worlds, capable of making their own decisions and not available for my manipulation or use. They are special. They are like me, and yet different. Insofar as they are like me I can relate to them in a way that is different from all other objects. Insofar as they are like me and yet different, I can be enriched by them and by their differences. They are basically different because they are personal centres of their own worlds, but they will also have many other differences, physical, psychological, cultural. I can learn from these differences and be enriched by them as I am introduced into the world of other persons. In this sense every person is potential gift for me. Whether that gift becomes real and actual for me depends on my own attitude and decision. To experience the gift, I need to accept it, and in order to accept it I must *recognise*, *respect* and *respond* to the other person, both as person, like me, and as other, different from me. When I respond with the response that is appropriate to this particular person and to the total situation (values, circumstances, consequences), I grow as a person, and I enable the other to grow. I must *recognise* the other as person, as centre of his or her own world, but also as different, so that I do not ignore or deny the difference, much less seek to obliterate it. To *respect* the other means to allow the other to be different, to be other, not to manipulate or change the other. To *respond* in the right way is to reach out to the other according to his or her particular need in a way that is appropriate to the situation.

But my response is not always positive. Precisely because the other person is different I may see that person as a *threat* rather than a *gift*. The differences can make me feel inadequate and insecure, and this provokes fear, which prompts me to withdraw into myself, to refuse to recognise, respect and respond positively. To withdraw into myself is a refusal to grow. To do this continually is to fail to respond to the basic challenge of human nature, which is to become actually what we are potentially, to become fully mature human persons. The moral challenge is to relate to others in such a way as to allow the gift element to predominate over threat, to go out to others for mutual enrichment. This challenge applies to all three moments of *recognition, respect* and *response*. Failure or refusal to recognise and respect others in their personhood and their otherness makes it impossible to find the appropriate way to respond.

Just as there is no such thing as 'no communication' between persons in contact in a particular situation, since refusal to communicate is communication of a negative reaction, refusal to respond to others is a negative response. There is no neutral ground. When a block of silver is rubbed against a block of gold, no change seems to take place, but a good physical chemist can show that tiny particles of each metal cross the barrier of separation and become embedded in the other block. In the same way, but on a much more subtle level, every person I have ever loved, or feared, longed for or run away from, is part of me, and I am a part of them. One does not need to be on a psychiatrist's couch to discover this. Personal reflection can bring home the truth of the principle that, as human persons, we are what our relationships make us, we are what they enable us to be. It is not an automatic determinism setting us into a mould, because we have a basic freedom of choice, not always about our encounters, but about how we respond. The responsibility is ours. In this sense we do not 'just grow,' but we shape our own character, we chart our own destiny.

The challenge to respond positively and creatively to others is an ongoing one, since we continually encounter different persons, and even with the same people the situation and circumstances are constantly changing. Each of the people I meet is part of a network of relations with others (married, single, vowed, parents, children). That network is not a static entity, but a fluid, flexible relationship relating to past and future, and we are all related to the material world we inhabit. When it is said that the human person is at the centre of morality, it is not the individual, isolated person, but the person in society, in history, in cosmos, and none of these elements should be neglected in assessing a situation and discerning the responses that are appropriate. In this sense there can be no static, unchanging code of ethics to solve problems in advance, and mature moral decisions must of necessity include a healthy situation ethic, as the best of our Catholic moral tradition has always done. Morality must take account of the process of change and development, in individuals and in society.

Personal growth
The relational model of morality has a ring of truth insofar as it does not emphasise obedience to imposed rules, but focuses on the personal growth of individuals to moral maturity. This growth is not only a refinement of our moral sense, but also a development of our total personality. Thus, to *recognise* the other person as person and as other develops our own self-identity, insofar as we define ourselves by our differences, and it is only through contact with others who are different that we grow in *self-identity*. Likewise, to *respect* others in all their differences, accepting and appreciating those differences as an enrichment of our experience, helps us to grow in *self-acceptance*. This growth in self-identity and self-acceptance also comes from the recognition and affirmation we get from others. In fact, in our experience of relationships, the friendships of our lives are not just experiences we have, but factors that shape who we are, the kind of person we are becoming. Finally, to *respond* to others in each new situation with the appropriate response enables us to grow in *self-transcendence*. To transcend self, to go beyond self may sound strange, but in fact it means reaching out to others in a way that enables us to grow beyond the narrow, childish or selfish self that we are so often tempted to remain, and develop into the higher self we are called to be. In this way, when we *allow gift to predominate over threat* in our relationships, there is a mutual enrichment of all the parties in relationship. Our creative response to those who cross our path is creative of our own selves as well as creative of others. It has been said that there is a destiny that makes us brothers and sisters, none goes his way alone; all that we send into the lives of others comes back into our own. Counsellors know only too well how *self-identity, self-acceptance* and *self-transcendence* are the essential bedrock of mature human personality.

Lest the above sound like mere pop psychology, it would be worth reflecting on the growth and development of the human personality of Jesus of Nazareth, the perfect human being, the model of mature humanity. He experienced fear and had a bloody dread of what lay in store for him because of the kind of person he was and the message he was trying to preach, but it did not prevent him from reaching out across the cultural barriers of his time to mix with all kinds of people, strangers, outcasts and sinners. It was this experience, together with his intimacy with his Father, that enabled him to grow in self-identify and gradually clarify his mission as Son of God. Because he was at home with all these people, he had no psychological problems with his self-acceptance. On the cross he showed his self-transcendence, where he was able to go beyond the ordinary human self to a higher level where he could draw all things to himself, where, like the lightning conductor on the tall building, he could soak up all the hatred and evil around him and neutralise it in the deafening silence of his acceptance.

For the sake of clarity we have taken the simple case of the one-to-one relationship between two individuals, but the same principles, challenges and dynamics are to be found in other relationships, between families, groups, nations, and between individual and group, and group with individual. On the eightieth anniversary of the Battle of the Somme during World War I, it was very moving to hear the reflection of a 103-year old survivor of the carnage in which over a million men were slaughtered. With great vehemence he said that all war is madness, that there can be no justification for such savagery when people can meet around a table and sort out their differences in dialogue and sharing.

From all of the above it is clear that the answer to the question: 'What is morality?' must focus on the centrality and uniqueness of the human person. Morality has to do with what befits or does not befit persons as persons. One cannot be moral, as distinct from a-moral, without a profound experience of the value and the sacredness of the human person. It is precisely this that marks us off from the rest of creation. This is the most basic of human experiences, the reason why we recognise and accept obligations to other human beings, from the simple commitments of fidelity to promises, repayment of debts, telling the truth, to the extreme manifestation of concern in giving one's life for others. Our most human attitude is that of wonder, awe and gratitude before the mystery of the human person. Our appreciation of the value of persons leads to respect for the sacredness of life, first in persons and then in all living things. Reverence for the mystery of the person is the basis of morality, and morality is the living out of this, discerning what is right in terms of what befits the person as person, and seeing wrongdoing as what is not right and fitting.

Rules still needed
In the relational model of morality there is still room and need for principles, norms and rules, but these serve only as guidelines in the discernment process. The real moral call is centred in the person or groups to whom we respond. It is the business of ethics and moral discernment to discover what is the appropriate response in the various relationships, situations and circumstances, so that gift will predominate over threat and all involved will be enabled to grow. We need to discover what is the appropriate, and therefore right and morally good, response in the various fields of justice, truth, sexual behaviour, marriage and family, politics, economics, technology and medicine. We still have to work out the values, principles, norms and rules to guide us in deciding how to treat life from conception to death, and in identifying our responsibilities to our environment and to the future generations who will inherit the earth that was entrusted to our stewardship.

As mentioned already, the basic question in morality is not so much what should I do, but how should I live, what should I become. By our free decisions we create our own moral character, and by our response to others we affect their growth as well as our own, encouraging and developing it or stunting and blocking it. In all of this it is important to remember the element of process, of growth. There can be no static morality, so the impact of change on our understanding of morality is not a reason for panic. We need to balance the various models of morality so that we are not entrapped in any one narrow view. They each have their advantages, though some may be less helpful than others. To evaluate them properly we need to ask: to what extent are they faithful to the scripture message and to all that is best in our Christian tradition, how do they relate to the experience of today's good-living people in their daily lives, and how useful and effective are they in helping us to see our way through the complex moral issues of our day?

Thanks to the waning of the legal model that dominated so much of our moral tradition, and the development of new approaches, it is no wonder that there is now less unanimous agreement with official Church teaching on many moral subjects, especially when it comes to details. The basic values remain the same and traditional moral principles continue to apply, but in a different context they can lead to conclusions that are at variance with some official teaching. This is quite normal in today's world. Vatican Council II states explicitly that laity must not imagine that Church leaders can readily give a concrete solution to every moral problem, 'or even that such is their mission.' In practice this means that we must relativise our false absolutes, control our lust for certainty, and learn to live with a certain degree of uncertainty. An essential element of maturity is the ability to live creatively with tension. Some of our official teaching would have far more credibility and carry more ring of truth if it were presented a little more tentatively, with a little more humility.

4

MORALITY AND RELIGION

One of the reasons why so many people imagine that morality cannot really change is that they see it as intimately connected with God, the Almighty, the All-wise, the Eternal. Moral truths must be eternal truths. But this is an over-simplification. As a human experience, religion itself changes as it grows and develops, from its primitive, prehistoric form to the sophisticated religions of today. The same growth and development is to be seen within the various religions. Change is a normal and natural human phenomenon. St Teresa of Avila assures us 'Let nothing upset you, let nothing frighten you. Everything is changing; God alone is changeless.' Most religions believe that God does not change, but our understanding of God and our relationship with God in religious experience is constantly changing, for the simple reason that we ourselves are continually changing. Because of the link between morality and religion, the way we think about God influences what we think about morality and *vice versa*. In this context there are three questions worth reflecting on: the changes in religion and in our Catholic tradition, our changed understanding of the 'law of God' as revealed in the Bible, and the precise relationship between morality and religion. An important question discussed by theologians in recent decades has been: is there a specifically Christian morality, and in what way is it special as distinct from ordinary human morality?

The nature and growth of religion
How religion came about in the historical development of human beings is a matter of conjecture. Experts in archaeology, palaeontology, anthropology, psychology and sociology do not agree on any one theory, for the simple reason that we can never know, on purely scientific and historical grounds, what the emergence of human consciousness was really like. The earliest records on which to speculate are burial sites about 60,000

years old and cave drawings of Europe and Africa, dating from 35,000 years ago. We cannot be dogmatic about when and how human beings became aware of themselves through the power of speech and discovered their capacity to change the world and plan their future. This new self-consciousness would have made them aware that they were part of the world of nature, but at the same time that they were different, that they could reflect on their experience and ponder on its deeper meaning.

It seems that there was a spiritual dimension to human experience from the very earliest times. Our early ancestors saw the world as shot through with unseen, magical forces, spirits and gods, but without making any distinction between the material and spiritual aspects of the world. They developed the notion of the Holy, the sacred, and many primitive cultures had a belief in some sort of High God. Certain objects were regarded as sacred and could only be handled by sacred persons, such as priests. There was veneration of the spirits of the dead, and these were treated with respect and awe. Elaborate burial rites indicate a belief in the after-life. There are many mythological stories in which primitive peoples sought to interpret the world and how they came to be in it. Variations of the biblical myth of creation and of a great flood are to be found among widely separated peoples. Some primitive tribes believed that the Great Spirit built a bridge from this world to the next, and that the rainbow is the bridge. Their belief in immortality was linked to moral obligations for this life, so that the good would prosper in the next life.

Anthropologists claim that these various beliefs show the spirituality of our early ancestors, who responded to God in various ways for at least 50,000 years before the rise of formal religion. This spirituality gradually found expression in a religious system of gods, priests, worship and sacrifice. It became a world of shared meaning and eventually developed into formalised religion. Hinduism was the first world religion to arise, about 2000 BC, followed by Shinto 500 years later. Judaism appeared next, with Abraham in 1850 BC and Moses in 1250. Zoroastrianism, Taoism, Confucianism and Buddhism arose during the seventh and sixth centuries BC. Christianity came in the first century AD, Islam about 600 AD, and Sikhism about 1500 AD. From this brief outline it is clear that religion is by no means a simple phenomenon, and that its growth and development involved significant changes over thousands of years. Religion is always coloured by the culture and experience of its believers and practitioners. One could also say that there are different kinds of religion. As Cardinal Newman pointed out, there is the religion of a warlike people, and of a pastoral people, a religion of rough times and a religion of civilized times, superstitious religion and sophisticated religion, a religion of the philosopher, the scholar and the gentleman. There can be different manifestations of the same basic phenomenon. Here again, change is a normal part of life.

Dimensions of religion

Morality is only one dimension of religion, and not necessarily the most important one. Ninian Smart, in his classic work, *The Religious Experience of Mankind*,[1] lists six different dimensions to every religion worthy of the name. They are: the ritual, the mythological, the doctrinal, the ethical, the social and the experiential. A brief explanation of these and of the changes that have taken place in each one in the Catholic tradition may help to clarify the place of morality in religion.

The ritual dimension

The *ritual* or *ceremonial* dimension is the most obvious to outsiders. This is to be seen not only in special religious buildings such as temples and churches, but in various rites of worship like prayers, offerings and gestures. There can be elaborate religious ceremonies like High Mass, but ritual activity also includes simple gestures like genuflecting, closing one's eyes or bowing one's head in prayer. The outer activity expresses an inner attitude, like reverence, thanksgiving or supplication. These ritual actions are a means of being in touch with the unseen world, the spiritual and the divine, and they express, through acting out the ritual, basic truths of a religion's belief-system. Christian baptism or the Eucharistic celebration recall and re-present truths to which the believer is committed, and the meaning of the ritual cannot be understood without reference to the faith-context in which it is performed. Major events of human life, such as birth, marriage, reconciliation, healing, death and burial are celebrated ritually to give them a sacred meaning. It can happen, however, that the actions will be performed without any reference to their meaning, in which case they become empty formal gestures that are religious only in appearance. It was for this kind of outward but empty religious practice that Jesus criticised the Pharisees.

In Christian religion the ritual dimension is called liturgy (from the Greek, meaning public work). Down through the centuries the Church has developed strict rules for the major celebrations, particularly the official celebration of the sacraments, and popular piety created a variety of practices for others. Practically all of these have been culturally conditioned, and have changed considerably through time. Some, like the change to the vernacular languages in place of Greek and Latin, took centuries. The Second Vatican Council was responsible for considerable change in this area of Church life.

The mythological dimension

Religion has to do with the invisible world, and this is symbolised in what is called the *mythological* dimension of religion. The word 'myth' here is not used in the sense of something which is not true. Originally the word meant 'story,' and in the religious context it refers to a story or tradition that reveals to people a fundamental truth about the world and about themselves. It tells them who they are, what is good and bad, and how they are to organise themselves to maintain their self-identity. The mythological stories may not be literally true as referring to historical fact, such as the Genesis account of the creation of the world, the Garden of Eden and the banishment of our first parents to a world of cruelty and pain. Although recognised by some as unhistorical stories, they are believed as myths or stories carrying fundamental truths valuable for life. But some myths in a religious tradition refer to historical events with a religious meaning. The Passover ritual for Jews re-enacts the historical deliverance of their ancestors from slavery in Egypt. Likewise the Last Supper for Christians was an historical event in the earthly life of Jesus, but the story has a deep religious significance which is re-enacted in the liturgy.

In this area too there have been some radical changes in the Christian tradition. For long centuries the foundation-myths of the Bible were taken literally, and scholars thought that the age of the universe could be calculated by adding together the ages of the patriarchs. This was the official teaching of the Church for most of its history. Only in this century did it allow for the possibility of interpreting the seven days of creation as long periods of time, and it was just over fifty years ago that it went a step further and accepted that the first chapters of the book of Genesis need not be taken literally as historical fact. There are Christians who still take a fundamentalist attitude to the Bible and have great difficulty in harmonising their faith with modern science. But the newer understanding of our religious myths brings out more clearly their deeper meaning. The basic truths of faith remain, and they are enhanced by our treating the Bible as a collection of religious writings rather than as a book of history or of natural science.

The doctrinal dimension

The foundation myths of religion are simple stories which carry a deep meaning: they give life and feeling to people's faith and conviction. But the human mind has a hunger for truth, an unrestricted desire to know, so it is only natural that people will want to know what those mythical stories really mean, not just in the past, but in the here and now, and in practice. The reflection and discussion to which this hunger gives rise is *theology*, or *doctrine*, which is a rational analysis of religious faith. A clear example of the difference between mythological, symbolic story and theological doctrine is the contrast between the simple account of creation in the first chapter of the Bible and the scholarly philosophical treatment of the same topic by Thomas Aquinas. The strength of theology is that it tries to present a total picture of reality, a coherent vision which encompasses all of human life and destiny. But theology does not take place in a vacuum, independently of human experience: it is always understood and expressed in terms of people's culture. The theology expressed in the biblical texts of the Old Testament reflect Hebrew thought and culture, but a different theology emerged when the early Christian theologians re-interpreted it in Greek philosophical terms. Further change occurred when the Church's intellectual life was influenced by Roman culture, and this influence increased when the western Church forged closer links with Roman civil authorities.

Greek and Roman theology dominated the Church's life for most of its history, but considerable change has occurred in recent times. In the earlier centuries there were differing theologies, but from the Middle Ages onwards the Church prided itself on a single, uniform theology with only slight variations, stemming from the monumental work of Thomas Aquinas, saint and doctor of the Church. The uniformity was artificially sustained through rigid censorship and control. But the scene is now totally different. Though there is an essential agreed core of doctrines, nowadays one must speak of Catholic theologies in the plural, such as Indian, Asian and African theologies, black theology, feminist theology and liberation theology. Some Church members and leaders find this disturbing, even threatening, but others see it as quite natural, indeed as an enrichment. Once again, we are faced with the phenomenon of change, even radical change, as a normal part of life.

The ethical dimension

The fourth dimension of religion is the *ethical*. World religions are not simply a matter of stories and doctrines: they all have a moral or ethical dimension. Beliefs are not simply abstract thoughts, but a coherent vision of reality and life that should be lived out in practice. The early Christians were first described as followers of *The Way*. Religion is a way of life, with practical implications. Even if the moral obligations and standards are not always lived up to, they are an important element in every religion. Because of their beliefs, believers are committed to follow a particular pattern of behaviour, to accept a certain code of ethics. Down through the ages, religions have been influential in moulding the ethical attitudes of the society to which they belonged. The Indian way of life is significantly different from that of the Chinese, both influenced by their respective religions, and much of the western world shows the influence of Christianity. In practice, however, followers of a particular religion may well fail to live up to its ideals. For example, love of neighbour is central to the Christian faith, but in spite of being the most Catholic country in Africa, Rwanda gave a shocking example of genocide. The inhuman slaughter of whole populations in the former Yugoslavia seems to have been aggravated, if not actually caused, by religious differences. Northern Ireland has one of the most church-going populations in the world, but this did not prevent mindless sectarian killings over many decades. Religions are often institutionalised, so that a particular religion is part of the life of the community, and can have a dominant role in setting rules for community behaviour.

To list the ethical dimension of religion in fourth place could give the impression that religion is primary and morality is secondary, that morality is a consequence of religion. In fact, the opposite is true. Many people presume the primacy of religion because their first experience of moral teaching and obligation was in the context of religion. Parents and other authority figures were accustomed to invoke God as the great enforcer, and they threatened punishment from God for failure to obey what were presented as moral precepts. But religious experience is not logically prior to moral experience. Belief in God develops from other experiences, including moral experience. Moral experience begins in the visible and tangible world, with the experience of freedom and responsibility, and this comes before any religious interpretation of reality. Logically, religious experience comes later; it is the discovery of the deeper meaning of all reality. In the past, and unfortunately still in the present, too many people speak glibly about 'God's will' as though they had a direct insight into the divine mind or could read off a clear and unambiguous code of ethics in the Bible that would bypass the process of discerning right and wrong through human experience. Though intimately connected, morality and religion are two different realities.

Many of the changes that have occurred in the ethical dimension of religion come from the growing separation of Church and state and the development of a more and more secular ethic, cut off from religious influence. This is not necessarily a bad thing, insofar as it challenges religious believers to live by conviction even when not backed up by civil legislation. The Church has an ambiguous history in this regard. When Catholics were in a minority in a country they claimed the right to toleration and fair treatment, but when they were a majority, as in Spain during the Franco regime, they paid scant attention to the rights of minorities, on the grounds that 'error has no rights.' Behind the abstraction of 'error has no rights' it was often forgotten that *people* always have rights to be respected. The modern world, in which concern for the dignity of persons is expressed in openness, consultation, collaboration, accountability and due process, finds it difficult to recognise gospel values in the way in which the Church sometimes exercises its authority over its members.

The social dimension

Each religion is a system of beliefs shared by many individuals and groups. For survival in their own self-identify they need organisation and structure, in which they acquire a communal and social significance. This *social* dimension of religion is to some extent influenced by the group's beliefs and ethical practices. But it sometimes happens that believers modify their beliefs in response to the situation in which they find themselves; for example, Christians can interpret the command to love our neighbour in a way that allows for war for the sake of patriotism. While the first four dimensions of religion express convictions about the nature of the visible and invisible world and indicate how people ought to live their lives in conformity with their beliefs, the social dimension shows how in actual practice people live out their beliefs and how religious institutes operate.

Catholic faith maintains that certain sacramental actions can only be performed by a priest, and this conviction leads the Church to maintain a strict division between priests and laity. The hierarchical structure of the Church is traced back to the intention of Christ and the experience of the early Christians, but in the culturally different climate of today's world there is more emphasis on the Church as the people of God and less concern about clergy as a sacred and privileged group. A renewed appreciation of baptism gives more responsibility to laity. This new responsibility requires that laity be fully involved in the life of the Church, no longer treated as passive receivers of whatever the clerics pass on to them. In today's adult world, the Church cannot afford to continue its traditional paternalism or male-dominated attitudes. So in this area too the Church is in process of change as a normal part of life.

The experiential dimension

The final dimension of religion has to do with its very essence. Religion not only has ideas about the invisible world and practical guidelines on how to approach it, but it also promises an actual experience of that world. This is the *experiential* dimension of religion. The Buddhist monk expects to reach nirvana, a state of deep peace giving special insight into the transcendent. When Christians pray it is not simply to implore some material benefit from God, but also to experience his presence, peace and consolation. All of the great religions began with the religious experience of an individual person, in which they were overcome by awe and devotion. St Paul had a special experience of God in his conversion on the way to Damascus. What made Jesus particularly special was the unique intimacy he enjoyed with his Father in heaven. Mystics down through the ages have described their religious experiences. But on a humbler level very many people, even those with little contact with formal religion, admit to having experiences that can only be described as religious. Religious experiences are not simply the ordinary perceptions of seeing, hearing and touching the material world, but a special awareness of the reality of an invisible world that lends a new depth to ordinary events of everyday life.

Our Catholic tradition shows a long history of religious experience among the mystics and saints and in the lives of ordinary believers. But in recent centuries official documents of Church teaching warned against the dangers of experience, pointing to the aberrations to which it could lead. Too much emphasis on the rational nature of theology made it almost rationalist, leaving little or no room for the imagination, for emotion, for feelings, which were to be mistrusted. In recent decades, however, thanks largely to the charismatic movement, there has been a rediscovery of this important dimension of religion. Although God cannot be put under a microscope for scientific analysis, it is recognised that religious experiences can and do put us in touch with a personal God, and that we can have some discernment of his will through our inner experience.

Once again, it is clear that considerable change has occurred in all dimensions of our religious tradition through the centuries, so new perceptions of morality should cause no surprise. These changes have not been the result of decrees by some religious authority, but natural developments in human experience. They have come about through changes in the surrounding culture. But the Bible itself is not immune to the influence of culture, and it too changed through time. The Jewish-Christian Bible is not a direct revelation as if dictated to human writers by God. A more accurate description of the collection of texts which we call Bible is that it is the *written account of the religious experience of the people of God*. The writing was the final stage. What came first was God's initiative in choosing a small group of nobodies to become his special people. They became his people simply because he chose them, and down through their history he did explicitly with them what he does implicitly in a variety of ways with all people, with the whole human family. The Jewish experience of God was coloured by their developing, changing culture, and when it came to be written down and accepted as biblical text, the text reflected these changes. For this reason a text chosen out of context can only have a distorted meaning, and every text needs careful interpretation.

What does the Bible say?

For many people, morality is rooted in God's law, and the prime source for this is God's revelation in the Bible. But does the Bible give us grounds for thinking that the moral law is a fixed, static entity that comes to us in revelation? Does the Bible give us a code of revealed morality, God's own list of what is right and wrong? Many Christians would say at least an implicit 'Yes' to this question, and some official statements of Church teaching give the impression that a biblical quotation can resolve moral problems like masturbation, homosexuality or contraception, although it is quite clear that the biblical writers had no idea of how these topics are understood today. Pope Pius XI's 1930 encyclical on marriage, *Casti connubii*, is a good example of this, referring to Genesis 38. The text says:

> Those who, in performing the conjugal act, deliberately deprive it of its natural power and efficacy, act against nature and do something which is shameful and intrinsically immoral. We cannot wonder, then, if we find evidence in the sacred scriptures that the Divine Majesty detests this unspeakable crime with the deepest hatred and has sometimes punished it with death, as St Augustine observes: 'Sexual intercourse even with a lawful wife is unlawful and shameful if the conception of offspring is prevented. This is what Onan, the son of Juda, did, and on that account God put him to death.'

The Bible text referred to here describes how Onan, in fulfilment of the Mosaic law, should have raised up children for his dead brother by sleeping with his sister-in-law, but instead spilled his semen on the ground every time he had intercourse with her. Scripture scholars have long since shown that this text says nothing about sexual morality as such; it condemns Onan for his failure to carry out his duty to his dead brother. In fact none of the more recent documents of the Church on the subject of contraception quote this scriptural argument.

The mere fact that a particular point is described in the Bible as 'God's law' does not mean that it is still binding on today's Christians. Indeed those who believe that the moral obligation of a law comes from the fact that it is 'in the Bible' will have difficulty in explaining how God can command behaviour that would nowadays be regarded as highly immoral. In the Genesis story Onan is condemned by God for not doing his duty, namely to produce children for him, but this would mean having an adulterous relationship with his sister-in-law, Tamar. Furthermore, God's design in the story is realised by Tamar tempting her father-in-law into having intercourse with her by pretending to be a prostitute. This is only one of the many cases in the Bible where incest, fornication, polygamy and deceit are presented as part of the divine plan.

The book of Deuteronomy has two unusually harsh texts. Moses, in God's name, commands that 'If two men are having a fight and the wife of one tries to help her husband by grabbing the other man's genitals, show her no mercy; cut off her hand' (Deut. 25:11). In the matter of obedience to parents, Moses, again in God's name, lays down the law:

> Suppose a man has a son who is stubborn and rebellious, a son who will not obey his parents, even though they punish him. His parents are to take him before the leaders of the town where he lives and make him stand trial. They are to say to them: 'Our son is stubborn and rebellious and refuses to obey us; he wastes money and is a drunkard.' Then the men of the city are to stone him to death, and so you will get rid of this evil. Everyone in Israel will hear what has happened and be afraid. (Deut. 21:18–21)

It is difficult to imagine such texts being proclaimed today in a liturgical ceremony, with the reader adding: 'This is the word of God.'

There are passages in the New Testament that have the appearance of straightforward moral commands, which no modern Christian would accept as binding without considerable interpretation. Jesus tells his apostles to have neither gold nor silver nor purse nor more than one tunic. He invites his followers to turn the other cheek when they have been struck, but when he himself received a blow he asked for the reason. He says that eyes should be plucked out and hands cut off if they happen to be an occasion of sin. St Paul taught that a woman who prays without covering her head dishonours it. He admonished slaves to be obedient to their master and asked masters to be kind to their slaves, but at no point did he criticise the institution of slavery, which today's Church condemns in the strongest possible terms.

These few examples make clear that the quotation of a passage from the Bible cannot be taken as the literal word of God, expressing his precise will for moral behaviour. To understand any text, from whatever source, one must ask certain questions: what does it say (language), what does it mean (context and culture), is it true and in what sense is it true, and in the case of a law for action it must be asked: how is it applied? Until we have answered these questions satisfactorily in the case of biblical texts, we cannot proclaim them as God's word with any real meaning for people's lives today. To accept and enforce them literally in a fundamentalist manner can lead to the most terrible results, like amputating the hand of convicted thieves.

Were the commandments revealed?

There are Christians who like to think that the ten commandments, the foundation-stone as it were of Jewish and Christian morality, were given directly by God to Moses on Mount Sinai amid thunder and lightning, and that they were immediately carved on two tablets of stone. Hopefully most people are aware that this is not to be taken literally. But what is the point of the story if it is not true in the literal sense? In fact, scholars have shown that most of the ten commandments were widely known centuries earlier by non-Israelite peoples, and were the common law of Mesopotamia. Some of them can be found in the code of Hammurabi, five centuries before Moses. The Israelites formulated their laws over a long period of time, and in doing so they drew on the accumulated wisdom of the surrounding peoples as well as on their own experience of what was needed to keep a people together in peaceful harmony. In the early history of Israel, the common law concerning marriage was not very different from what it was in the neighbouring civilisations. Polygamy, legalised concubinage and divorce prevailed there as elsewhere. The Jews were no different from the rest of the Near East.

Yet there was a difference, namely the religious meaning of the laws.

For the Israelites, they were seen in a totally new light. They were accepted as consequences of the great mystery of God's covenant with his people. The Deuteronomy text says:

> Moses called together all the people of Israel and said to them: 'People of Israel, listen to all the laws that I am giving you today. Learn them and be sure that you obey them. At Mount Sinai the Lord our God made a covenant, not only with our fathers, but with all of us who are living today. There on the mountain the Lord spoke to you face to face from the fire.' (Deut. 5:1–4)

This covenant between God and his people was the source of unity between the mixed multitude that Moses led out of Egypt, and it provided the basis upon which early Israelite history was organised. The commandments became more than simply laws imposed from without by an earthly sovereign. They described the kind of ethical behaviour that should characterise the life of God's people, so the commandments would become inner personal attitudes. They would be obeyed out of gratitude for God's goodness and not out of fear evoked by threat of punishment. In this way, the commonsense rules necessary for social harmony were no longer simply ordinary laws of society, but essential elements of the covenant relationship between God and his people. They took on a deep religious meaning.

Much the same is true of the New Testament. Jesus left no detailed code of morality, so Paul and the early Christian communities simply fell back on the moral codes current at the time, which happened to come from the Stoic philosophers. The lists of virtues in Paul's letters are largely the household rules common in his time (Col. 3:18–4:1; Ephes. 5:22–6:9; 1 Cor. 6:9–10). But in the biblical text they take on a new meaning, a religious meaning. What were simply considered vices in the Greek world were now used to describe what is opposed to 'life in the Spirit,' and virtues became the 'fruits of the Spirit.' It may be disappointing not to be able to find 'new bits of morality' laid down in the Bible as information revealed by God, but it does not follow that the Bible need have no place in our moral discernment. It is still a valuable resource to enlighten us and enable us to live morally good lives, if we know how to understand and use it.

Insights from scripture
There are many things we find in scripture to inspire and guide us in

deciding moral issues, namely basic truths that provide a wider and deeper context for our reflection, and insights that can throw a totally new light on situations, such as: God's fatherhood and the consequent brotherhood and sisterhood of all people; the goodness of creation; the world entrusted to our stewardship and responsibility; God's care for all people, especially the weak; the dignity of each human person, created in the image of God; God's patience and never-ending forgiveness; the example of Jesus in his intimate relationship with his Father and his total availability to people; his attitude to evil and his acceptance of the cross; the sermon on the mount; the beatitudes. These insights will not give us an immediate solution to a concrete moral problem, but they can sensitise us to certain values, and colour our attitude to daily life. We can also be helped by studying how God's people in both Old and New Testaments dealt with particular problems in the past. But their solutions cannot be the last word for us, since we live in a different culture.

Reference to a different culture is not simply a matter of a difference between the Bible and our modern world. Change is an integral part of both. As mentioned already, the Bible is the written account of the religious experience of the people of God. That experience was a lived reality that grew and developed over centuries, so that within the Bible itself very considerable changes are to be seen. There is an obvious growth in moral sensitivity and refinement from the time of the patriarchs to the time of St Paul. The wholesale slaughter of men, women and children carried out in God's name and with his approval that was common in earlier times would be totally out of place in the New Testament. The early parts of the Bible show concern about some basic human values, the same values to which we subscribe today. But some of the decisions made by the patriarchs about how to safeguard and promote these values are quite abhorrent to the moral feelings of today's world. For example, we believe that hospitality is an important value in human life, but we shrink from the way Lot sacrificed his daughters for the sake of it. When the men of Sodom wanted to have their way with his two visitors, Lot entreated them:

> Friends, don't do such a wicked thing. Look, I have two daughters who are still virgins. Let me bring them out to you, and you can do whatever you want with them. But don't do anything to these men; they are guests in my house and I must protect them. (Gen. 19:7–8)

A similar incident is described in the book of Judges (19:20–28). We can have many human values in common with our early ancestors of the Bible, but we rank them differently, and we have some that were unknown or not important to those of an earlier time, such as democracy, the rights of women, equality between the sexes. When the Old Testament spoke of a man violating a woman, there was little indication that it was an offence against the physical integrity and personal dignity of the woman; the harm was to her husband if she were married, or to her father if she were unmarried, and it was to these men that compensation had to be paid.

These brief comments on the complexity of biblical texts should warn against a too facile recourse to scripture in the hope of discovering 'what does God say' about a particular moral problem. St Paul mentions that homosexuals are excluded from the kingdom of heaven (1 Cor. 6:9), but he had no knowledge of homosexuality as we know it today. He knew it only as a perversion and it is possible that he was thinking of temple prostitutes. Moreover, if his words were to be taken as the final argument against homosexuals because 'it is God's law,' then why not use another Bible quotation for the world of fashion, in which the sacred writer says: 'Women are not to wear men's clothing, and men are not to wear women's clothing: the Lord your God hates people who do such things' (Deut. 22:5)?

To sum up, the Bible is important, but it is not absolute. It contains no revealed code of moral behaviour that we can take literally as 'God's will.' The morality we discover in the Bible had to be discovered gradually and formulated by the people of God in the light of God's covenant with them, and on the basis of their experience, an experience that changed over time. What we find in the Bible, therefore, is culturally conditioned and needs careful interpretation. But our interest in the Bible should not be reduced to a search for practical solutions to moral problems. In fact, there are no infallible, divinely-revealed, not-to-be-questioned solutions to our moral problems. The inter-dependence between morality and religion is much deeper than that. A Christian making a moral decision needs to take account of the whole biblical and Christian tradition of beliefs, stories, myths and symbols. This provides a Christian vision, leading to basic attitudes and dispositions which are bound to colour one's evaluation of situations and finally one's decisions.

Is Christian morality different?
When we search the Bible for God's will, Jesus stands out as the one in whom all God's revelation is fulfilled, the perfect Word of God, God in

human form, God made visible. The previous chapter mentioned discipleship of Jesus as one of the models of morality, and indeed Christians see him as the norm for all morality. To remember Christ and to contemplate the significance of his words and work is part of making moral judgments in the Christian life. The figure of Jesus provides Christians with a source of illumination and a criterion of judgment in moral problems. He gives insight and direction, he shows something of the way in which his disciples are to follow. However, this does not mean that Christians are morally superior to others, nor that only Christians can recognise what is morally good. But it does mean that those whose lives are genuinely nurtured by the Christian community, who are called to faith in God through Jesus, and who commit themselves to him in discipleship are given illumination and guidance from him in their moral lives. Those who follow him will not allow their lives to be determined by their own powerful desires and interests, nor by mere loyalty to family, group, or nation, but first and foremost by Christ. Everything must be evaluated in the light of Christ as norm. But accepting Christ as norm does not solve the difficult problem of deciding what is morally right or wrong in practice. A factual analysis is needed to show what forms of human behaviour can be labelled as genocide, adultery, cruelty to children, exploitation, or immoral medical interventions, etc. This is the business of ordinary human reason. But does it follow that there is a special Christian morality specifically distinct from general human morality, that there is some plus factor over and above what non-Christians think of as morality?

This question has been much discussed in recent decades and most theologians would say that in terms of *material content* there is no difference between Christian and non-Christian morality. There is existentially only one morality common to all human beings, rooted in their very humanity and responsibility. Christian morality is not distinctive in its basic goals or its fundamental principles, since these are shared with all serious-minded people of all traditions. This is not a novel position. Already in the thirteenth century Thomas Aquinas held that the law of Christ of itself adds no new particular moral prescriptions to what can be perceived by human reason alone. On the basis of common humanity it should be possible for all human beings to dialogue together in a common search for what is genuinely human, and therefore morally good, and to recognise what is morally evil. All could agree on a generally valid natural morality.

But at the same time it must be recognised that Christian faith does make a difference, indeed a significant difference. What is different is the special context in which the moral life is perceived and the special place given to Jesus Christ and his teaching, not for mere external imitation, but as the criterion and inspiration for a whole style of life. When a Christian performs a morally good act, it is not done simply in obedience to a law or in relation to God as the Absolute, but the person relates to God as Father, who gives us his love and salvation in the person of Jesus his Son, even when the action seems at first to be merely conduct conforming to human morality. The new context comes from the fact that in faith the Christian accepts certain realities unknown to others: the person of Christ, the Holy Spirit at work in people, the Christian community of the Church, the sacraments, and the special guidance that comes through the teaching authority of the Church. It is these beliefs that make us what we are as Christians and they must be reflected in our actions. The influence of these beliefs will be at the level of deeper and richer motivation. We may do the same things as others, but with a special awareness and a deeper motivation.

The Vatican Council's document on *The Church in the Modern World* states that 'faith throws a new light on everything, manifests God's design for our total vocation, and thus directs the mind to solutions which are fully human' (n. 11). It goes on to say that 'Only God, who created us in his own image and ransomed us from sin, provides a fully adequate answer to these questions. This he does through what he has revealed in Christ his Son, who became man. To follow Christ, the perfect human being, *is to become more human oneself*' (n. 41). If we are invited to consider today's problems 'in the light of the gospel and human experience,' and if faith directs us to solutions that are fully human, we gradually develop a Christian outlook and disposition that enable us to discern the truly human with greater facility and depth. If we believe that God's grace can come to the aid of our human weakness, purify our hearts and clarify our vision in our search for what is truly human, and therefore morally good, this is what is distinctive of Christian morality.

Religion and sin

Sin is the word used to describe moral evil when seen in the context of religion, as distinct from ethics or civil law. The Christian ideal is to do everything as done to the Lord, so shortcomings are considered as against a divinely given law, as grieving the Holy Spirit. Sin is primarily a religious and theological reality, a symbol which expresses our alienation from God. As a symbol, it was subject to historical and cultural development, from biblical times to the present day. The cultural conditioning of past centuries was so strong that the word sin has almost become trivialised in today's secularised world. The popular press often uses it to refer to sexual misconduct, but seldom applies it to economic oppression or the abuse of power. It is still a reality, but needs a better presentation to make sense in today's world. For many centuries the emphasis on personal sin left many people with a crippling fear of self and a doubting of their own self-worth. A more balanced approach has developed in recent times. As mentioned earlier, we are most like God in our freedom, and we are created to be free, to grow and develop into the fullness of the maturity of Christ. We do this by saying 'Yes' to the world, to life, to our neighbour, and in and through all of this, to God. To say 'No' is to sin, to alienate ourselves from the world, from life, from our true selves, from our brothers and sisters in the human family, and ultimately from God who created us for life, for friendship and love. If the glory of God is the human person fully alive, sin can be seen as anything that violates our human dignity, anything that restricts or blocks freedom, in ourselves or others.

The Genesis story of the fall of our 'first parents' is not historical fact. It tells us nothing about what happened at the beginning of time, but describes what is happening to people all of the time. It needs to be read, not in the past tense, but in the continuous present, with Adam and Eve standing for all human beings of all times. It describes the psychology of all sin, which is the human self-assertion of those who want to be God, who want to go their own way in deciding what is right and wrong. The Garden of Eden is a beautiful picture of how God meant us to live, in harmony with ourselves and the surrounding world, in partnership with others, not ashamed of being fully known because we have nothing to hide, and enjoying intimacy with God walking with us in the garden. Sin means saying 'No' to all of this, and thus becoming alienated from our true selves, from our closest companions, from our environment which now seems hostile, and most of all from God, from whom we hide in guilt and shame. This kind of approach speaks more to the condition of today's Christians. It makes sense of their experience, but especially it gives them consolation and hope. Our human story begins, not with sin, but with God's infinite and intimate love, which we can never lose. Sin is something that happens along the way. In a sense it is statistically normal.

Irish theologian Gabriel Daly makes the very important point that sin is not another name for crime, felony or misdemeanour. It is a religious term for something which may also have those other labels, but is seen differently in the context of religion and faith. The word sin always always implies hope, the possibility of a change of heart, of conversion, expiation, and most of all God's forgiveness and the consolation and challenge of a new start. The English mystic, Julian of Norwich, says that Jesus told her that 'sin is necessary, but all will be well, and all will be well, and every kind of thing will be well.' St Paul assures us that 'Where sin increased, God's grace increased much more' (Rom. 5:20), and when he said that 'all things work towards good for those who love God,' St Augustine added: 'Yes, even sin.'

New sins?

For centuries the Christian examination of conscience was fairly stereo-typed, with the same list of sins against the commandments. But when the concept of sin is broadened to include all the ways in which we can say 'No' to God by saying 'No' to life, to the world, to ourselves and others, it is not so easy to draw up a list. When sin is seen as the refusal to grow in humanity and into the likeness of Christ, how do we measure? When sin is seen as inhumanity, how do we recognise what counts as sin? In how many ways can we be inhuman, to ourselves and to others? Honesty and justice are easily measured in one-to-one personal relations, but they are more difficult to assess in the world of corporate business. Are we not sinning when we allow our concern for the poor and the deprived to wither away through inaction, indifference? How many inhuman regimes in history have come to power through the inaction of good Christians who failed to see that politics is about the common good and is within the scope of morality. The unjust and oppressive social structures that condemn millions of people to slavery are now seen as sinful, and a challenge to conscience.

Men can now recognise how they sin in discriminating against women, offending their personal dignity. But some women theologians have highlighted new sins by pointing to forms of sin which may be more peculiar to women than pride or lust for power, such as triviality, distractibility, dependence on others for their own self-definition, sentimentality, gossipy sociability and mistrust of reason, which can amount to under-development or denial of their own self-worth. Sometimes self-denial for the sake of others, not wanting to have any real self oneself, may seem like virtues, but they could be real sins because they are saying 'No' to their own God-given self-worth.

Perhaps the new sins that are least recognised, least acknowledged and seldom repented of are those committed by Church officials against human freedom and human dignity in their abuse of power. These sins are all the more serious for being done in the name of God. It is not necessary to go back centuries to the Inquisition to find examples. In several areas of today's world the Church has not been gospel-like, for example in its silence in the face of massive injustice, and bishops who sided with, and at times even defended, cruel dictatorships were inadequate images of Jesus the Good Shepherd. In the gospels, the real sinners for Jesus were those members of the religious establishment who blinded themselves to his message, who arrogantly behaved as though God were their own private possession. All who have influence and authority in the Church have a heavy responsibility in how they use it. Does their leadership and administration free people to grow into the fullness of the maturity of Christ, or do they prefer to keep people passive and subservient? Do they listen to lay women and men who have the authority of their own knowledge and experience, and involve them in the common search for deeper truth, especially moral truth in the areas of sexuality, marriage, bio-technology? Are they sensitive to the suffering caused to conscientious dissenters by harsh treatment and sometimes blatant injustice in official procedures that fall below the standards now common in the outside world? It is no service to the credibility of the Church to pretend that its structures and officials are beyond question. One can be totally loyal to the Church and love it passionately while admitting that all its members, including its various officials, are ordinary human beings.

A new context, new ideals
Just as the religious faith of the people of God in the Old and New Testaments saw the obligations of human morality in a new context, in the context of the covenant relationship with God and as a consequence of the new life in Christ, our faith today enables us to view the demands of being fully human as a response to the call of God in Jesus. Our faith provides us with a new stimulus and motivation to act morally, puts before us the attractive, impressive and challenging model of Jesus in his humanity, and through his Holy Spirit gives us the power to cope with our sinfulness and respond to his call. His teaching and example make us more sensitive to ideals above the normal moral obligations, like turning the other cheek, going the extra mile, forgoing our rights, loving our enemies, and they remind us of a theology of suffering, of failure and the cross. Likewise our belonging to a Christian community can make

demands on us like participation in the Eucharist and celebration of sacraments. Our belief in an intimate personal relationship with God can make us sensitive to invitations in a certain direction that will be ours alone. All of this is special to Christians.

The most fundamental moral obligation for humans is to become actually what we are potentially, to grow to the fullness of our humanity, to the full maturity of a responsible human being. If as Christians we are called to follow Jesus, who is not only God in human form, but also the perfection of humanity, the more Christ-like we become, the more fully human we become. But the opposite is also true: the more fully human we become, the more Christ-like we are. As St Irenaeus puts it: 'The glory of God is the human being fully alive.' Although Christians have the special privilege of an explicit knowledge of Christ, they will meet many non-Christians who are Christ-like. This is a reminder that Christians have no monopoly of salvation, any more than they have a monopoly of morality, of truth or goodness. Morality and religion are distinct but inter-connected. Hopefully the above reflections may clarify the relationship and show that neither one is a fixed, static reality. Both are living, changing human experiences, and change is something that is natural to both.

5

DOES NATURE CHANGE?

When the Church solemnly pronounces on matters of morality it quotes Scripture whenever possible, but quite often bases its reasons on 'nature' as an indication of God's law for human beings. The reference to nature points to a reality beyond personal whim. It is taken as an objective standard for moral behaviour, a criterion or measure for deciding what is morally right or wrong. In the midst of so much change it seems that the natural law provides an unchanging centre for morality, a reliable continuity behind the surface changes of culture. Since nature is a God-given fact and not a human creation, what we discover as the laws of nature can easily be seen as the laws of God. This notion has been central to Catholic moral theology, which claims that its teaching can be applied always, everywhere and for everyone because it is not linked to a single culture, or even to directly revealed truth, but is an expression of nature itself, which is universal. Because Catholic teaching is rooted in nature and does not come from any religious revelation, it should make sense not only to believers but to all people of good will. In fact, some of the most important recent encyclicals have been addressed to this wider audience of the whole world. The word 'natural' is often used to mean normal, common, non-artificial, words which point to a stable, easily recognisable reality not subject to major change. But is it true that nature does not or cannot change?

Natural law
In fact, the long history of moral discussion shows that there has always been an acceptance of something like natural law as a foundation or reference point for all other laws. People have always appealed to a justice higher than law, against which all law must be judged. It is spoken of as the unwritten law, the natural moral law, the law of God. St Paul says that the gentiles have this law written in their hearts (Rom. 2:15). Human

beings are not a law unto themselves, the sole arbiters of right and wrong, but they are dependent on God, their creator. As mentioned in the previous chapter, the Bible has no new code of morality revealed by God. Whenever it presents moral laws that are binding in today's world, they are no more than the precepts of natural law. For well over two thousand years, right up to our own times, all the major writers on morality, in spite of wide differences, have held some version of natural law, a law rooted in the very nature of the human person.

However, although the term 'natural law' was generally accepted in a long tradition, it is not quite accurate as a description of the reality. The natural law is not 'natural' in the sense of the physical, chemical, botanical, and zoological laws of the human and subhuman world, laws which describe how the natural world works unless interfered with by humans. It is a *moral* law, which is essentially different. Nor is it a 'law' like the written laws which carry penalties for disobedience. Indeed the term has a variety of meanings, and different elements have been stressed in the course of history. This means that there is no single understanding of natural law universally accepted as such, although there is consensus on the need for, and indeed the existence of, a natural law to underpin morality and all just laws. The Greek Stoics seem to have been the first to stress the importance of nature in morality. They recognised nature as a well-organised structure of which human beings are only a part, and humans can thrive only by respecting the order of nature. Aristotle, in the fourth century BC, developed this notion further, but emphasised not so much the overall structure of the world as the driving force within individual beings striving towards their natural activity and their own perfection. Since reason is the distinctive feature of human nature, morally good actions are those which are guided by reason towards their natural end.

Nature before reason

In the first century BC the Roman writer Cicero continued this idea of action guided by reason, but added a new emphasis in terms of establishing social order, taking account of interpersonal relations and the needs of society. In the third century AD the development of natural law theory took a new turn with the Roman jurist Ulpian, who spoke of natural law as what nature teaches all animals, and not just humans. It is almost like instinct. This was an unfortunate turn insofar as the specifically human element of reason took second place to the physical faculties of people, and these were linked to similar powers in animals. The emphasis on physical nature seemed to give more objectivity to natural law as something 'given' or laid down by the Creator, which human beings could not and should not manipulate, whereas the emphasis on reason seemed to leave more room for flexibility and variety, and therefore something less fixed and absolute. This approach gave primacy to the dictates of physical nature, with less attention paid to elements that are essentially part of human personality, like reason, freedom, affectivity and personal relationships. One would like to think that this upside-down view of natural law as a source of morality were a mere parenthesis in the history of moral theory, but in fact it has played a central role in Catholic teaching down to the present day and its influence is one of the main reasons why non-Catholics and indeed very many Catholic theologians have problems with some current teaching of the Church.

Thomas Aquinas tried to accommodate both views of natural law, when he defined a human right as 'the rational ordering of a natural inclination.' The natural inclination refers to the basic thrusts or appetites of human nature: towards life, food, clothing, shelter, sexual activity and reproduction, care and upbringing of offspring, human relations, friendship, intellectual inquiry, social organisation, and religion. These form the basis or foundation of moral obligation insofar as they are indications of the Creator's will as to the shape of human life. Those that are found in the animal kingdom are regulated by instinct, but in human life they need to be regulated by reason, and it is this combination of basic natural inclination and the regulation by practical reason that leads to the formulation of human rights and obligations, or moral imperatives, which ultimately are recognised as natural law. The twelfth-century St Bernard said that a person born with reason and not using it is no better than the beasts; for the beast who does not rule himself by reason has an excuse, since this gift is denied to him by nature, but humans have no excuse. Natural law, therefore, can be said to combine an order of nature and an order of reason, and it is reason which works out the various commands which govern practical moral living.

Blueprint, maker's instructions

The logic behind this position is to be found in the 'blueprint' or 'maker's instructions' theory of natural law that for centuries was the main approach of Catholic moralists. When one buys a motor car or other piece of machinery it usually comes with a handbook of rules on how to use it properly. They are not arbitrarily made up by the seller, but they are a careful description of the machine and how it functions. By following the rules carefully one can get the best out of the machine, because they are a description of its nature, and it is only by respecting its nature that one can benefit from it fully. To ignore or disobey the rules by using the wrong kind of fuel or mishandling brakes or gears can lead to serious or even tragic consequences. It pays to respect the specific nature of the machine. The handbook of rules is in fact the law to be obeyed. But if one had never seen the rule-book, it would be possible to get a clever mechanic who by studying the machine and the inter-relation of its various parts would be able to arrive at a knowledge of their function, and as a result of his study and experimentation be able to re-write the handbook for the guidance of those who use the machine. In the same way, nature (the complex world of living and non-living beings, plants, animals and humans) is an expression of divine intelligence, and from careful examination of its various components human beings can arrive at an idea of how God intended them to function, and so discover what is right and wrong, what is God's law, natural law.

The basic insight here would seem to make sense, but the blueprint or maker's instructions theory of natural law was exaggerated to the point that it has given rise to serious misunderstanding, and is responsible for much of the confusion in contemporary Catholic discussions of moral issues. Because the nature of human beings can be studied and described in the same way as the nature of animals, plants or non-living things, the natural moral law is often compared to the laws of physics, chemistry, physiology, etc. – clear, fixed, stable, needing only to be read off or 'discovered' in human nature. But this is to leave out of account the most distinctive feature of human nature, namely our creative intelligence and free will. Although our basic human needs remain the same, our human nature is not something static and fixed for all time. The human person is a being of possibilities, and we create our nature as we choose among these various possibilities. We change inwardly each time we adopt a new image of ourselves, or get a new understanding of ourselves. For example our understanding of our bodies, of our sexuality, or of our relationship to the material universe is radically different from what it was in primitive times. There was a time when justice demanded that every family or group have its own cave, whereas nowadays we are outraged that anyone should have to live in a cave. We change outwardly insofar as we fashion instruments and create technology which become extensions of ourselves, and with the help of these we can change the world we inhabit. Until recently the moon was an object of contemplation, whereas nowadays it is a place that can be visited. Many of our inventions, like

3M SelfCheck™ System

Customer name: Stephanie Coffey

Title: soul's journey into God ; The tree of life ;
The life of St Francis
ID: 0101122834
Due: 03/10/2017 21:50

Title: problem of evil : a reader
ID: 0101332129
Due: 03/10/2017 21:50

Items that you renewed

Title: soul's journey into God ; The tree of life ;
The life of St Francis
ID: 0101122834
Due: 03/10/2017 21:50

Title: Does morality change
ID: 0101144515
Due: 03/10/2017 21:50

Title: problem of evil : a reader
ID: 0101332129
Due: 03/10/2017 21:50

Title: new Jerusalem Bible
ID: 0103615420
Due: 03/10/2017 21:50

Total items: 6
19/09/2017 13:09
Checked out: 4
Overdue: 0
Hold requests: 0
Ready for pickup: 0

Thank you for using the
3M SelfChe

printing, motor and air travel, bring about a whole new phase of civilisation, as was mentioned in Chapter 2. Thus, change is an essential part of human nature. It is a mistake to imagine that God created an original human nature in an earthly paradise at the beginning of time, to which any subsequent development must be considered merely an addition, something almost artificial.

Physical nature

This fundamentalist understanding of human nature tends to give an exaggerated importance to physical and biological nature in determining moral norms. The impression is given that we can best discover God's plan for us by studying the human functions in their natural state, prior to any intervention by human intelligence. Thus, speech is for communicating knowledge, eating for the conservation of health, sex for reproduction. But this simplistic approach ignores the fact that these activities are *human*, and have their full human meaning only in a human context, which includes our intelligence, free will and the whole world of culture, of shared meaning. The laws governing these activities insofar as they are physical are not moral laws. We may not wantonly ignore them in our moral evaluation of situations, but they tell us little or nothing about how these activities are to be used for our responsible self-development and growth as persons, and this is what morality is all about.

What can be read directly in our physical or biological nature is nothing more than facts (like the law of gravity, etc.), namely how nature works spontaneously. For example, nature causes ovulation to be suspended during the early stages of lactation in a woman who has given birth (among people who use only breast-feeding), and the same effect is produced by taking contraceptive pills (which follow natural laws in their manufacture and in the way they work in the human system). Both of these are *facts of nature*. Many contraceptive pills could be ruled out as immoral because of their dangerous side-effects, and this would certainly rule out abortifacients. They are wrong because of their effects, not because they are artificial. Indeed for a person with an unusually delicate stomach or a blood clotting problem it could be morally irresponsible to use otherwise common and safe medicaments, likewise because of the effects.

The fact that the contraceptive pills involve human intelligence and skill to produce the appropriate chemicals in the laboratory does not make them less natural, since the ingredients combine and function according to the laws of chemistry and physiology, and the human intelligence that manufactured them is itself part of the same God-given nature. But 'nature' does not tell us whether it is morally better to make use of one rather than the other of these facts of nature. That one is considered 'artificial' is not sufficient ground for moral condemnation, otherwise tranquillisers and most of the techniques of modern medicine would be immoral. The patient undergoing serious surgery, whether pope or pauper, will want the most qualified and effective anaesthetist possible rather than one who uses only so-called 'natural' methods. To understand what is morally good, we need an understanding of the meaning and importance of the particular activity or fact of nature in the totality of the human person as such. Thus, which method of birth control is morally right for a couple in the exercise of responsible parenthood will depend on a variety of factors, and not simply on whether it is 'artificial' or not. This will be considered in more detail in a later chapter.

The priority given to the 'order of nature' over the 'order of reason,' which has had such a negative influence on Catholic moral theology for centuries, dates from St Thomas, who argued that the former comes directly from *God* as the author of nature, whereas reason comes from the *human person*. The clear implication is that God takes precedence over the human person, who is simply his creature. Thomas concluded that 'in matters of action it is most grave and shameful to act against things as determined by nature.' On this principle he explained that sexual activities which exclude procreation (which is the God-given purpose of sex) are more serious than those which do not exclude it. Thus, masturbation, contraceptive marital intercourse, homosexuality and bestiality, in which procreation is not possible, are against biological nature and are therefore more serious than sins which do not exclude procreation, like fornication, adultery, incest. The former go directly against God's will, manifested in biological nature, whereas the latter are more in keeping with that nature.

Nature versus reason

This traditional approach is open to many objections. It claims that the order of things is dictated by God's providence, that this order can be discovered from the regular and uniform physical laws of nature, and that it is our duty to follow this order as God's will. But this approach confuses human biological structure with human nature, and assumes that nature is something static, unchanging. It ignores the fact that our God-given creative intelligence is also part of the divine plan, and that since the beginning of time human beings have been altering nature, trying to remedy its defects and improve its potential. Should we remain passive in the face of deformed new-born babies? For several decades now infants born with defective heart valves have been saved by surgery, which is a major interference with nature, and therefore artificial. If the physical and biological understanding of 'nature' were to be taken to its logical conclusion, the natural law would be broken by people who shave, cut their hair, trim their nails, travel by air, walk on their hands or stand on their heads. One might well ask: 'Is it natural to wear clothes?' These examples may be dismissed with a smile as bordering on levity, but the reality is that the miracles of modern surgery or medical technology, which save millions of lives, are artificial. They are the result of human intervention in the order of nature. In fact, it is more and more difficult to find anything in daily life that is is not artificial, and that can be described as purely natural.

Unfortunately the simplistic reasoning behind the blueprint theory of natural law is still at work today. In discussing the morality of helping a husband and wife whose only possibility of having a baby is through *in vitro* fertilisation, official Church teaching allows intervention only 'to assist the normally consummated act to achieve its objective.' In the 1950s this was interpreted by some theologians to mean that if a syringe were used to collect the semen deposited in the course of normal intercourse in order to inject it further along its natural path, the physical separation from its 'natural' contact with the female body by having it even momentarily in the syringe, would make the procedure artificial and therefore unlawful. Physicians wonder how moralists can think up such theories. Present Church teaching holds that the *place* where ovum and sperm are helped to combine must of necessity be the Fallopian tube and not the laboratory. The tube is indeed the 'more natural and normal' place, but if this is physically impossible why should recourse to the *in vitro* procedure be ruled out as artificial, unnatural and therefore immoral, provided all abuses have been avoided? This weakness of the blueprint theory will be discussed more fully in the chapter on responsible parenthood, an area where the condemnation of everything labelled 'artificial' has lost so much credibility for Church teaching.

Examples from the past

It is sobering to recall some of the practices that in past centuries were condemned as unnatural. The Eastern Church prohibited third and fourth marriages as against natural law. The writers of the early western

Church forbade even killing in self-defence on the same grounds; it was left to St Augustine to define the distinction between justifiable homicide and murder. Clement thought both ear-rings and nose-rings equally forbidden by the laws of nature. Tertullian could not bear the actor's make-up or the garland of flowers, because they were unnatural, and he reminded us that 'ours is a God of nature.'

St Albert the Great, the professor of St Thomas Aquinas, is an interesting example of how 'nature' was quoted to determine what was lawful or sinful in sexual intercourse. After a detailed explanation of how appropriately God had designed the shape and location of the male and female sex organs in human beings in order to achieve their procreative purpose, he concluded that

> nature teaches that the proper position for intercourse is that the woman should be on her back and that the man lie on her belly . . . and women conceive more easily in this position than in others . . . Intercourse sideways is a minor deviation from this, sitting is greater, standing is greater still, and greatest of all is from behind, like beasts of burden. Some people have said that this last is a mortal sin, but I disagree with this. (Sentences 4.31.24)

Albert is simply reflecting the common teaching of the Church, not only of the thirteenth century, but for centuries before and after his time. He is a good example of the mind-set which focused on physical nature as a criterion of morality, because he was no lightweight, ivory tower theologian. He was one of the outstanding thinkers of his time, often described as the 'universal teacher,' and his works were both voluminous and encyclopaedic. As well as biblical and theological works and sermons, he wrote on logic, ethics, metaphysics, astronomy, physics, chemistry, biology, geography, geology, botany, and human and animal physiology. He did experimental work in many of these fields, and he is outstanding for his recognition of the autonomy of human reason. But his view of 'what nature ordains' in this area simply reflects social custom and the culture of his time rather than God's will. Committed Christians reflecting on 'nature' in today's culture would smile at his idea of nature, since they have no scruple in believing that whatever husband and wife do to each other in their lovemaking is morally good as long as it is mutually acceptable and is not offensive to the human dignity of either one.

As recently as 1931 Pius XI wrote an encyclical on Christian education in which he condemned co-education as against nature. His reference to natural law would seem to make this an absolute statement valid for all time. But how absolute is absolute? The Vatican in 1954 decreed that religious could run co-educational schools if they had a specific permission from Rome, but in 1971 decreed that it was sufficient if the local bishop gave his permission. If paragraph 14 of *Humanae Vitae* (on artificial contraception) is to be used as a test of orthodoxy, loyalty or fitness for ecclesiastical office, then why not also this paragraph 78 of *Divini Illius Magistri*, the encyclical on education, since both appeal to 'nature' as the basis of their condemnations?

Louise Brown, the world's first test-tube baby, is now eighteen years old. Just before his election, Pope John Paul I applauded the achievement and thanked God for this miracle of modern science that enabled a childless couple to complete their married happiness with a baby. His reaction found an echo around the world insofar as one in every seven marriages are sterile, although not all are caused by blocked Fallopian tubes. Shortly after his comment, the *Osservatore Romano* published an article by a Vatican theologian condemning the procedure as artificial, against the natural law and therefore intrinsically evil, something that could never be justified. The writer judged the procedure immoral because the semen was procured by masturbation, the combination of male and female elements in the laboratory was totally artificial, and the whole procedure made the new baby a factory product. Since then there have been 15,000 such infants throughout the world, born to couples who see their babies as the fruit of their love. Of course there are a number of quite serious and complicated problems attaching to the procedure of *in vitro* fertilisation that raise moral questions, but an *a priori* condemnation on the basis of its being against nature is not convincing to modern adults. The technology has improved considerably over the years, but the industry that has grown up around it gives very serious cause for concern, and indeed many aspects of it deserve outright moral condemnation. However, for a moral evaluation of the procedure, all of these factors need to be considered together, and not simply the fact that it is described as artificial.

Basic needs and values

Criticism of the blueprint theory does not mean that there is no such thing as natural law. It is simply to warn against expecting God to communicate his will through a particular channel like the nature of human sexuality, expecting to be able to read off specific precepts of moral law from an examination of people's biological, physiological, psychological or sexual make-up. All that can be read like this in human nature is our

capacity to ethicise, our ability to make decisions about right and wrong
and to feel bound by them. What those decisions will be in specific areas
will depend on a variety of factors, but they cannot be determined in
advance by simple biological facts.

However, we can accept a modified version of the maker's instructions theory insofar as we discover basic human needs and potentialities
in human nature that simply cannot be ignored, and these give us some
general insight into values like freedom, responsibility, sociability, love,
etc. In striving to preserve and promote these values, experience and
reflection will enable us to formulate some general principles like: treat
others as you would wish to be treated yourself; some arrangements
should be made for the preservation of life, for the regulation of the sex
instinct, for the organisation of the family and of society. These may seem
somewhat vague, but they are the basis on which we work out more
detailed norms for moral behaviour. The more general these norms are,
the more universally they will be accepted. But concrete, detailed norms
will vary according to changing historical circumstances, both because
the same basic value may be served in different ways, and because our
understanding and appreciation of some values may change.

Does nature really change?
It is easy to recognise the physical changes that take place in a human
being between birth and death, but the human person undergoes much
deeper changes in the course of a lifetime, and the human species has
been continually changing for thousands of years. To focus on physical
human nature as we know it today as an indication of God's will to distinguish moral good and evil seems inadequate in the overall context of
change. What is natural is change itself, and the challenge is to understand it and learn from it. History is an essential part of our human
nature, and history means change. An individual person grows slowly
through childhood, adolescence and adulthood, and in the process there
is a recognisable development of reason and moral autonomy. A similar
process can be seen in the human race, as it progresses from tiny groups
almost totally concerned with survival to more developed societies with
leisure to develop their culture and the things of the spirit. Prehistoric
human beings were undoubtedly human, but they would have great difficulty in relating to their brothers and sisters in today's human family.
Substantial changes occurred in the human race in response to people's
needs and to changes in the environment. These were not simply physical changes like brain size and skin pigmentation, but also psychological

and spiritual changes in human understanding and self-awareness.

The human person is not an isolated, independent being. Nobody grows alone and nobody is totally self-sufficient. What any person is at a particular time is the result of heredity, culture, social conditioning, physical environment, personal psychic dynamism and especially personal choice, decision and initiative. The human body is initially the product of heredity, the material received from many generations of ancestors, each adding its negative or positive contribution to the make-up of the individual. Depending on its health and capacities or its weakness and defects, this body sets the boundaries for the individual's development as a person. All through life, the body can influence the emotional, intellectual, moral and spiritual responses of the individual. Brain lesions and the influence of various drugs can bring about a total change of personality and limit effective freedom. Such changes can happen by accident (naturally?) or as a result of conscious decision. It is said that over a third of human conceptions are spontaneously aborted, sometimes even without the mother being aware of it. It is claimed that five to ten per cent of people are homosexually orientated prior to any personal choice on their part. These facts suggest that we ought to be a little less dogmatic in our assertions about nature and its laws. It is interesting that human sperm were first seen under the microscope in 1677, but it was only in 1827 that the ovum was first observed to be present in the menstrual flow.

Cultural variation
Human nature is affected not only by physical changes but particularly by cultural changes. Every human being belongs to a particular culture, which is part of the person's identity. Culture is people's whole way of life, their social symbols and rituals, art, language and literature, social relationships and groupings. Culture is a whole complex of shared meanings, all of which condition people to be who they are. Cultural anthropologists have shown us significant differences between cultures and groups of people. What is accepted as normal in one culture can shock people of a different culture. One tribe in Papua New Guinea abhors any sign of self-assertion, aggressiveness or anger, whereas in a neighbouring tribe the ideal is violence. In another tribe the traditional roles of the sexes are reversed, with the men being meek and passive while the women are aggressive and domineering. In many cultures the colour white is for joy whereas in others it is for mourning. Given the great variety of human cultures, it is unreal to expect all peoples to reach

the same conclusions in solving moral problems. The Jewish people were nomadic, agrarian and urban at different periods of their history and this is reflected in the different laws to be found in the Bible.

Not only cultural, but also social conditioning shapes individuals and groups. There are considerable differences between rich and poor, educated and uneducated, those in secure employment and those who have no opportunity to work. One could also list the psychological pressures that weigh on people. These various differences are mentioned not in order to show that there is no basic and common human nature, but to draw attention to the great variety of its concrete expressions. Such differences might lead us to ask whether in some cases what we quote as 'human nature,' indicating God's plan for moral behaviour, may be so culturally conditioned that we cannot quote it as universal, or as an indication of God's mind. Our perception of reality is conditioned by our own personal and cultural experience, and this may be quite limited.

The practical conclusion from all of this is that human nature does indeed change, and our perception of what counts as 'natural' likewise changes. For example it would be wrong to imagine that our modern notion of marriage as a partnership between equals is really the norm intended by nature, when in fact marriage and family life have until very recently been regarded in the context of the tribe, clan or extended family. Marriage has been understood and lived in so many different ways in history that sexuality has always been characterised by a certain vagueness, openness and flexibility, so that it needed to be given form and definition by society. This was admitted by Thomas Aquinas in answer to the question of whether marriage is permanent. He explained that marriage is natural in the sense that there is a natural inclination in human beings towards marriage, but in fact marriage takes place in the concrete through human freedom. Thomas maintained that human nature is not unchangeable, and he accepted the multiplicity of concrete forms in which marriage had expressed itself at various stages of human history. His conclusion was that it is of the very nature of marriage to be historical. Thus, in a given set of economic, social or cultural circumstances, polygamy might be the best norm for family life, whereas nowadays we look on monogamy as best serving the values of human dignity, family relations and equality between the sexes. This means that it is not possible to make any single historical or cultural form of marriage absolute as the norm for all. The Christian message has to remain open to all cultures and to all historical change, and it is enlightening to see the considerable changes that have occurred in Church teaching about marriage through the centuries.

Do we still need natural law?

With so much talk of variety, change and development, the question arises: do we still need natural law? The answer must be a resounding 'Yes,' absolutely. First of all, it would be irresponsible to ignore the accumulated wisdom of millennia of human history and discard the concept of natural law, a concept that is at the very core of civilisation. But more essentially, natural law is our very nature as human beings, free agents capable of creating our own destiny, of shaping the future of the world, but we can do this successfully only if we respect our own human nature and the basic structure of reality.

As indicated above, human beings have always recognised the need for law to provide the framework for their freedom and flourishing. They learned from experience that in the long run might is not right, that in order to guarantee their own rights they must respect the same rights in others, that rights and obligations go together. But underlying this experience of practical decisions lay a more basic insight, that there is an objective unwritten law that is the touchstone and foundation of all other laws, of moral obligation itself. This insight was tellingly expressed by the Greek poet Sophocles in the person of Antigone, who was aware that in transgressing the human law and being crushed by it, she was obeying a higher law, the unwritten and unchangeable law, the law that did not come about today or yesterday, but which lives always and for ever, whose origin is unknown to us. Five hundred years later a similar protest was made in the New Testament by Peter and the other apostles: 'We must obey God rather than men.' Down through the centuries philosophers, theologians, statesmen and especially prophets have appealed to this law as the foundation for all laws, in their protest against unjust laws, and in their cry for justice.

The modern world has learned from the tragic experience of uncritical liberalism, shallow legal positivism, and cruel dictatorships in so many parts of the world, that it needs to recover the notion of natural justice and natural law. Something of this is reflected in the United Nations Declaration of Human Rights in 1948, and it is interesting to note that Japan, West Germany and Italy, countries which had experienced totalitarian regimes, made considerable use of the natural law concept in rebuilding their legal systems. Looking back over centuries of human history, one could well speak of the eternal return of natural law. That the ideal should have been imperfectly understood or badly applied for long periods of time does not take from the perennial validity of natural law, but simply acknowledges that human nature is not a finished product, that human beings can make mistakes, but they are at their best when they learn from their mistakes. In this context it will be a useful exercise to reflect on the natural law in the changed circumstances of today's world. What does it mean today?

The New Testament gives us the assurance that the natural law does indeed exist, and that it is an important reality. This is clear in the first two chapters of St Paul's letter to the Romans, where he explains that although the pagans do not have the Torah or Jewish law, in their reason they are brought before God through the medium of the created world, and in their conscience they realise that they are bound to obey his laws. For Paul, the moral law is simply this claim of God on human beings. He believed that the pagans knew the precepts of the moral law that regulate relationships among human beings, and they knew this in their hearts, by nature. Paul insists that in spite of their not having the Jewish faith, the pagans are quite capable of telling good from evil (e.g. 1 Thess. 4:12; 1 Cor. 10:32; Col. 4:4; 1 Tim. 5:14; 6:1). Moreover, many concrete moral norms are common to Christian, Jewish and pagan societies. Anthropologists and missionaries working with primitive peoples previously untouched by Jewish or Christian influence (e.g. in Papua New Guinea) discovered that tribal laws already contained the essentials of the ten commandments proclaimed by Moses. In fact, the more we study moral codes, the more we find that they do not differ in major principles. The precise concrete details are culturally conditioned in all cases, but the basic fact of moral obligation is something common to all humans. This is the essential meaning of natural law. This law is discerned through human experience without reference to revelation or to the testimony of an external authority. Precisely because it shines by its own light and its own intrinsic witness and intelligibility, it can serve as a criterion to recognise how specific laws are culturally conditioned (even in sacred scripture) and need careful interpretation. Natural law is basic human reasonableness carried over into decision and action. It is a kind of practical wisdom which recognises the basic thrust of our human nature towards certain goods or values which enable us to flourish as human beings, and then decides what actions are most appropriate to achieve, protect and promote these values.

Nature and reason

In spite of the criticisms expressed in the earlier part of this chapter, the traditional elements of natural law, namely natural inclinations and regulation by human reason are still essential, but they need to be seen in a correct relationship and in the context of modern culture. The maker's instructions theory still contains a valid insight, reminding us that there is an objective order in the universe, and that it is good to respect this order. The many nature films now available provide endless, quite extraordinary examples of this. When we speak of a good watch, a good tree, or a good horse we mean that they serve their purpose, they function as they *should*, in accordance with their nature. In the case of the tree and the horse the guidance is by instinct or natural inclination, since they are not free to do other than follow their nature. But in the case of human beings the *should* takes on a *moral* meaning and implies *moral obligation* because humans are free. With their intelligence they can see and understand what it means to be human and they experience natural inclinations towards what will benefit their well-being. The inclinations of human nature (towards life and the necessities of life, towards sexual relationships, the upbringing of offspring, and life in society) guide them towards decisions to satisfy those inclinations in a way that will contribute towards their growth as good persons. Among various options presented by their freedom they have to discern what is truly good in order to reject what is merely apparent good, to distinguish genuine natural and rational needs from mere wants. The reasoning involved in this kind of discernment is not mere intellectual knowledge working through abstract concepts, a kind of mathematical calculation, but a much deeper, vital, unsystematic and more vague knowledge involving feeling and imagination, an evaluative knowledge working through *inclination, connaturality* or *congeniality*, in which reason listens to the basic inclinations of human nature itself. In technical terms, the moral *ought* of what must be done as a good action is grounded in the *is* of our human nature, of what it means to be human. Natural law is a norm of responsible human conduct, a guideline that comes before all particular formulations of law.

The combination of reason and nature has always been the core of natural law, and was brilliantly explained by Thomas Aquinas, but after his time the main emphasis was on nature, often understood in a narrow physical sense, leading to the formulation of absolute norms intended to be valid for all people of all time. Some Church teaching, especially in the area of sexual and medical ethics, is still influenced by this inadequate approach to natural law. But the classical natural law is coming to new life in the context of recent cultural changes. There is no longer an artificial separation between nature and reason as two totally separate entities. Instead of being restricted to the laws of physics, chemistry and biology, human nature is seen as including our God-given creative intelligence, which is capable of interfering with physical nature without this interference being judged immoral. Other factors need to be considered to decide which interventions are morally justified and which are immoral. In the new approach, nature is no longer thought of in terms of an abstract human nature to be found in a univocal, universal and essentially unchangeable way in all human beings. There is more emphasis on concrete human nature seen in different historical periods and in specific cultural situations, and it is human nature in its totality, in all its dimensions, that is morally relevant.

This new approach is a result of the cultural change mentioned in Chapter 2, namely the change from *classical* to *historical* consciousness, one of the greatest cultural changes in human history, which has been going on for the past fifty years. We can no longer speak of an unchanging nature, because history and change are of the very essence of human nature and indeed of the cosmos. When intelligence is seen as an integral part of human nature it follows that the human person can take over from blind natural forces to provide a more human solution to specific problems. For example, in former times population control was a haphazard result of widespread fatal diseases and continual tribal warfare, whereas nowadays contraceptive technology gives a humanly better result. In this sense contraceptive techniques can be accepted as part of nature, although how and when their use is morally good requires further discussion. Church teaching has changed quite radically in the last few decades on slavery, punishment, women's dignity and rightful place in society (though not yet in the Church), sex, religious freedom and toleration. These changes did not come about as a result of divine revelation or mystical experience on the part of leaders and pastors, but simply as a natural consequence of changes in the surrounding culture. In spite of its claim to be a light to the nations, the Church was not always in the lead.

The person is central
An important element in today's culture is the primacy given to the human person. This is crucial in the area of morals. The concept of person has been central to Greek philosophy for centuries, but it has a deeper and more extended meaning in today's culture. The self-understanding of people today includes characteristics that are quite new and are extremely important in any consideration of morality. The person is spirit incarnate, enfleshed in a material body, subsisting in his or her own

right, never a means to an end, always open to the world, to other people, to God, not a static fact or a finished product, but a being called to self-realisation, and indeed self-transcendence, through personal freedom, choice, decision and action. The human person is essentially a changing, growing and developing being.

Nature and person are not quite the same. One *is* a person, but one *has* a nature in and through which one becomes fully a person. Therefore, not every interference with physical nature is a diminishment of the person. Personal development is a matter of reacting responsibly to the various human values discovered gradually by a community of persons through centuries of lived experience. These values are physical, social, cultural, personal and religious. There is no separate category of *moral* values, but moral value is constituted by the person's free choice and personal appropriation of each and all human values. In complex situations there can be a conflict of values, and in this case the choice must be left to the conscience of the individual person. There is a moral responsibility to judge which value may be postponed or sacrificed for the protection or promotion of another. In these situations it is necessary to decide which values are more important, which are more urgent, and whether the threat to a particular value is immediate or remote, certain, probable or merely possible. In this way, physical actions are relevant in the moral order only insofar as they are given *personal human meaning* by the intention of the person making the choice. Therefore natural appetites may be frustrated and physical evils (e.g. mutilation or death) permitted, provided there is a proportionate reason, namely a higher human value at stake (e.g. overall health of the person, or love of neighbour in the case of organ donors).

Canadian theologian Bernard Lonergan is one of those who first drew attention to the vast cultural change involved in the shift from classical to historical consciousness. He has written extensively on human consciousness and the human person. Although his approach links up with Aristotle's definition of the human being as a rational animal, his development of this is far more complex. For Lonergan, the physical, chemical, organic and psychic processes of human nature are essential to the existence and flourishing of the person, but they are *integrated into the higher world of intelligent consciousness*. Through this higher level of consciousness, humans can change their own nature and environment, but moral considerations limit what they *may* do as against what they *can* do, if they are to develop fully and responsibly as persons. At the same time, because of the integration of these lower and higher levels into the unity of person, the so-called lower realities take on new meanings that are quite different from what is seen in the animal world. Thus, physical activities like eating and burial have social and religious meanings, and are surrounded by special rituals, and human sexuality has a rich cultural meaning that goes far beyond its mere physical expressions.

Marriage is a good example of the Church's failure to recognise the importance of cultural meaning and its conditioning of moral norms. Because of the weight of the decadent tradition which emphasised physical nature more than it should, Church teaching for centuries insisted that the primary purpose of marital intercourse was procreation, while mutual satisfaction was secondary, whereas current teaching omits all reference to primary and secondary purposes and sees the unitive and procreative as equal, and it develops the unitive dimension beyond mere sexual satisfaction or 'alleviation of concupiscence' to a much richer understanding of its potential for affirmation, healing and growth of the partners and indeed of the children. But it is sobering to remember that this new insight was accepted by Vatican Council II in the face of fierce resistance by a considerable minority of the bishops.

A modern version of natural law

When asked about absolute norms in ethics, Lonergan summarised the fundamental precepts of natural law as: Be Attentive, Be Intelligent, Be Reasonable, Be Responsible, and whatever precepts are arrived at by obeying these four requirements. This is a perfect example of the move from nature to person, from laws of nature to laws of reason. It is a very sophisticated development of Aquinas' phrase 'the rational ordering of natural inclinations.' These four precepts describe the process of moral discernment, to discover what is morally right, to decide and do it. Briefly, the basic moral obligation is to see, to understand, to reason, to decide, and to act responsibly.

To be attentive means to be fully aware of all that is involved in the situation. It means getting the facts, as objectively and comprehensively as possible, and naming them factually, without moral labels. Thus killing is killing, a pre-moral evil, but to label it murder at this stage is to go beyond the facts and confuse the issue. To drive a car at 150 km an hour without knowing the condition of the car, the reliability of the brakes, or paying attention to whether the street is crowded, or noticing that one is agitated or sleepy, is morally irresponsible, and could be criminal, and in religious terms a sin. Being attentive means also being aware of possible consequences of an action, because these too are facts of the case.

To be intelligent means to understand the facts, not simply in their physical nature, but also in their cultural context, in their full human meaning. It involves understanding not only the immediate facts of a concrete situation, but knowing about the natural world, the processes of human reproduction, the delicacy of ecology balance, the complexities of medical diagnoses and treatment.

To be reasonable means to bring reflective, discursive reason to bear on the facts as understood, to discover their implications, the possible outcome of different courses of action, the possible options available for the solution of a problem, what values are at stake, the relative importance or urgency of values in conflict, etc. Reflective evaluation brings out which possibilities are reasonable courses of action because of the reasons behind them, and shows what is unreasonable because there are no convincing reasons to support it. This evaluation is not simply a question of indicating how one conforms to physical nature, but rather an analysis of all the human values involved, and showing when it is appropriate or imperative to intervene in the natural processes, pointing out which interventions enable people to flourish as human persons, and which activities block human flourishing.

To be responsible is to move into a higher level, from rational consciousness to rational *self-consciousness*, to the awareness of oneself as person, to the level of morality and personal responsibility. The final step in the process is to actually decide and act on what was discovered by intelligence and motivated by reason. This is the experience of *conscience*, the awareness of oneself as a responsible being, capable of changing oneself and affecting one's environment. The moral challenge is to have consistency between one's knowing, willing and doing, that we knowingly and willingly do what is right.

Classical and statistical laws

In the long history of natural law, a most important insight of Thomas Aquinas was unfortunately lost sight of. In the Catholic tradition, natural law was presented on a par with the physical, chemical and biological laws of nature, with the same uniformity and predictability, with the result that precepts of natural law were understood as absolute and universally binding. This is true for Lonergan's four precepts, which reflect the nature of our human consciousness, and for the most general precepts of the older tradition like: do good and avoid evil, treat others as you would wish to be treated; there are no exceptions to these. But precepts derived from them could not have the same universal binding force, because their formulation included variable elements of time, place and culture. Aquinas always maintained that, apart from the most general precepts, natural law applied or was valid *ut in pluribus*, only as a general rule. This insight was largely overlooked after his time, but it can be rediscovered and given new life in the context of Lonergan's approach.

When the encyclical *Humanae Vitae* was published, Lonergan raised the question whether the relationship between human insemination and conception is a statistical law or a classical law of one-to-one causality. If it is a law of immediate causality, the relationship would be sacred and inviolable, and all contraceptive interventions would be forbidden. Because Church teaching for so long was dependent on Aristotle's understanding of nature and its classical laws of cause and effect, and his claim that every act of insemination was procreative, and only occasionally, by accident, failed in its purpose, contraception was condemned absolutely, with no exceptions. But nowadays we know that as many as two million spermatozoa are discharged into the vagina for one conception to be possible, and that many couples can have intercourse up to a hundred or more times a year without any conception taking place. There might be two or three conceptions in six or seven years. It is clear from this simple fact of nature that the relationship between insemination and conception is not one of immediate causality, and therefore is not a classical law of nature, but a purely statistical one of probabilities. This point was taken up and argued in 1989 by Sebastian Moore, theology professor of Boston College in the United States. In 1967 Lonergan told him in conversation that contraception can never be proved to be against the natural law, for the simple reason that the relationship between coition and conception is purely statistical.

This involves a new way of looking at nature and its laws. The law of gravity and other laws of physics and chemistry are classical laws, in which there is a one-to-one relationship of cause and effect. Objects heavier than air *always* fall towards the centre of the earth, and chemical elements *always* combine in the *same* specific proportions to form new compounds. *Every time* I touch the piano keys they always produce the expected sound. But not every act of coition results in conception. Some couples using non-contraceptive intercourse can conceive in a few weeks, others in a few months and others still only after a year or more. This is how nature works. The frequency of intercourse against the infrequency of conception indicates a different kind of relationship, a different kind of law at work. It is a statistical relationship of probability, like the statistical laws that indicate the probability of a tossed coin turning up heads in a given number of throws. Classical laws govern natural cause-and-effect regularities, but statistical laws govern probabilities and the frequency of events. Both kinds are *equally laws of nature*, and therefore *part of natural law*. Lonergan would say that classical laws tell what would happen if certain conditions were fulfilled, but statistical laws tell how often the conditions are in fact fulfilled.

Both classical laws and statistical laws are equally laws of nature, reflecting nature at work in different ways. There is nothing to justify the claim that the former are more natural than the latter. To interfere with either kind of law is to interfere with nature. If it is against the natural law to use a physical or chemical preventative during individual acts of coition, then to interfere with the *probabilities* of conception by avoiding intercourse during fertile times, which is the natural family planning method, is equally against the natural law. *Both interfere directly with the laws of nature.* A number of people discovered this insight during the public debate on contraception around the time of the encyclical. Indeed most members of the papal commission set up to examine the matter, notably Dr John Marshall, changed their minds on this, coming to see that there is no moral difference between artificial contraception and so-called natural family planning. Both are equally an interference with nature. Therefore, if natural family planning can be morally good, then artificial contraception can also be morally good. If one or the other method is condemned as immoral, it must be for reasons other than mere interference with nature, and these reasons need to be evaluated for their reasonableness. The label 'artificial' has no moral significance. Church documents since Vatican II have quietly dropped the outdated Aristotelian biology on which the condemnation of contraception was originally based, but by retaining the ban on so-called artificial contraception in today's cultural context they create serious problems for the credibility of the teaching.

Conclusion

The answer to the question 'Does morality change?' should be obvious by now. The universe, our whole world, human nature and human culture are in a continuous process of change. Change is an essential part of our nature. For this reason we cannot speak of a natural moral law that is unchangeable or everlasting, especially if we think of it in terms of a set of rules. Human nature is not static, but open to growth, and it is part of a cosmos which itself is in a continuous process of development.

A natural law that is to make sense in today's world must incorporate this dimension of openness, growth and development, together with the element of continuity. Since, in Christian terms, we have been created in the image and likeness of Christ, the moral challenge is to grow more and more into that likeness. This is not an automatic growth that goes on independently of our personal free will. Nor does it imply that the human race is on a constant upward curve of improvement from primitive conditions to sophisticated levels of civilisation. The genocide of millions in Stalin's Russia, Nazi Germany, Rwanda and other places in our time should banish any simplistic optimism. Freedom and maturity are never achieved as a permanent acquisition, but need to be continually won over and over again, because human development is the result of personal moral choice, which is subject to error, selfishness and sin. The mustard seed will grow into a tree in obedience to the classical laws of nature, but human beings can only grow through personal acts of choice, and growth as a person is a kind of self-creation. Indeed to grow fully as a human being involves self-transcendence. This is the Christian paradox of death and resurrection. This is what morality is all about.

The fact that we change through history does not mean that there is no constancy or continuity, no discernible pattern to guide us as we strive to become more fully human. The natural law as outlined above provides us with mental procedures and general principles to discover the right direction of genuine human flourishing and to discern which actions are in keeping with authentic human growth. Our moral consciousness as responsible agents will alert us to wrongdoing through the experience of guilt. The next chapter will take a closer look at what conscience means. It must be remembered of course that in Christian tradition this exercise of looking to natural law does not rule out help from a higher power. We can count on the aid of the Holy Spirit in our discernment and moral struggles. We have recourse to God in prayer, asking that we be alerted to our prejudice, selfishness and blind spots, requesting the courage and strength to overcome these obstacles, and calling on divine assistance to help us be attentive, intelligent, reasonable and responsible. But there is no magic about prayer, and there is no divine revelation of answers. Friends can give advice and we can look to the Bible and to the tradition of the Church for inspiration and guidance, but it is a failure in maturity to expect these to provide a short-cut that would by-pass critical intelligence and reason, or to shield us from the need to find convincing arguments for our moral beliefs.

6

CONSCIENCE TODAY

The word 'today' in this chapter's title is simply a reminder that, like so many other elements of our human nature, conscience too has had its history. While it is an essential part of our human personality, it has been understood and experienced in different ways down through the centuries. It will be helpful to look at the ups and downs of this history in order to avoid unfounded generalisations about the past and to provide a context for an understanding of conscience more appropriate to today's culture. Church documents too often use the phrase 'the constant teaching of the Church' to support a particular position, when it is not clear that the teaching that was repeated was precisely the same all through its history. At times a tradition can be quoted with the implication that it goes back to early Christian times, when in fact the particular 'tradition' is hardly a century old whereas before it developed there was quite a different tradition with fifteen hundred or more years to support it.

Conscience a universal experience
The word 'conscience' has had such a complex, ambiguous history and has been used with so many meanings that it is difficult to confine it to a simple definition, yet it is central to any discussion of morality. In fact, no culture has yet been found in which conscience is not recognised as a fact. Ancient people spoke of 'heart' and 'loins' to describe the innermost nature of a person with reference to responsibility and morality. Down through the centuries there have always been people who did not conform, who refused to accept or obey because they responded to a higher law, the law of conscience. Socrates, Joan of Arc, Thomas More, Martin Luther King, Alexander Solzhenitsyn are just a few of the prophetic figures who incarnate conscience in dramatic fasion.

The Greeks were the first to reflect philosophically on the nature of conscience, and they described it as 'self-consciousness in its role of making moral judgment.' They did not restrict it to abstract knowledge of right and wrong, but recognised the influence of feeling and will, so they spoke of good and bad conscience, operative not only after the deed, but before and during it. The Old Testament uses the word 'conscience' only once (Wis. 17:11), but the reality of the internal voice as the voice of God continually calling for fidelity to the covenant runs all through. Genesis 3 is an excellent description of remorse of conscience. The term is not found in the gospels, but the teaching of Jesus moves the emphasis from external action to the heart, to interior disposition and the need for purity of intention. In the rest of the New Testament the word occurs thirty times. St Paul took over the popular concept and even the technical term he found in Greek culture and developed it as a central part of the Christian moral message. For the New Testament writers, conscience meant a consciousness of the true moral content of human life as seen by faith, the basic outlook on life governing all one's actions. But it involved also a prudent assessment of each human situation in the light of Christian responsibility and love.

Conscience always sacred

It would be unfair to imply that the sanctity of conscience was first discovered and proclaimed by the Second Vatican Council. In fact, it has been an integral part of Christian teaching from the beginning. Peter and John spoke boldly to the High Priest Annas and the other members of the council: 'You yourselves judge which is right in God's sight – to obey you or to obey God; for we cannot stop speaking of what we ourselves have seen and heard' (Acts 4:19–20). This was the voice of conscience. There are some traces of the recognition of the rights of conscience in pre-Christian society, particularly among the later Stoics, from whom the very word 'conscience' itself came into Christian use. A classical example of a conscientious stand was quoted in the previous chapter, from the poet Sophocles in the person of Antigone. But before the time of Christ in general there was little respect for personal conscience. For most of the ancient world, the law of the community took the place of individual conscience, and there was no room for dissent. It was the Christian message of the infinite worth of each human being, created in the image and likeness of Jesus, called to share in God's own creativity, and alive with the Spirit enabling people to go beyond mere law, which encouraged the Church to develop and maintain the principle of the sanctity and supremacy of conscience.

Though many of the influences affecting the Church in the first sixteen or seventeen centuries of its existence would have inclined it to put the community before the individual, its constant teaching was *Conscientia semper sequenda*, conscience must always be obeyed. The Church took over from the Jews the belief that it was the custodian of God's revealed law. It inherited from the Greeks a special respect for the 'natural law' enshrined in nature and in the consensus of civilised moral codes. It was subjected to persecution from without and heresy from within, and it had to hold its own against the Roman Empire and later against the national states. Under such pressures, it would have been quite natural for the Church to fight shy of any freedom of conscience that could encourage individualism, indiscipline or disruption. But in fact, the Church continually preached the supremacy of conscience as basic Christian doctrine. In the twelfth century the canonist Gratian collected an enormous number of patristic and papal statements on this point. Many of these refer to the situation of conscience having to say 'No' to a civil power, but the principle was also applied to nonconformity within the Church.

Even such an autocratic Pope as Innocent III could proclaim: 'You ought rather to suffer excommunication than commit mortal sin, even though you cannot prove to the Church that the sin would be mortal.' Theologians and canonists continually defended the principle that personal conscience must always be obeyed, even when it is in error. For example, Thomas Aquinas taught that it would be a sin to accept the Christian faith if a person believed it to be evil. One is always obliged to do what reason declares to be right, even if it means losing one's reputation, one's standing in the community, or even one's very life. No authority, no Church, no other person can take the place of one's personal conscience.

Theory and practice

In spite of this constant tradition, however, it must be admitted that the Church's record in practice obscured the principle to such an extent that many people today still find it difficult to accept the Vatican II statements on conscience as the teaching of the Church. The Inquisition is the most obvious example of the Church's failure to understand the full practical implications of its teaching, but the mentality that produced the Inquisition was not limited to one century or restricted to men of cruel bent. Pope Leo X declared, against Luther, that the burning of heretics was perfectly in accordance with the will of the Holy Spirit. Clement VIII condemned the notion of freedom of conscience and is quoted as saying that 'as for tolerating freedom of conscience in England, it would only do harm and make Catholics become heretics.' In the twelfth century, the great St Bernard of Clairvaux, a sensitive and most attractive character, could preach that errors should be refuted by argument, not by force, and he tried to persuade the Albigensian heretics of the error of their ways, but at the same time he offered them the grim alternative 'believe or die.' He insisted: 'If they prefer to die rather than believe, let them die.' In 1864 Pope Pius IX declared that freedom of conscience and religion was sheer madness, echoing the sentiment of Pope Gregory XVI who in 1832 spoke of 'the erroneous and absurd opinion, or rather madness, that freedom of conscience must be asserted and vindicated for everyone.' And yet this is precisely what the Second Vatican Council solemnly proclaimed barely a century later.

Pope Innocent III waged war on the Albigensians and urged his cru-saders to 'use cunning and deception as weapons, for in the circumstances deceit is no more than prudence.' The Albigensian cru-sade was the first major conflict of its kind within Europe and is important because of the precedent it set as to how wars of religion should be fought, and how fellow-believers in the divinity of Christ should treat each other when they disagree about their beliefs. The history of this war makes sad reading today. Enormous numbers of men and women were thrown to the flames, in batches of a hundred or more, and it continued for twenty years. It is true that the pope could not always keep the crusaders within the bounds required by the morality of war, and the soldiers were often spurred on by motives other than zeal for the faith. But the whole crusade was justified on the principle that a common Catholic Christianity was the basis of all western law and order; to challenge that was to challenge the very foundation on which society rested. In this climate of opinion it was easy to forget the claims of conscience and the essential freedom of the act of faith. When religion and civilisation were being defended, nonconformity and heresy were considered treason and had to be punished.

The use of torture
Pope Nicholas V in the ninth century outlawed the use of torture as a means to force heretics to confess, but the climate changed during the next three centuries to the extent that the Church came to justify it in prin-ciple and make use of it in practice. Canonists of the period recalled Old Testament texts which imposed the death penalty for blasphemers and idolaters. Even Thomas Aquinas justified capital punishment for

heretics because 'they are blasphemers of God and followers of a false law.' Since faith was considered the cement of the social order, any crime against faith was punishable as treason. The Church would judge the case and hand over the guilty ones to the civil authority. But when torture was used to extract confessions, although it was the civil power that was in charge of administering the torture, it was the ecclesiastic who ordered it, often controlling its intensity and duration until a confession was obtained. Torture was so generally accepted that often it was the people themselves who took the law into their own hands, lit a fire and snatched the accused heretics from the clerical tribunal to throw them into the flames. Burning at the stake was a common punishment for heretics who failed to retract, but confiscation of property, imprisonment and exile were also used.

In 1234 Pope Gregory IX set up a special tribunal, the Inquisition, to seek out heretics and bring them to trial. It was originally aimed against the breakaway sects of Cathari and Waldenses, but quickly extended its aim to include other religious groups, as well as witches, diviners, blasphemers, sodomists and sacrilegious persons. It was very much in the mood of the times. Even before the Church decreed any penalty for heresy, public opinion all over Europe had shown itself savagely hostile to heretics, who were often lynched without any trial. It was Emperor Frederick II who laid down capital punishment for heresy. The Inquisition travelled around from place to place, and gradually developed a whole new body of law and criminal practice to suit its purpose. It imposed death as a penalty for convicted heretics, usually by burning at the stake, and used torture in the examination of those accused. In the eighty years after 1254 as many as seven different decrees were issued by six different popes to justify and authorise the use of torture. In 1310 Pope Clement V (under pressure from Philip the Fair) ordered the reluctant King Edward of England to use torture on the Knights Templar to force them to admit to heresy, idolatry and sodomy so that Philip could confiscate their enormous wealth in France. In countries outside France, where torture was not allowed, the Templars were fairly tried and exonerated. But the Pope was furious at this and ordered retrials everywhere, with the use of torture until confessions were obtained.

Joan of Arc, martyr of conscience
In 1431 the illiterate, nineteen-year-old girl, Joan of Arc, was declared guilty of heresy by the university of Paris and tried by a tribunal made up of one cardinal, six bishops, thirty-two doctors of theology, sixteen

bachelors of theology, seven doctors of medicine and 103 other officials. She had nobody to defend her. To frighten her she was shown the torture chamber and the wooden trestle on which her limbs would be pulled and twisted out of shape. This did not change her mind, but she was so terrified by fire that when threatened that she would be burned alive she retracted and promised that she would be totally submissive to the Church. Immediately her conscience reproached her and she withdrew the retraction. She was burned in the presence of ten thousand citizens and close to a thousand English soldiers, accused of being a liar, sorceress, blasphemer, idolater, apostate, schismatic and heretic. It was not until five hundred years later that Pope Benedict XV canonised her as a saint, admitting that the tribunal that condemned her was unjust and the accusations nothing but calumny. It is sobering to realise that it took the Church five centuries to recognise the injustice.

Only a few years before the martyrdom of Joan, the Czech reformer John Hus was burned alive as a heretic. The Council of Constance condemned him to death as a heretic, on hearsay, without having read his books. His condemnation was the result of false witness, intrigues and corruption. He wrote: 'Christian faithful, seek the truth, listen to the truth, love the truth, say the truth, be attentive to the truth, defend the truth until death; because the truth will set you free from sin, from the devil, from the death of the soul, and at the end from eternal death.' The bishops had him dressed in his priestly vestments, and then stripped him of them one by one as they cursed him and told him that they were entrusting his soul to the devil. They refused him a last confession. He had told the Council that he could not retract, since he never made the statements he was falsely accused of, and to say otherwise would be a lie in the sight of God and make him offend his conscience and the truth of God. It seems that a movement among scholars and some ecumenical bishops in Poland is now working for the rehabilitation of John Hus.

The Spanish Inquisition

At the end of the fifteenth century, at the request of the Catholic Kings, Pope Sixtus IV established a new tribunal, the Spanish Inquisition, much worse than its predecessor. Even making allowance for the intellectual, religious, sociological and political climate of the time, it is one of the darkest and most shameful chapters in the Church's history. Its particular target were the Jewish converts to Christianity, who were inclined to revert to some of their Jewish practices such as wearing a clean shirt on the Jewish Sabbath, refusing pork, or reciting the Psalms without adding the *Gloria* as a conclusion. Those who confessed to these 'crimes' were humiliated, while others were simply put to death. Nearly three hundred went to the stake in Seville, while others got life imprisonment, heavy fines or disgusting public penances. As a five-year-old boy, Alonso Sánchez, who became the father of St Teresa of Avila, was among the two and a half thousand who were paraded through the streets of Toledo half naked or in garments of shame. A generation later, St Teresa herself, who was declared a Doctor of the Church in 1970, was under suspicion of heresy during her lifetime, and only considerable diplomatic manoeuvring on her part enabled her to avoid trial and punishment. The tortures used to extract confessions were horrendous, and some witnesses described them sadistically as 'exquisite' and 'incredible.' Exact figures of those who were put to death are not available, but historians estimate that at least two thousand were burned alive by the Spanish Inquisition alone. It was permanently suppressed in 1834.

The Inquisition in Rome led to a real reign of terror in the city in the period immediately after the Council of Trent, under the Popes Paul IV and Pius V. Heresy was considered a plague of the soul, to be fought as ruthlessly as any physical plague, with imprisonment, torture and death by fire. Paul IV, even at the age of eighty-two, would never miss the weekly meeting of the inquisition tribunal. Pius V was even more fanatical, trying to turn the city into a monastery by rooting out heresy wherever it was suspected. Individuals were falsely accused and under horrendous torture confessed, only to be beheaded or strangled and then burned at the stake. When Pius V was canonised in 1712 it does not seem that any serious question was raised about his incredible record of cruelty and lack of respect for conscience. In 1540 Pope Paul III had established a special Congregation of the Inquisition to oversee procedures. In the 1908 reorganisation of the Roman Curia this became the Congregation of the Holy Office, and in 1965 this in turn became the present Congregation for the Doctrine of the Faith.

Double standard

The casual reader of Church history is puzzled by the inconsistency between this savage behaviour and the Church's teaching on conscience. But the two attitudes that seem so contradictory existed side by side not only within the Christian community, but even within individual minds. It is obvious in the case of St Bernard and Pope Innocent III, quoted above. Eight centuries before, St Augustine, one of the most outstanding of the Doctors of the Church, taught that the act of faith must be totally free, not coerced, that no one could believe against his will, but at the same time he was in favour of the civil coercion of heretics. His reason for this was that coercive measures could help them towards faith and true freedom. But of course his notion of freedom excluded the freedom to dissent or to be wrong.

Thomas Aquinas had a different approach. He made a distinction between Jews and pagans, who never belonged to the Church, on the one hand, and heretics and apostates, who once accepted the faith and later renounced it, on the other. He taught that the former may never, in any circumstances, be forced to accept the faith, nor should their children be baptised against the wishes of their parents. He argued this on the basis of the essential freedom of the act of faith and on the grounds of natural justice (the rights of conscience in the case of adults, and parents' rights in the case of children). 'Forced faith' is a contradiction in terms, a human impossibility. But, in the case of heretics and apostates it is assumed that they cannot be sincere in rejecting the true faith, since there is no objective reason strong enough to justify leaving the faith once one is a believer. Thomas says that they should not merely be banished from the Church by excommunication, but handed over to the secular power to be banished from the world by death. He argued that the life of the soul is much more precious than that of the body, and since it is a capital offence to counterfeit money, which is necessary for temporal life, much more so, anyone who corrupts faith, which is the life of the soul, deserves death. This makes strange reading today, when the death penalty has been abolished in so many countries, and is finally frowned upon by the Church itself. But equally strong is Thomas' view that parents' rights over their children must never be violated, even at the risk of the children's eternal salvation (as was then thought), whereas for heretics the rights of conscience are not so sacred.

Conscientious objectors

Among the reasons for this apparent inconsistency in Aquinas' logic is the very objectively-orientated theology of the time, with its emphasis on 'objective truth,' and reality 'out there' almost independent of the thinking subject, its experience of a monolithic world of faith, so different from our secular society of today, its paternalistic notion of authority, its concern with the 'common good,' law and order, hence its suspicion that the nonconforming individual must be bad willed or stubborn (apart from the invincible ignorance of pagans and Jews). Something of this attitude can still lurk in the subconscious of people even today. The Church's high-handed treatment of some dissenting theologians, with not even a token attempt at dialogue and scant concern for pastoral care or basic justice, can be a scandal to people in today's very different world.

During the first four centuries of the Church's history there was a strong rejection of war and military service, and something of this spirit continued in later centuries. St Maximilian Martyr was beheaded for refusing military service. St Martin of Tours withdrew from the army and St Jean Vianney was a deserter from the forces of Napoleon. After the conversion of Constantine the theology of the 'just war' was developed, and this seemed to exclude conscientious objectors. Indeed, Pius XII declared in 1956 that a Catholic cannot invoke conscience in order to refuse to serve his country as the law dictates. On the level of official teaching, the Church recognises the rights of conscientious objectors, but until very recently the recognition was quite limited in practice. Until the 1960s, textbooks of moral theology dealt with the question in a footnote to the treatise on war, and even though the principle was admitted that such people could not be coerced against their conscience, it was pointed out that in modern times it is almost impossible for the private citizen to solve doubts concerning the justice of a war. The implication was that the government, with more information at its disposal, was more likely to be right than the private individual. When the Austrian peasant, Franz Jägerstätter, went to his death in a Berlin gaol in August 1943 rather than act against his conscience by joining the Nazi war, his parish priest, his bishop and most of his friends tried vigorously but in vain to persuade him that he had no right to be a conscientious objector because he did not know the wider context and was in no position to judge. It was long after the war before his prophetic and heroic stand was recognised and applauded. At a memorial Mass celebrated in his honour by the Archbishop of Vienna in 1996, the Dominican Peace Action group from Britain declared that, like St Catherine of Siena, Jägerstätter had washed the shame from the Church's face. The real shame is that so few of the bishops at the time could match his courage. It seems that procedures have begun for his beatification.

Error has no rights

Another area in which the Church was ambiguous with regard to conscience was that of Church-State relations. With some justice it could be accused of Machiavellian policies insofar as it tended to demand freedom for itself where its adherents were in a minority, but refused the same freedom to other religious communities where it was in a majority and could influence legislation through the civil authorities. Whenever non-Catholic minorities were tolerated in Catholic countries, it was more for the sake of the common good of the civil community than out of respect for the sanctity of conscience. John Courtney Murray's writings on Church-state relations and religious freedom in the 1940s and 1950s were constantly criticised by the Roman authorities until they were finally vindicated by Vatican Council II. The enlightened Pius XII, when explaining that non-Catholics should not be forced to embrace the faith against their will, did say that the Church considers their personal convictions a reason for tolerance, but he emphasised that it was not always the principal reason.

The justification for this kind of intolerant attitude was the oft-quoted principle that 'error has no rights.' This sounded right in the neo-scholastic mentality of logical principle, but cannot stand up to critical examination in today's culture. Rights belong to persons, not to statements, whether true or false, and all people have inalienable human rights independently of civil or ecclesiastical law. Freedom of conscience and expression is one of these rights and cannot be infringed, although the freedom *to act* on one's beliefs may be restricted for the good of others. Thus a Jehovah's Witness is free to hold that blood transfusion is immoral, against God's law, and he or she cannot be forced to accept transfusion, but most civilised states would not allow parents' beliefs to prevent their under-age children from receiving transfusion when their lives are at stake. The spurious principle that 'error has no rights' was finally repudiated by Vatican Council II when it condemned all violations of the integrity of the human person, such as mutilation, physical and mental torture, undue psychological pressures, and went on to explain that 'we must distinguish between the error (which must always be rejected) and the people in error, who never lose their dignity as persons even though they flounder amid false or inadequate religious ideas. God, who alone is the judge and the searcher of hearts, forbids us to pass judgment on the inner guilt of others' (*Church in the Modern World*, 27, 28).

Freedom enslaved

Many Catholics will be shocked at these shameful forgotten truths of our history, but the Church's attitude to slavery, which is a major crime against personal freedom, was even more inglorious. St Paul exhorted Christian slaves to be obedient to their masters and advised masters to treat their slaves kindly, but he never questioned the institution of slavery itself as contrary to the gospel. Since none of the biblical writers criticised it, the early Christian theologians tried to justify it. They claimed that although all people are created free and equal, slavery is the result of sin and is part of God's plan of salvation, so that it is neither unlawful or inappropriate. In the Middle Ages canonists went further and tried to justify it as useful to society, and it was accepted by the Church until the eighteenth century. In fact, the Church itself was a slave-owner. Popes, bishops, monasteries and parishes owned slaves for centuries. Slavery was part of the social structure, simply taken for granted without question. Four General Councils of the Church (Lateran III in 1179, Lateran IV in 1215, Lyons I in 1245 and Lyons II in 1274) approved slavery and saw no objection to its being used as a punishment or deterrent. The practice of keeping Christian slaves may have died out in the fourteenth century, but it was common for Christian families to have many Turkish or black slaves. Pope Nicholas V gave full permission to the King of Portugal to invade and conquer all the lands owned by Saracens, pagans, infidels and enemies of Christ, and to subjugate the inhabitants to perpetual slavery. In 1493 Pope Alexander VI granted to the Catholic Kings of Spain full rights over the lands recently discovered in America, with the injunction to subject the natives. Five years earlier King Ferdinand of Spain made a gift of one hundred slaves to the previous Pope, Innocent VIII, who distributed them among the Roman cardinals and nobles.

Of course, some popes forbade the practice of keeping Christian slaves, but did not really condemn the institution itself. The great Dominican Bartolomé de las Casas spent much of his life defending the rights of the Indians in South America, but rather remarkably he suggested that Negro slaves be used instead of Indians. When Rome asked the colonists to respect the Indians because of their immortal souls, the colonists argued that there was no declaration about Negro souls, so they imported Africans. In the mindset of the times Negroes were identified with Moors, and therefore infidels, and this justified the double standard. In 1639 Pope Urban VIII decreed excommunication against those who enslaved Indians, but at the same time he bought Negro slaves for himself. Other popes continued the same practice and as late as 1799 the popes used slaves to power their galleys, chaining them at night and during rest periods, even though major European countries had long since given up slavery. Over a century earlier the anti-slavery movement began in England among the Quakers. The Catholic Church was quite late in catching up, but in the present century it has spoken out against the practice, describing it as odious, destructive, infamous, a scourge and a poison.

Lessons to be learned

The above reflection on Church history is not intended to embarrass the Church (though there is ample room for embarrassment and a crying need for repentance), but simply as a reminder that the Christian community has not always been faithful to the gospel. God's word needs to be inculturated, to take root and be expressed in each culture, but as prophetic utterance it must also be counter-cultural, identifying and condemning those elements of a culture at variance with essential gospel values. In the areas of torture, slavery and lack of respect for conscience, the Church has signally failed to be a light to the nations, and has sinned grievously. The lesson to be learned is that we need to be critically aware of how powerfully a religious and socio-political culture can blind theologians and Church leaders to certain implications of the gospel. It took Bartolomé de las Casas, the young chaplain to the *conquistadores* in South America, several years to realise how racist the Spaniards were in assuming European superiority and how counter-gospel the Church was in tolerating the destruction of entire cultures in the name of Christ. In fifty years the native Indian population was reduced from sixty-five millions to barely nine million. During the eighteen centuries in which the Church accepted and practised slavery it simply imbibed without question the surrounding culture and the existing social order, and indeed strengthened them with its own justification and example. The lesson to be learned is that the Church needs to be continually challenged by the gospel, because both its statements and its practice are always influenced by the surrounding culture, even apart from the sins of its members.

Strangely enough, the phrase 'freedom of conscience' does not appear anywhere in the Vatican II documents, but the concept is solidly enshrined in its teaching (*Church in the Modern World*, 27, 28). It was one of the most hotly debated issues at the Council, and the document on *Religious Freedom* marks a radical change of emphasis when it declares that 'the right to religious freedom is based on the very dignity of the human person as known through the revealed word of God and by reason itself' (n. 2). It explains that this freedom means that everyone should be immune from coercion by individuals, social groups and every human power, so that, within due limits, no men or women are forced to act against their convictions nor are any persons to be restrained from acting in accordance with their convictions in religious matters, in private or in public, alone or in association with others. It insists that this right to freedom is based not on subjective attitude, but on the very nature of the human person, and this right continues to exist even in those who do not live up to their obligation of seeking the truth and adhering to it. This is in stark contrast to the statements of Clement VIII, Gregory XVI and Pius IX. Even allowing for the theological and historical circumstances that made those earlier statements understandable to some extent in their day, they could never be justified nowadays, and there is no denying that official Church teaching on freedom of conscience is now radically different from what it was in the past. Quite simply, the Church got it wrong in the past and now sees things differently. This total reversal of a teaching accepted and practised for centuries should warn us against absolutising similar statements that are conditioned by their time and culture. There can be no timeless, a-cultural pronouncements, absolutely binding in all places and times.

What is conscience?

Since the worldwide debate provoked by *Humanae Vitae*, more people nowadays feel free to follow their conscience even when their decisions are at variance with what the Church expects. They may be encouraged by the above examples from Church history about torture, slavery, conscientious objectors and lack of respect for individual conscience, which show that Church pronouncements were not always in line with the gospel. But because of this crisis of authority and obedience people can too easily claim to follow conscience when in fact they do not have a mature understanding of what conscience really is and may end up just doing what they please. To say this is not to join the ranks of those unhelpful Church leaders who say 'Yes, one must follow conscience, but it must be an informed conscience,' with the implication that Church teaching will provide the information. Intelligent laity are angered by such statements, and say that in practice this amounts to 'We know best, do what you are told.' They wonder why conscience should be mentioned at all if it is simply a matter of obedience. When large numbers did not accept the encyclical's ban on artificial contraception because they were not convinced by its arguments, authority reacted with the primitive response of most authorities under attack, namely by insistence on obedience, in some cases backed up with sanctions. The mystique of obedience set in motion in the Church during the sixteenth century still colours official thinking in today's Church, and it is often presented as the core of morality. On the other hand, confessors who were confused by the debate and insecure when they found their personal common sense out of step with official teaching, simply told penitents to follow their conscience. This well-meant advice led to confusion among laity insofar as many people had seldom been told this before, and few had ever heard a comprehensive, adult explanation of what conscience really is and how it functions.

The present official teaching of the Church is quite clear in the documents of the Second Vatican Council. The first chapter of *The Church in the Modern World* gives a beautiful description of humanity created in the image of God, and speaks of the essential unity of human nature, of the dignity of human intellect, of truth and of wisdom, of the sanctity of conscience.

> Deep within their consciences men and women discover a law which they have not laid upon themselves and which they must obey. Its voice, ever calling them to do what is good and avoid evil, tells them inwardly at the right moment: do this, shun that. For they have in their hearts a law inscribed by God. Their dignity rests in observing this law, and by it they will be judged. Conscience is the most secret core and sanctuary of the human person. There people are alone with God, whose voice echoes in their depths. By conscience that law is made known which is fulfilled in the love of God and of one's neighbour. Through loyalty to conscience, Christians are joined to others in the search for truth and for the right solution to so many moral problems which arise both in the life of individuals and from social relationships. Hence, the more a correct conscience prevails, the more do persons and groups turn aside from blind choice and endeavour to conform to the objective standards of moral conduct. (n. 16)

The document goes on to emphasise the importance of freedom for a true exercise of conscience.

> It is only in freedom that people can turn themselves towards what is good. People today prize freedom very highly and strive eagerly for it. In this they are right. Yet they often cherish it improperly as if it gave them leave to do anything they like, even when it is evil. But genuine freedom is an exceptional sign of the image of God in people. For God willed that men and women should be left free to make their own decisions, so that they might of their own accord seek their creator and freely attain their full and blessed perfection by cleaving to God. Their dignity, therefore, requires them to act out of conscious and free choice, as moved and drawn in a personal way from within, and not by their own blind impulses or by external constraint. (n. 17)

These words confirm the assertion of the first chapter above, that we are most like God in our freedom.

What conscience is not

First of all, conscience is not a special faculty or power distinct from ordinary reason. A conscience decision is made by the same human reason that we use to decide which model of car to buy or where to go for a holiday. Likewise, although some decisions of conscience can involve quite deep feelings, like agonising guilt when we deliberately act against them, conscience is not to be identified with mere feeling or emotion. Furthermore, it is not to be confused with the Freudian notion of 'super-ego.' Freud noticed that his mentally disturbed patients often had the delusion of being watched, even when they were alone. They believed that people were waiting for them to do something forbidden, for which they could then be punished. From this he formed the idea of a self above the normal self, a super-self or super-ego judging the self as an object. In early life this super-ego is formed by internalising the attitudes and rules of parents, and as time goes on the young person accepts these personally, together with the conventions of society, and gradually the super-ego takes on all the functions of early authority figures: observing, accusing, punishing or rewarding. The mature conscience outgrows this, but the childish, immature conscience of some people has many of the characteristics of Freud's super-ego. True conscience is quite different.

It is often said that conscience is the voice of God, but this is only a half-truth. When a Christian has to make a difficult decision in a complex moral situation, it is natural to ask God for help, and the discernment process can be helped by reflection on the truths of revelation, by grace and by one's personal life of prayer. There is no question of private revelation providing easy answers, but there is a strong presumption that one who is habitually in tune with God through fidelity to the gospel will have a special sensitivity towards Christian values and a healthy awareness of personal weakness, blindness and sin. This can be a real help in responsible discernment. On this level it can be said that conscience is the voice of God. Even in difficult, unclear and messy situations, when one is genuinely seeking to do God's will, there is an experience in which morality and mysticism meet. But it is not true that the final decision is *literally* God's will. It is traditional Catholic teaching that we can be sure of God's will only in general. When it comes to specifics there is no absolute certainty. Those who claimed that Franz Jägerstätter was not justified in his conscientious objection to the Nazi war were just as convinced that their assessment of the situation was God's will as he was of the opposite. In short, it is not quite true that the voice of conscience is the actual voice of God, but it is absolutely true that God's will is that we follow our conscience, always and ever. We may never hand it over to another.

Conscience needs to be formed

The Church's current teaching on the dignity and sanctity of conscience and on the need to be free in order to act from personal conviction is a significant change from a long history dominated by the attitude expressed by Pope Leo X in 1520 when he spoke of obedience as the strength of the Church's discipline and the source and origin of all virtues. This tradition left little room for personal responsibility and creativity in moral decision-making. The weakness of this attitude was castigated by the French novelist Georges Bernanos when he said that the sabotage of that sublime faculty of the soul known as judgment can only lead to catastrophes, that people trained to blind obedience are those who are also prone to sudden blind disobedience. If rules are not internalised and personally appropriated, they lead either to passive and external conformity, or to revolt and anarchy. The mystique of obedience that was such a strong feature of Church teaching in the past has now given way to a more balanced approach. When people looked to the Church for guidance, the response was to provide answers to moral questions and lay down rules for moral conduct. There is still a place for this pastoral concern to instruct the faithful, and it is right to insist that only an instructed, well formed conscience is a sure guide to be followed. But more is required for the formation of conscience than giving information and rules.

From infant to adult

Since conscience is an exercise of reason, there can be no question of conscience in children who have not come to the use of reason. The human infant is born with the potential or capacity to reason, but the child cannot use it until it begins to use the word 'because' in a significant way, namely when it is capable of giving reasons for its actions. And yet long before reason becomes active on this level, parents begin to train their children in patterns of right living. Initially the young child is totally self-centred, a little bundle of instinctive needs, the most basic of which is the need to be loved, to be accepted, to be approved. The darker side of this is the fear of rejection by the parents, even if objectively this is no more than a frown on the parents' face. The child quickly learns which behaviour brings approval, acceptance and love, and which actions earn disapproval and cause feelings of rejection. This learning extends all the way from toilet training to table manners and the right and wrong way to relate to brothers, sisters and others. Parents lay down the rules on what is right and wrong, and children obey them simply in order to retain the approval and love of the parents. When the child disobeys, it experiences guilt feelings, not because of any appreciation of the wrongness of the actions, but simply because of the fear of rejection.

This kind of conditioning is perfectly normal and healthy; it is all the child can understand in its early years. The child learns that 'good' behaviour brings approval and love, 'bad' behaviour brings feelings of badness, guilt, rejection. Children conform on the basis of reward and punishment, pleasure and fear. This is a *pre-moral* level of behaviour. But gradually, as the child begins to reason, it discovers that life is more pleasant when it is organised, so it pays to obey the rules laid down by authority. Although reward and punishment may still influence decisions, morality gradually becomes equated with *obedience to social and religious authorities*. Some psychologists claim that the majority of people remain at this level of conscience, which explains their preoccupation with law and obedience. But a higher level is reached by those who accept and obey laws, but are more concerned with the values which the law seeks to protect and promote. People on this level act on the basis of *personally accepted moral principles*. This is the level of mature conscience.

These stages are a logical development of conscience, but they are not watertight compartments with a sharp transition from one to the next. In fact the earlier ones are integrated into the later ones and provide the underpinning for the more developed stage. The felt emotional states inculcated in childhood and early adolescence are quite healthy in themselves and prevent us from doing many anti-social acts. This kind of psychological conditioning frees us from various irrational impulses. Because we are conditioned to reject these impulses spontaneously, we do not have to do battle with them each time they arise, and so we can give more attention to serious matters. Likewise, since we have been conditioned to obey the law without too much questioning, we do not have to puzzle everything out for ourselves, but we trust the authority of others. However, the morally mature person does not accept this conditioning uncritically. Conscience grows towards maturity by internalising and making its own certain *values* and *principles*, and it is these which determine how moral decisions are made. The mature conscience recognises that conditioning which limits us in some areas of freedom is accepted for the sake of the greater freedom it provides in the more important matters of life. This basic conditioning frees us *from* irrational impulses, endless discussion and unnecessary worry, and so frees us *for* the ordinary business of living, and for the serious moral decisions that require more concentrated discernment.

Levels of conscience

Today's world provides us with an enormous range of options. Never before in human history have people had such a variety of choices available to them in so many areas of life. The problem is to know how to choose wisely. Morality is about choice. People become aware of conscience when they have to choose between different courses of action and the question arises: what is the morally right thing to do? Conscience is concerned with the concrete *decision* about what is to be done here and now.

But conscience is more than just decision. The word is also used to describe the background from which the decision is made, namely the deeper level of consciousness which is a person's general knowledge of moral principles about right and wrong, good and bad. Depending on the individual, it can be more or less extensive. It includes the basic principles: do good rather than evil, treat others as you would wish to be treated yourself, and it can extend to the ten commandments and specific developments of them. This is more than neutral, abstract knowledge. It calls to something deep within our nature, and leaves us with the conviction that we must obey it if we are to be true to ourselves. In this sense, conscience is more than just intellect and will, knowledge and consent. On this deepest of all levels, conscience is the core of our being as free persons. Here it can be said that 'conscience is the whole person.'

In moral terms, an individual is a certain kind of person and has a special pattern of life because of acceptance of, and fidelity to, a set of values like respect for persons, truth, sincerity, integrity, justice, love of God. In this sense, conscience is a *special kind of self-awareness*. It is a consciousness, not only of what we are doing, but of what we are and of what we are becoming. It tells us the kind of person we are, but at the same time it also tells us the kind of person we ought to be. It is not only a mirror or indicator, but also an invitation and a summons, commanding us *to become* and *to be* what we are meant to be, to continually grow into our better selves. In Christian terms it can be said that God, the author of our human nature, calls us through the basic thrust of that nature, towards self-transcendence, through the irrepressible appetites of mind, heart and body, a call which we recognise in the experience of conscience.

It is to this conscience that the words of the prophet Jeremiah apply, when he spoke in God's name: 'I will put my law within them, and write it on their hearts' (31:33). Ezekiel spoke of the transformation of conscience with the words 'I will give them a new heart and a new mind.' St Paul makes it clear that God's call is not restricted to a particular religion, but applies to all human beings when he said of the gentiles that 'what the law commands is written in their hearts.' He is referring to the experience of conscience. This insight of Paul is echoed by the Second Vatican Council, speaking of the salvation of non-Christians: 'Those who, through no fault of their own, do not know the gospel of Christ or his Church, but who nevertheless seek God with a sincere heart, and, moved by grace, try in their actions to do his will as they know it through the dictates of their conscience – they too may achieve eternal salvation' (*Constitution on the Church*, n. 16).

Conscience is knowledge of a special kind, namely the awareness of being obliged by a law not of our own making, yet not imposed from without. It is an experience of mind and heart, the innate thrust of our human nature to love the good and avoid evil. This directive of our nature is permanent and ongoing, but not specified in detail as to what precisely is good or evil. Conscience still has the task of discernment, or deciding day by day what is right or wrong.

Levels of consciousness
The levels of conscience just mentioned are:

1. *decision* (this I must do), flowing from
2. *judgment* (this is the right thing to do in this situation), which is made after
3. *assessment of the facts of the situation* and *an habitual knowledge of moral principles and laws*, which come from
4. one's education and experience and ultimately from *the core of one's personal being*, the kind of person one is morally.

But these levels of conscience are part of a wider context of human consciousness. The most immediate and basic level is *empirical consciousness*, which is that of the five senses (sight, hearing, touch, taste and smell), and of memory, imagination and perceiving. *Intelligent consciousness* involves the use of intelligence, in inquiry, insight, understanding, formulating ideas or concepts. A third level is that of *rational consciousness*, involving reflection, reasoning and the making of judgments about reality. The fourth and highest level is that of *responsible consciousness*, involving deliberation, decision and action. This is the level of *moral consciousness* or *conscience*. This fourth level is distinct from the other levels taken by themselves, but is never separated from them. The lower levels are integrated into the higher, so that the human person is all at once empirically, intelligently, rationally and morally conscious, as a whole. Conscience is the highest level of human consciousness. It is the awareness of our personality as a whole and especially of our freedom and responsibility.

These levels of consciousness link up with what was said of the precepts of natural law in the previous chapter: be attentive, be intelligent, be rational, be responsible. These are the basic moral imperatives, essential for all moral decisions and actions. To ignore them is to be irresponsible, and therefore immoral. To be fully faithful to them one needs to recognise and beware of the darker side of our human nature: the risk of ignorance, bias, inauthenticity and sin. To struggle against these requires continual conversion on the intellectual, moral and religious levels. This means that formation of conscience is an ongoing challenge all through life.

Mature conscience is the ideal, but the term is misleading if used in an absolute sense. We can speak of physical, psychological, moral and religious maturity as distinct dimensions of human personality, but they need to be in harmony. One could be psychologically mature and morally immature, or morally mature and religiously immature. A more realistic term would be 'maturity at age.' A person of twenty who is mature for twenty would be immature at forty if no moral growth occurs in the intervening twenty years. There is always room for further growth. It is a lifelong process. There can never be a complete set of ready-made answers, nor can one fall back on slot-machine morality. Moreover, development of conscience is more than just increasing one's knowledge. A crucial element is *fidelity to conscience* and *continual openness* to future development. Conscience can be flawed through habitual neglect, but it may also cease to grow, through routine drifting, through uncritical acceptance of outdated theology, of solutions from the past that no longer respond to new situations. It is the role of prophets, through their words and actions, to shake us out of our complacency and to alert us to new calls on conscience. Human rights activists and liberation theology are in this prophetic tradition.

Both in the formation of conscience and in the use of conscience, it is important to stress that more than mere knowledge is involved. Intelligence and reason are needed to make moral decisions, but feeling and imagination are also important. Pragmatic decisions can be quite cold-blooded and calculating, but moral decisions involve *evaluative knowledge*, since they are a *response to values*. This means that the heart as well as the head is involved. For moral conviction, appeal must be made not only to the intellect, but to the imagination and affectivity. Hence the importance of heroes and saints to fire the imagination and stir the heart. It is important to develop the affective memory in childhood, when, already before it reaches the use of reason, the child is formed in basic trust. It learns to trust its parents and others, to discover that the world is basically good, that it need not fear or be ashamed. Training in morality requires a delicate balance of affection, discipline and explanation. The affective dimension develops through relationships, and the young person eventually becomes what its relationships enable it to be. Feeling and imagination come into play when it is necessary to put oneself in the shoes, if not the skin, of others in deciding what is the moral response to them in different situations.

Peace or guilt

When faced with a moral decision, conscience presents us with the call to do the right thing, and our better self is attracted in that direction, so that part of our being is ahead of the rest. This is a healthy tension, the experience of being stretched towards the good. When we finally do what conscience commands, the rest of us catches up with the better self, the tension is relieved and we experience peace and wholeness, a sense of at-one-ness with ourselves. This is the peace of a 'good conscience.' When we ignore or refuse to do what we know we should, the tension remains, so we lose our basic oneness, we are torn within ourselves, separated from our better self, and we experience alienation and guilt. When there is inconsistency between our knowing and doing we become divided within ourselves. We may make excuses and rationalise our failure, but the very attempt to give 'reasons' for something which is really against reason only aggravates the tension, and we feel guilty. Guilt is the experience of a 'bad conscience.' This lack of inner peace can spill over into our relationships, and we become alienated from our fellow human beings and even from our material environment.

Guilt is the awareness of having acted against conscience. The inconsistency between knowing and doing causes a break in inner harmony,

and since conscience is the very core of the whole person there are repercussions in mind, will, body and emotions. Guilt brings feelings of
shame, and remorse. This is perfectly normal and healthy, body-lan-
guage reacting to something that is not right. The remedy is to admit,
accept and adjust, by acknowledging the wrongdoing, asking forgiveness and repairing the damage. Inner peace can be restored. But guilt is
morbid, neurotic, irrational, and unhealthy when the feeling is out of all
proportion to the wrong done, or is unrelated to any real wrongdoing.

Mature conscience

Elements of unhealthy guilt can be felt at times by mature people, but
they are not upset by it. They have a balanced outlook on life. They can
respect law and authority, but their lives are governed more by freely
chosen values. Theirs is a morality of responsibility rather than of per-
missions. They see God as a loving Father and Mother interested in their
growth and happiness rather than a taskmaster measuring guilt. They
are more concerned about their basic attitudes and the overall pattern of
their lives than about isolated bits of behaviour, although they are not
careless about individual actions. They can accept responsibility for fail-
ures and sins, but they do not torment themselves about them. They can
forgive themselves and feel loved and worthwhile. They believe God
loves them in spite of sin, loves them for their own sake and not simply
because they have earned his love by their good behaviour. In repentance
and trust, they can leave the past to God, live fully in the present and look
confidently to the future. Morally mature people know their own limitations and weakness, but they are constantly open to new information,
new insights, new values, and they want to grow in sensitivity and willingness to do good. Their life is not tied to a rigid set of laws, but they are
flexible, aware that growth is a slow process, that things take time.
Though conscious of the danger of mediocrity and complacency, they do
not get into a panic over the occasional lapse as long as they are
doing their best. They know that God listens to sentences rather than to
isolated syllables.

  Mature people know that conscience is their secret core, the very centre of their personality, their sanctuary, a sacred place where others can
enter only by invitation. God alone has access to this sanctuary and it is
here that they find their deepest peace. Because of their experience of this
sacred space within themselves, they try to respect the same mystery in
others. They can appreciate the feeling of Moses at the burning bush,
when he took off his sandals because he was on holy ground. Conscience,

even in the least of our brothers and sisters, is indeed holy ground, truly a sanctuary, a sacred place that must never be violated in any circumstances or under any pretext.

Mature people believe, with Vatican II, that when they come face to face with God on their own personal last day, they will not be judged according to rules learned by heart, or according to the views of their parents, or Church documents, or laws from the Bible, but according to their own personal conscience, not according to whether they did the right thing, but basically according to whether they did *what they saw and understood* as the right thing. They are bound to follow the guidance of conscience, even if they later discover that it was mistaken, that they acted in ignorance, but in good faith.

The mature conscience can understand St Augustine's words: 'Love God and do what you will.' Theologian Bernard Lonergan was echoing this thought when he said that the continual formation of conscience is as simple and as complex as falling in love. If you really love somebody, you do not have to be constantly referring to laws and rules written somewhere outside of you to guide you in your behaviour towards your beloved. Of course we can be, and often need to be, helped by the experience of the wider community of family, friends and Church, in order to discover what counts as truly loving behaviour, especially in serious and complex matters. Conscience is always personal, but it cannot be isolated from community. The next chapter will take a closer look at the process of discerning right and wrong, discovering how conscience works in practice.

7

Moral Discernment

The phrases 'good and evil' and 'right and wrong' are sometimes used loosely as if they were equivalent. In fact, there is an important distinction between them. Good and evil refer to the moral goodness or badness of persons, whereas right and wrong refer to the moral rightness or wrongness of a person's behaviour. Good and evil are primary, right and wrong are secondary. The two sets are connected, but not to be confused. The person who does what is right and avoids what is wrong is not necessarily morally 'good.' He may be doing the right things, not because they are right but simply for notice, to win approval. St Paul lists many admirable virtues and gifts but warns that, without love, they are of no avail. On the other hand, a person who sincerely follows a conscience that has been responsibly formed but happens to be mistaken, is morally good. Of course morally good people will do their best to 'do the right thing,' but what *is* the right thing? This is the function of conscience, to discern between right and wrong in moral behaviour, to discover what is the appropriate response to people and situations in order to act in a morally responsible way. This is something that has to be discovered, in response to the precepts: be attentive, be intelligent, be reasonable, be responsible.

Today more than ever people are faced with serious, indeed at times agonising, choices. Science and technology have enormously increased the available options. Couples decide for or against conception, whether to continue or to abort a pregnancy, whether to try *in vitro* fertilisation if natural conception fails. People have to choose whether to accept or refuse expensive, complex medical treatment for certain illnesses or simply let nature take its course, whether certain situations justify actively speeding up the dying process, whether they commit themselves in marriage for life or decide for themselves when to end it. In today's culture people insist on the right to make their own decisions, without interference from others. When proclaiming this right to self-determination, they claim to be following their conscience. But it is misleading to say 'Let conscience be your guide' if this implies that I can decide arbitrarily by myself, that I can do whatever I feel is right. Conscience can never be a matter of personal whim or caprice; it must be guided by objective criteria. Moreover, it cannot abstract from the network of relationships to which every person belongs. As social beings whose welfare contributes to, and is dependent on, the common good, we cannot make major life-decisions in isolation. Moral discernment can be a demanding exercise.

Principles and rules

A large part of the classical Catholic tradition saw discernment in terms of applying universal moral principles to specific human situations by a process of deductive reasoning. The principles were derived from scripture, tradition and natural law, and were proposed or affirmed by the teaching authority of the Church. But people nowadays realise that norms and principles can seldom fully capture complex moral situations, nor can human problems be neatly summarised in the minor premise of a logical argument. Principles and norms can certainly enlighten conscience in the process of discernment, but they can never take the place of conscience. Formerly the Church's pastoral concern to help people in the formation of conscience was to provide the principles from which to draw practical conclusions in concrete situations, and to list the rules that almost dictated the conclusions. It seemed a simple exercise in logic. Little room was left for personal responsibility, and for many people morality was no more than obedience. Today's culture rejects such a simplistic approach and the Church now has the more difficult task of helping people to make informed moral decisions in the light of their own experience. The Church does not help them by doing their theologising for them. The walls which the Church built around them in the past to keep them safe from error can easily become a prison to prevent their growing in freedom and responsibility.

Moreover, although the discernment process must be intelligent, reasonable and responsible, it is not simply an exercise in intelligence and logic. The whole person is involved, not the isolated individual person, but the person who is part of a network of relationships, the person in society, in history, in cosmos. Thus the discernment process will be affected by the individual's personal identity and integrity, abilities, obligations, past experience, insights, affections, outlook and perspective, dispositions, intentions and creative imagination. Conscience will likewise be influenced by cultural conditioning and religious faith. In the case of Christians, their beliefs about God, Christ, Church, creation, human life, community, sin and forgiveness can have a significant influence on the way they interpret facts and assess values. Virtuous people, who have qualities such as peace, joy, gentleness, sensitivity, fairness, generosity and patience are more likely to be objective in their judgments of conscience. As Aristotle put it, the criterion of moral good is the morally good person.

The morally good person is one who has *become* good through good moral choices flowing into morally good actions, not occasionally, but habitually, a person who has consistently followed a responsibly formed conscience. While such a person develops a certain moral *sensitivity* inclining one in the direction of moral good, and acquires a certain clear-sightedness from habitually choosing the good, the basic precepts of the previous chapter still need to be obeyed: be attentive, be intelligent, be reasonable, be responsible. Moral instinct may incline one in the general direction of the good and hint at the morally responsible decision to be made, but it is still necessary to *discern*, to *discover*, rationally and responsibly, what should be done in the concrete situation. In the discernment process one can be helped by insights from scripture, from Christian tradition, from the life of Christ and the example of the saints, and advice can be had from a variety of experts. Guidance can also be had from moral norms, coming from positive law, from the moral teaching of the Church, and from the moral wisdom of the human community. All of these are *authorities*, to be listened to with respect and to be evaluated for the contribution they can make. But the discernment process in each situation must begin with the *facts*, because facts have their own authority. The obligation to follow conscience refers to an *informed* conscience, and clear knowledge of the facts is absolutely essential. As Aquinas was wont to say, *Contra factum, nullum argumentum*; there is no arguing with facts. Analysis of the facts of a situation has always been an integral part of moral reasoning. There are excellent presentations of this kind of analysis in the books of Daniel C. Maguire, *The Moral Choice*,[1] and Richard M. Gula, S.S. *What are they Saying about Moral Norms?*[2] They speak of 'reality-revealing questions' and stress the crucial need to determine the facts of the case before rushing to judgment. These questions need to be answered by the individual making moral decisions for personal action, but they are also needed for groups discussing moral issues, to enable them to formulate norms for individual guidance, and to clarify community thinking about values and particular types of moral/immoral action.

Facts and values

The first step is to be attentive to the data, to get the facts right. *What* is the situation? Precisely *what* action or omission is being considered to resolve the dilemma? For a fuller picture of what is involved, one needs to ask: *Why* is this particular course of action being considered, what is the motive? *How* will the decision be implemented? *Who* is the person going to carry it out? *When? Where?* What are the *foreseeable effects* of the action or omission? Are there other possibilities, *viable alternatives* to what is being contemplated? These questions need to be answered clinically, clearly, and as fully as possible before a responsible decision can be made. Much of the confusion and disagreement in moral discussion comes from careless use of language. This concern for clarity of perception and expression, however, does not mean that conscience cannot decide unless it has absolute certainty about the rightness of a decision. The certainty of mathematics or physical science is not to be expected in moral reasoning. There are situations in which contrary options seem almost equally reasonable and responsible. While doing our best to be attentive, intelligent, reasonable and responsible, we have to live with the imperfection of human knowing and curb our lust for certainty. There is no obligation to do the absolute best, if we could ever recognise it, but only the best in the circumstances, and on an 'objective' scale this might well be second-, third-, fourth- or more best. However, the 'best in the circumstances' cannot be discerned until we have a clear picture of all the circumstances, of the total situation, and this is not possible without satisfactory answers to all of the above questions.

When all of the facts have been assembled to give a total picture of the situation, they need to be *evaluated*. This gives rise to another series of questions. What are the *values* at stake in the situation (life, health, truth, justice, fairness, fidelity to obligations or promises, etc.)? If there is a *conflict of values*, where values cannot be equally safeguarded or promoted (e.g. save the marriage or respect the natural rhythm of reproduction, tell the literal truth or save innocent life with an untruth), which value is the more important, which is the more urgent? If there is *risk of harm* involved, how serious is the *risk* (remote, probable or certain), and how serious is the *harm* (to life, reputation, or mere comfort and convenience, etc.)? Only when the total situation has been clearly grasped and all of the factors involved have been evaluated and balanced one against the other is it possible to make a responsible moral choice and decision. A final step in the search for objectivity, to curb the temptation of self-interest, is the question: what if everybody in a situation like this were to choose the same solution, would it be a good thing? After all, morality is not only about private decisions, but involves the common good.

Need for clarity
The first of the reality-revealing questions is extremely important. *What* precisely is being discussed? This needs to be answered factually, clinically, with a non-moral description of what is involved. Words like murder, lying, stealing, cheating, etc. cannot be applied to physical actions in the abstract, without reference to motives and circumstances. These are *moral* terms, which include motives and circumstances, factors over and above the physical activity. To begin a discussion on abortion with the assertion that 'abortion is the murder of a human foetus or embryo,' is to confuse the issue from the start, and to bias all further discussion. One should begin with the statement of fact, that abortion is 'miscarriage of birth, especially if deliberately induced.' Abortion means killing. The point of the discussion is to decide whether or not it is murder, when and in what circumstances, but this cannot be decided until the total situation is evaluated. Thrusting a knife into a living human body is a clear physical fact, but it can have a variety of human meanings, e.g. murder, homicide in self-defence, or surgical intervention for the good of a patient. Speaking a falsehood may be lying or preserving a secret to save a life or reputation. An act of human intercourse might be an expression of married love, rape (even within marriage), or hatred of women. These are essentially different human actions, not the same action plus different motives or circumstances.

Moral judgment requires that we know exactly *what* is in question. Thus, one cannot make moral judgments about communism, capitalism, racism, etc. unless it is clear what is meant by these labels. The meaning of certain realities can be clouded by misconceptions and prejudice. For example, for several centuries textbooks of Christian morality condemned masturbation in the strongest possible terms without examining *what* it really is. This attitude was not the creation of the Church, but simply reflected the prevailing culture. In the medical profession up to the last century masturbation was commonly believed to cause insanity, and the first American textbook on psychiatry declared that it brought about impotence, pulmonary consumption, vertigo, epilepsy, loss of memory and sometimes even death. This kind of perception blurred all rational discussion of the subject by condemning it in advance of any serious examination. A somewhat different assessment of it today is that of the woman who discovered masturbation at the age of eighty and asked a newspaper counsellor if twice a week was excessive. Likewise, a discussion of the morality of war, and the concept of the just war, would be significantly different depending on whether the context is that of nuclear power or of so-called conventional arms.

The first step in moral assessment is to be clear about *what* is involved. The next question is '*Why?*' Actions cannot be given a moral label apart from their full human meaning and this comes primarily from the intention of the person acting. It is the free decision of the agent which makes an action moral. Hence the importance of *motive*. Without knowing the motive, actions like speaking, walking, taking another's property, or killing cannot be described as moral or immoral. Watching a film of the amputation of a human limb, it is impossible to make a moral judgment of the action, because the motive is not clear, and the action could be either a health measure or an immoral mutilation.

Intrinsic evil?

Because the same physical action can have different human meanings, and therefore different moral evaluations, it is confusing to go on using the traditional description of certain actions as 'intrinsically evil,' meaning that they are so evil in themselves that no motive or circumstance could ever justify them. The phrase is misleading because the word 'evil' is ambiguous, with two different meanings. An evil is a non-good, a disvalue, something harmful like ignorance, poverty, suffering, disease, injury, death. Whatever good consequences they may occasionally have, they are bad or evil in themselves. Since they are disvalues, we have an obligation to avoid or combat them as far as possible, and failure to do this can be immoral. But in themselves they are not *moral evils*, whether they are caused by chance, by natural causes, or by human action. Even when caused by human action, in themselves they still remain *non-moral* or *pre-moral* evils. The word *moral* attaches only to free human behaviour. These pre-moral evils do not become moral evils until they are willed for their own sake, without proportionate reason. In this case, they still remain pre-moral evils, bad things to happen, but they are also *moral evils*, immoral actions for the persons bringing them about. Thus, killing a person with no justifying reason is a moral as well as a pre-moral evil. Killing in self-defence is still evil, a bad thing to happen, something to regret and to be done only with great reluctance and when no other option is available, but it is not *morally* evil. Where the killing is justified as self-defence or in defence of one's neighbour, it is still a bad thing even though it is part of a morally good action. Too often in the past Christians marched into battle and killed with gusto simply because the war was considered just.

It serves no purpose to speak of pre-moral evils as 'intrinsically evil,' giving the impression that there are never situations in which they may be necessary as part of a good action, and therefore morally justified. For example, it can be said that artificial contraception is a disvalue insofar as most people would prefer spontaneous love-making, untrammelled by interventions which may have negative side-effects, and in this sense artificial contraception could be labelled a pre-moral evil. Some Church documents speak of it as intrinsically evil, which implies that it could never be justified in any circumstances. But as a matter of fact, while contraceptive pills are condemned as a method of responsible parenthood, they were allowed by the Vatican for nuns threatened with rape in the Congo, and they may be taken for therapeutic reasons, e.g. to regularise the cycle (*Humanae Vitae* explicitly says this). All three cases involve the same pills, working in the same way according to God's chemical and physiological laws. Since the main difference is the intention or motive, it cannot be the 'artificial contraception' as such which is evil. If there are exceptions according to motive and circumstances, the description 'intrinsically evil' has little meaning when applied to physical actions. To continue using this expression, and expect that it be accepted, is a failure to respect people's God-given critical intelligence. That the phrase could be profitably dropped is shown by the fact that the Holy See's *Declaration on Abortion* (1974) makes no use of it whatever and yet presents a very convincing moral argument, whereas the *Declaration on Sexual Ethics* (1975) uses it freely with reference to masturbation and homosexuality and signally fails to prove its point.

Traditional moralists spoke of contraception, sterilisation, masturbation, direct killing of the innocent, divorce and remarriage as intrinsically evil, as evil in themselves, in all circumstances. For this to be true, however, it would be necessary to know fully in advance all the possible combinations of those actions with intentions and circumstances, together with the various pre-moral values and disvalues involved in each case. This is obviously impossible. A moral judgment of an action can be made only when all three elements are considered together (action, motive, circumstances), and this is possible only with concrete actions, not with whole categories of actions in the abstract. It can be said that murder, lying and stealing are intrinsically evil, but these are already moral terms and can only be applied to the total concrete actions. They are meaningless when applied to physical actions in the abstract. Murder is killing, but not all killing is murder. Lying is falsehood, but not every falsehood is a lie.

A good example of the need to consider action, motive and circumstances together in order to judge the moral rightness or wrongness of a particular activity is the meaning of human sexual intercourse. Church teaching and common wisdom hold that its natural purpose is to express and promote marital love and provide the possibility of offspring, of responsible parenthood. When this relationship is present in a given set of circumstances, and not deliberately hindered or blocked, the act of intercourse is morally good. But if the couple foresee that they are not in a position to provide proper upbringing for the child, the same physical activity is irresponsible and therefore morally bad. Thus, the use of 'natural' methods can be morally good or bad depending on whether or not there is a proportionate reason for using them. Similarly, the use of 'artificial' contraceptives can be morally good or bad depending on whether or not they promote marital love and are used in the context of responsible parenthood. Consideration of the physical activity on its own cannot provide a moral evaluation. It makes no sense, therefore, to speak of 'intrinsically evil actions,' actions that are evil in themselves regardless of motive and circumstances. Few moralists today use this expression.

Double effect

Traditional moralists explained cases like killing in self-defence with the notion of direct and indirect effects and intentions. It is never lawful to intend killing directly, but there can be situations where death is foreseen as an indirect result of a morally good action, as in self-defence. This became known as the *principle of double effect*. In its strict application the good and evil results should flow separately from the action, because where the evil is a means to the good it would be directly willed and therefore immoral. The classical example was the ectopic pregnancy or the cancerous womb, where the removal of the Fallopian tube or of the womb, with the certain death of the foetus as an indirect result, would be justified on the grounds that the primary concern is to save the mother, and the death of the foetus would not be directly intended. The principle sounds logical enough, but it could lead to bizarre results. For example, it would condemn the surgeon who, after excising a benign tumour in the womb also removed a three-month-old foetus in order to save the woman from bleeding to death because the presence of the foetus dilated the womb and made it impossible to stop the bleeding. Since the removal of the foetus was directly intended as a means to an end in this case, it could not be justified. In classical double effect thinking, what he should have done was to remove the bleeding womb, with the foetus inside, to save the mother's life, and then the death of the foetus would have been an indirect effect, not directly willed. The strange consequence of this way of thinking is that the 'lawful' procedure would leave the woman without a womb and no chance of ever conceiving again, whereas the 'unlawful' procedure would not only save her life, but also her fertility. Bernard Häring once put the principle very graphically to Richard McCormick with the reminder that the tubes are for the woman, not the woman for the tubes. This is rather an extreme case, but it shows up the inadequacy of the direct/indirect distinction in the principle of double effect.

Proportionate reason

Most Catholic theologians today (whom the traditionalists criticise as 'revisionists') claim that a more satisfactory solution is to say that in a dilemma where both options involve pre-moral evil, one should choose the lesser evil. It still remains an evil, a bad thing to happen, but it is not morally evil because there is a *proportionate reason* for causing it or allowing it to happen. Moralists of this school are described as 'proportionalists' and at times harshly criticised as 'consequentialists' (even in official Church documents). The criticism is that so much emphasis on consequences gives the impression that moral discernment is simply a matter of pragmatism, deciding which option will produce the greatest amount of good with the least amount of harm. It is claimed that goods cannot be quantitatively measured or compared. But in fact, attending to consequences has always been an essential part of moral discernment. Too many do-gooders are oblivious to the appalling consequences of some of their well-intentioned but misguided actions.

It is obvious in the example just quoted that it is better to save both the mother's life and fertility rather than just her life, and where the choice is between saving the mother or losing both lives it is better to opt for the

mother's life. In fact, the Belgian bishops say that in this situation of distress the Church has always allowed surgical intervention, even when it
involves the loss of one of the two lives one is attempting to save. They
say that the moral principle here is that where two lives are at stake,
while doing everything possible to save both, one should attempt to
save one rather than allow two to die. But it is important to stress that the
weighing up of consequences is not a mere mathematical calculation of
'more or less' in quantitative terms. It has been objected that the principle of proportionate reason could justify the decision of a judge who is
willing to frame an innocent man in order to avoid the riots threatened
by a raging mob of hundreds. On a larger scale some would justify the
killing of a hundred thousand people in the Nagasaki atomic bombing
in order to avoid many times that number of deaths in a continuation of
the war with conventional weapons. But the principle of proportionate
reason is not simply one life versus a hundred, or a hundred thousand
versus millions.

These objections have been answered by a leading proponent of the
proportionate reason principle, Richard McCormick, S.J., probably the
most outstanding Catholic moralist in the English-speaking world. He
is careful to stress that a proportionate reason is not just any reason at all,
and the assessment of values is not just a quantitative measure of good
and bad results. For him, proportionate reason means that the value
being sought is at least equal to the one being sacrificed, and that there is
no less harmful way of protecting the values here and now. In assessing
proportion the following points need to be kept in mind: the social
implications and consequences of the action must be considered insofar
as they can be foreseen; the question should be asked: what if everybody
were to behave like this; be alert to the bias and possible prejudices of the
local culture; pay attention to norms formulated by the community in
the light of its accumulated wisdom; consult others, especially those
with experience in the field; and let one's religious beliefs throw light on
the situation and on the discernment process. Although the decision of
conscience is intensely personal, it should never be made in isolation
from the community. Serious attention should be given to norms that
reflect community discernment down through the years, although they
can never take the place of personal conscience.

In response to the suggestion that framing the innocent person to
avoid murderous mob rioting, or the atomic bombing of the Japanese
city to shorten the war, could be justified under the principle of proportionate reason, it needs to be asserted that there is no parallel

whatsoever, except in superficial appearance, between these cases and the abortion that is justified to save the life of the mother. In the latter case the abortion is intrinsically and necessarily connected with saving the mother's life, part of a single action as a means to an end. The decision to save the mother's life in this situation is morally good, supported by a really proportionate reason, because in the circumstances it is the lesser evil. In the other two cases there is no intrinsic connection between the immoral actions and the hoped-for good result. The mob is made up of people of free will and they should cease their evil actions irrespective of the judge's decision. To yield to their demands almost denies their own freedom. Moreover, while the judge may intend only to avoid bloody riots and possible deaths, he is in fact causing the death of an innocent person and also seriously harming the institution of criminal law and the framework of justice that are so necessary for social harmony. His action is immoral and could never be justified as a means to a good end. Similarly in the case of the bombing of non-combatants in Japan, there is no intrinsic or necessary connection between the bombing and Japan's stopping its unjust aggression. The bombing is a deliberate killing of innocent people, an action that is complete in itself and immoral because there is no proportionate reason to justify it. A morally bad action can never be a means to a good end, but an action that involves a physical evil may be part of a morally good action like self-defence.

Conflict situations

The 1995 encyclical, *The Gospel of Life,* makes this latter point when it speaks of cases in which the right to protect one's own life and the duty not to harm someone else's life are difficult to reconcile in practice. It says that 'no one can renounce the right to self-defence out of lack of love for life or for self,' and goes on to say that 'legitimate defence can be not only a right, but a grave duty for someone responsible for another's life, the common good of the family or of the State.' When it explains that this may involve taking an aggressor's life, it states that this is justifiable even though the aggressor may be morally innocent because of insanity (par. 55). But this principle applies equally to the situation in which the presence of the foetus is a direct threat to the mother's life. Unfortunately, the encyclical in par. 58 clouds the issue when it describes every procured abortion as murder, stressing the *innocence* of the foetus. It says that 'no one more absolutely innocent could be imagined' than the foetus. But the innocence is not a determining factor, since the insane aggressor, in the words of the encyclical itself, is also morally innocent. In more careful terminology, neither the insane aggressor nor the foetus which is a direct threat to the life of the mother is innocent. In the original Latin, *innocent* means harmless, *in-nocens*, not harmful. Both the aggressor and the foetus in these two cases are anything but innocent. Each one is *nocens*, harmful, a threat to life. For this reason, both cases are covered by the principle affirmed by the encyclical, 'Certainly, the intrinsic value of life and the duty to love oneself no less than others are the basis of a *true right to self-defence*' (par. 55).

Does the end justify the means?

Motive is absolutely central to morality, but not to the extent that 'the motive or the end justifies the means.' Noble purposes like the defence of religion or national security can easily be invoked to justify torture and other infringements of human rights. The Church itself was not always immune to this temptation, as we see from the Crusades and the Inquisition. Too often means and ends are confused; a means towards a good end can become an end in itself, pursued for its own sake. For example, a government needs to stay in power to work for the common good (which is a good end, a good intention), but the staying in power sometimes takes precedence over the common good and unjustified and immoral abuses are resorted to for this purpose. Similarly, a sufficient supply of modern arms is necessary to defend a country, but the arms race can take on a life of its own, so that the means towards a good end becomes an end in itself. Not only is the economy damaged and things like health and education neglected, but other countries are provoked to compete in the same immoral direction. The proper proportion between means and end becomes distorted.

If an action is *morally* bad, it can never be justified in any circumstances as a means to a good end. But for a proportionate reason we may *permit* a moral evil to come about (like the sin of another person), whereas in the case of a *non-moral* evil we may directly will it and directly cause it if there is a proportionate reason for doing so.

However, there is a sense in which it can be said that the end *does* justify the means, namely when the means in question is morally neutral or only a pre-moral evil. Walking, speaking, etc. are morally neutral, and when they are part of a morally good act they are morally good, just as they are morally bad when part of a morally bad action. When it is a question of a pre-moral evil, a disvalue (inflicting pain, telling an untruth, etc.), it remains evil, a disvalue, but if there is a proportionate reason (in the sense explained above) for causing or allowing it, then it becomes an integral part of a morally good action. On the other hand, to cause or allow a pre-moral evil to come about without a proportionate reason is morally evil, no matter how good the intention. When pre-moral evils or disvalues are involved, the key criterion for judging the morality of an action is proportionate reason, or due proportion between the good that is intended and the harm that is caused or allowed to happen. Due proportion is also lacking when a value is sought in a way that ultimately destroys it; thus, to ignore traffic lights in the name of freedom is to destroy freedom.

Absolute moral norms?

Given that the expression 'intrinsically evil actions' is considered unhelpful in moral discussion nowadays and that the principle of proportionate reason can justify exceptions to the fifth commandment, it is natural to wonder what force traditional moral norms can have in today's world. In fact, the ten commandments and many other norms formulated by the accumulated wisdom of the Church and human community down the centuries retain their validity. The process of moral discernment is always carried out in the context of a particular culture and tradition and is significantly helped by the norms developed by the community in the light of its values and experience. These are not rules to be blindly obeyed, but clear directives and guidelines to help discernment and decision. There are *transcendental norms* that are absolute in the sense of having no exceptions, such as the four imperatives mentioned in the context of natural law: be attentive, be intelligent, be reasonable, be responsible; and others like: do good and avoid evil, respect life, be just, be truthful, be chaste, be merciful, respect conscience; and for the Christian: live the gospel, obey God, love your neighbour. These are not conclusions of a reasoning process, but expressions of our self-understanding as moral and responsible human beings, and as Christians. They express what it means to be human, to be Christian, but they do not describe the material content of actions. They are always before us as the moral challenge to become actually what we are potentially. But they do not spell out for us which concrete actions are loving, just or merciful. Because they are so general they are universal and absolute.

There are other norms, referred to as the *concrete material norms of morality*. These norms warn us about, and prohibit, pre-moral evils or disvalues, telling us that we should not kill or injure people, speak falsely, or exploit others, etc. The commandments are good examples of such norms: thou shalt not kill, steal, bear false witness, covet your neighbour's wife or your neighbour's goods. They could be summarised in the general formula: you shall not bring about (by your actions) nor tolerate (by your omissions, your failure to act) pre-moral evil or disvalue. Concrete material norms do not take the place of conscience and the discernment process, but they are a help in the moral life insofar as we do not have to re-invent the wheel in every situation requiring a moral decision. When faced with a dilemma and a temptation to kill, my conviction about the fifth commandment leaves me with a negative feeling towards killing, a strong presumption against killing, and only the most serious reasons would move me away from this. Since these material norms of morality refer to pre-moral evils, and these can occasionally be part of a morally good act, the norms admit of exceptions. In this sense they are not absolute. Given the complexity of human life, it is impossible to avoid all disvalues in our actions, and it is the business of moral discernment to judge when there is proportionate reason to justify exceptions. But the basic moral challenge is to limit the pre-moral evils as much as possible. These material norms are clear when they speak of pre-moral evils, but when norms use 'synthetic' words like murder, stealing, lying and cheating, these already include motive and circumstances, but they do not say which kinds of killing qualify as murder, or when speaking a falsehood is a lie.

Deontology and teleology

Although material norms generally allow for exceptions, there are some which, for all practical purposes are almost absolute. Thus, for example, it is impossible to envisage situations that would justify rape, the direct killing of non-combatants in warfare, sexual abuse of children, medical experimentation on a person without the patient's informed consent. Some moralists today still hold that many more actions can be described as intrinsically evil, regardless of consequences or other considerations. They argue for an absolute prohibition of masturbation, contraception, direct sterilisation, artificial insemination, homosexuality and extramarital sex, because all of these are against nature and therefore can never be justified in any circumstances. It is our *duty* to avoid them. For these thinkers, norms are *deontological* (from the Greek *deo*, meaning 'I ought'), stressing duty, and norms are given a central place in moral reasoning. The majority of moralists, however, in line with a solid centuries-long tradition, take a *teleological* approach (from the Greek *telos*, meaning 'end' or 'goal'). While giving due attention to norms as important guidelines, they make more room for the finality or purpose of actions, examining their human meaning and context, and they are particularly concerned to foresee and evaluate their likely consequences. They recognise that in the world as we know it, pre-moral evils cannot be totally avoided without banning most human activity, since even the best actions can have unwanted side-effects. The challenge is to minimise the evil in cases where it cannot be avoided, and to formulate principles to discern how this may be done responsibly. The advantage of this approach is that it can make allowance for cultural change, and for growth and development, which encourages an ongoing rethinking and refinement of norms.

From the above discussion it might seem that moral discernment is all about justifying exceptions, and that exceptions are frequent, but this is far from being the case. It is really about an ideal, the ideal of human flourishing, of personal growth towards what it means to be a person and of respecting and enabling that in others. It means working towards that ideal world where there will be less and less need to focus on evil and more concern for promoting the good in all areas of life, for individual persons, for communities and for international relations. The *positive, transcendental norms* are a constant reminder of this ideal of human striving: do good, avoid evil, be just, be truthful, be merciful, etc. The function of the *concrete material norms*, in their negative form, is to warn us against all that gets in the way of the ideal: thou shalt not kill, steal, etc. These norms are relative insofar as they only forbid us causing or allowing to happen pre-moral evil which exceeds what is absolutely unavoidable in our striving for the good.

The milder approach

Church documents in the past were inclined to stress 'objective morality,' 'absolute norms,' 'intrinsically evil actions,' to the extent that Catholic moral teaching could seem harsh and unbending. In practice, of course, it was tempered by 'pastoral concern,' when a pastoral solution would be found to soften an intractable problem. But even apart from 'pastoral solutions,' the teaching itself had a more human side, making room for flexibility and common sense. This can be seen in what theologian Donal Harrington in an excellent book, *What is Morality?*[3] has described as 'the small print in theology.' Under this heading he stresses the fact that in many instances the only answer to a question about the morality of an action is: 'It depends . . .' because a black and white answer is not possible in a grey area, and so many factors have to be taken into account. There were various ways of doing this. One was the system of 'probabilism,' to interpret general principles when applying them to individual cases. Unfortunately, the word acquired the pejorative sense of a subtle way of justifying otherwise blameworthy acts, but the principle in itself is good. We find it used in the New Testament to deal with cases like the observance of the Sabbath, the paying of taxes, eating sacrificial food, marriage and virginity; and the early Church used it with regard to military service, wealth, dress, lying and persecution. Down through the centuries it became a fine art of balancing the opinions of experts to discover which was more probable, and it was accepted that in some cases it was lawful to follow an opinion that was probable, although not the most probable. In today's context of a clearer distinction between pre-moral and moral evil, and the critical assessment of 'proportionate reason,' the casuistry system would seem to be less needed in making decisions of conscience, but the study of cases can still be quite helpful as a method of analysis, especially in medical ethics.

Equity is another concept that helped to soften the impact of a too rigid law, especially in situations where obedience to the letter of the law would be against its spirit and defeat its purpose. This applies not only in the case of positive laws of Church or state, but even to precepts of the natural law. Some of these can be so culturally conditioned that when the culture and the situation change, the precepts need to be re-formulated for the new situation. Closer attention to *viable alternatives* can be helpful here. For example, although the Eskimos valued and respected life, in primitive times when food was critically scarce, it was customary for some elders to wander off and die of hunger in order to allow the others to survive. They felt this was a moral obligation since there was no viable alternative.

Wrongdoing and sin

Another consoling element of the traditional teaching is the important distinction between the objective and subjective aspects of moral action, the difference between wrongdoing and sin. People who do something objectively wrong are the cause of the action and of its bad consequences, but they are not morally or subjectively guilty and blameworthy unless they were fully aware that what they were doing was wrong, unless they did it freely and there were no circumstances that might lessen the guilt or remove it altogether. The traditional formula for serious sin was: serious matter, full knowledge and full consent. A diminution of any one of these would lessen the guilt. Today's culture is much more sensitive to the many factors that can dull our understanding, limit our freedom, and restrict the number of viable alternatives. Too often in the past a pregnant girl resorting to abortion would be denounced by clergy, family and friends and the man responsible for her situation would disown her. Having her baby and giving it up for adoption may have been an alternative in the abstract, but in her situation it was often beyond her ability. Her abortion was still wrongdoing, but in many cases there would be little or no subjective blame. Those who drove her to it could be far more guilty.

A similar case is that of the married woman with young children whose violent husband threatens to abandon her if she becomes pregnant again, but will not discuss the possibility of any kind of contraception, saying that it is her responsibility, and yet insists on having his 'rights' as and when he feels like it. So-called 'natural family planning' is not a viable alternative for her, so she resorts to some 'artificial' method. It is an insult to speak to her of the danger of a contraceptive mentality, when in fact she is taking the only means possible to save her marriage, which is necessary for her own welfare and that of her children. In cases like this some moralists might speak of an evil action being justified because of the good motive and special circumstances. Others would prefer to look on the human meaning of the action as a whole, and see it as a morally responsible and therefore good act. The wife might well prefer some other way of saving her marriage, but in her circumstances she has no choice. The classical example of circumstances changing the total meaning of an action is the starving person taking another's property to stay alive. It looks like stealing, but the traditional judgment was that in such an extreme situation property is no longer private, but common, belonging to all, with preference for those in dire need to save life. Another way of putting it is that life is a greater value than property and must therefore be given preference when it comes to a choice. Self-preservation is not stealing.

Perfectionism

The gospel is a high ideal and the Church has a long and healthy tradition of preaching ideals. We need ideals to fire the imagination and stir up enthusiasm and commitment. But at times the focus on perfection ('Be ye perfect as your heavenly Father is perfect') can develop into a perfectionism leading to scrupulosity and unhealthy guilt feelings. It is good to feel a sense of unworthiness in the presence of God's infinite goodness, but an awareness of that goodness should affirm people's own sense of self-worth, so that in spite of being sinners we can still realise how infinitely precious we are in God's sight. Commentators have noted that we have a well-developed theology and spirituality of perfection, but perhaps this needs to be balanced by a theology and spirituality of imperfection. This is not to lower our ideals, but to give us the patience and courage to accept our imperfection, to be at peace with the fact that we are ordinary people. It might also help us to cope with the highly complex, ambiguous and imperfect world in which we live. In our moral discernment it is fine to focus on the ideal, but an ideal which for certain individuals is totally unattainable is simply unreal. An impossible ideal is a crucifixion that can hardly be in keeping with God's loving will.

A simple but very topical example is that of homosexual people, a not inconsiderable proportion of the human race throughout the world, who through no fault or personal choice of their own, but by nature (from God?) are homosexually orientated. The Holy See's 1976 document on sexual ethics says that 'sexual relations between persons of the same sex are essentially disordered and may never be approved in any way whatever.' This was a blow to homosexuals, who have the same need for sexual love as heterosexuals, and for many of whom celibacy is an impossible ideal. One of the three authors of the Vatican document, Fr Jan Visser, explained after its publication that when people are so deeply homosexual that they will be in serious personal and perhaps social trouble unless they attain a steady partnership within their homosexual lives, one can recommend them to seek such a partnership, and this relationship can be accepted as the best they can do in their present situation. A responsible committed relationship is so much better than a life of casual encounters. He justified this on the ground that one can pastorally and positively recommend the lesser of two evils as the best thing in their situation. Moralists who agree with his conclusion justify their position in a variety of ways: theology of exceptions, principle of compromise, secondary natural law, proportionate good in a situation affected by sin, ontic or pre-moral evil. The most positive and satisfying approach would seem to be the *principle of the practical ideal*, proposed by Irish theologian Ralph Gallagher, C.Ss.R, in 1979. This is not an abstract ideal, but the ideal that is practically possible to the individual in a given set of circumstances. Homosexuality is quoted here simply as an example. It deserves much fuller treatment, but a problem is that our Catholic tradition in this area is more a morality of marriage than a morality of sexuality. It is still an area of great confusion.

The Holy Spirit and reason

Those impatient with the intricacies of moral reasoning need to be reminded that although conscience can be helped by prayer, by advice from experts, by the tradition of the human community and the teaching of the Church, none of these can take the place of personal conscience itself. The assistance of the Holy Spirit which Jesus promised to his Church works no magic. In fact one of the signs of that special help of the Spirit should be the good arguments which make Church teaching convincing. One of the reasons why so many items taught by the Church for centuries have now been quietly dropped or replaced by something totally different is precisely because the arguments supporting the former teaching are now seen to be inadequate. Catholic tradition emphasises that reason must be informed by faith, but faith can never oust reason in the process of moral discernment. In fact, to go against reason is to act against conscience. Hence the need for critical analysis to test the soundness of arguments. It is in the give-and-take of discussion between moralists that the flaws in reasoning show up.

Flawed reasoning can be caused by unconscious, unexamined assumptions and variations in methodology. Richard A. McCormick, S.J., lists some of the cultural factors which influence moral reasoning: the growth of an educated laity; different notions of God and his providence in the world; cultural liberalism; different concepts of authority in the Church; different models of Church; confusion about law and morality; cultural attitudes towards individualism and membership of society; pluralism of theologies; relevance of experience and the findings of the human sciences; over-simplifications in the use of scripture; rhetoric instead of genuine argument; and begging the question instead of proving the conclusion.[4]

Critical mind, sensitive heart

The above discussion of the discernment process may seem rather complicated, but in fact for most decisions of everyday life it can be quite simple. However, there are occasions when more careful analysis is needed, when the advice of competent people must be sought, and recourse is had to appropriate authorities, but ultimately the decision is made by the person concerned. That decision is the voice of conscience. In the more complicated problems, and especially in the new challenges coming from our fast-changing culture and high-powered modern technology, ordinary people can feel out of their depth. Professional moralists, with the necessary time and expertise, will argue the issues and try to formulate norms which the community may come to appropriate as guidelines to help individuals in their own soul-searching. But whether it is a matter of personal discernment or the give-and-take of professional discussion, it is essential to be faithful to the basic norms: be attentive, intelligent, reasonable and responsible. Although it is not possible to have mathematical certainty in moral matters, responsibility requires that we acquire as much certainty as possible that what is decided is the morally right thing to do. Uncritical thinking and sloppy arguments are irresponsible. Feelings on their own can lead us astray; they are notoriously blind and self-centred. There is no substitute for alert, critical intelligence, not only to convince others, but to convince ourselves that we are acting in good conscience.

Moral discernment, however, is not simply a question of intelligence and logic. Blaise Pascal reminds us that 'we know truth, not only by reason, but also by the heart.' The basic insight of all morality, namely the mystery and uniqueness of human persons and the awe and respect they call forth in us, is an affective knowing that is deeper than logic, and the values which we find make life worth living, like truth, goodness, justice, etc. are realities that are grasped by the heart as much as by the mind. Of course the effort to discover in practice what it means to be truthful, good, just, etc. requires critical intelligence, but guidelines alone will not yield moral discernment. We must always pay attention to 'gut' feelings and sensitivity, that can not only help us to discover the right thing to do in a given situation, but enable us to find how best to do it and when to do it. Such affective perception and intuition can also alert us to healthy changes in our culture that call for adjustments and new moral reactions.

The affective insight that comes from constant fidelity to conscience is not unlike the 'knowledge by connaturality' spoken of by the mystics. Once again we return to Aristotle's claim, that the true criterion of goodness is the morally good person. We become what we think, what we love and what we do. By constant fidelity to conscience we acquire the morally good habits called virtues: prudence, justice, courage, temperance and a host of associated human qualities that are the characteristics of the morally good person, such as compassion, gentleness, sensitivity. Since conscience is our deepest level of consciousness, the very core of our personality, it follows that the whole person is involved in a decision of conscience. The more rounded, balanced and mature the personality, the more likely it is that the decision will be responsible and objective. Morally mature people would be 'happy in their own skin,' having a healthy awareness of their own personal worth, but with respect and reverence for others as persons, people who can accept themselves, others and the world in which they live, people not preoccupied with self, people who can be detached and private but not cut off from others, people open to new experiences with the capacity to learn from them, people with democratic attitudes capable of working with others, people with a deep inner security able to accept criticism, people who have personal convictions about right and wrong. Of course, this is an ideal, but one worth striving for if morality is about human flourishing, about becoming actually what we are potentially.

Moral maturity is not a once-for-all acquisition, but a continual process of growth. As with any journey, there can be setbacks and deviations, but these simply remind us of the need for vigilance and self-criticism to recognise not only when and where we have gone wrong, but also to know when routine takes over, when we settle for the familiar and fail to see new challenges. Conversion is an important factor in the process of moral growth: intellectual, moral and religious conversion. This involves the recognition that we have gone astray and that we need to convert, to 'turn around,' to get back on track, in our thinking, in our value-system, in our moral attitudes, in our relationship with God and the world of the sacred. It is not a once-in-a-lifetime dramatic experience, but rather an ongoing process occurring at appropriate intervals along the path of life. The challenge is to be continually open to such occurrences, calling us to a change of mind and heart. This too is the call of conscience, telling us not only to form it, but to go on forming, and reforming, it, if we are to be faithful to it. Conversion may involve a going out of self, out of the narrow, selfish, sinful self which can trap and hold us back, the self that we are expected to go beyond in self-transcendence; but in another sense it means coming back to our true self, our better self, to the core of our personality, to the sanctuary where we are alone with God. Conscience is the call of God inviting us back to the path of truth, goodness and beauty whenever we stray, not only calling us, but also helping us from within through the power of his grace.

8

RESPONSIBLE PARENTHOOD

The previous chapter discussed moral discernment in general, on the level of principle, but it may be helpful to take a concrete example to see how it applies in practice. The topic of responsible parenthood is chosen for the reason that in the almost thirty years since the publication of *Humanae Vitae* the majority of Catholics have seldom heard this responsibility discussed in its full moral context. For the average Catholic, the encyclical condemns artificial contraception, and Church leaders have been repeating the condemnation ever since, often in the same breath as abortion and divorce. Any debate on the subject quickly moves on to the question of authority and obedience, and acceptance of the teaching is often seen as a test of loyalty to the Church. Sadly, responsible parenthood itself gets lost in the process. Conscience, moral discernment and responsibility often seem to be by-passed, even in official statements by Church leaders. *Humanae Vitae* was certainly a watershed for the Church. Some would see the fall-out from the encyclical as a disaster, while others maintain that in spite of the deep suffering it has caused to so many devout Catholics, the overall effect has been positive in helping people towards a more mature understanding of conscience.

The overall context
One paragraph of the encyclical lists what is forbidden, but most of the document is a positive treatment of married love, with insights of lasting value. The opening passages speak of conscience faced with new problems arising from the many changes in the world, and they admit that one question being asked nowadays is: must moral rules change when it is felt that one needs to be heroic in order to observe them, since married couples need love-making to keep their marriage intact? The document is open and realistic in acknowledging changes: the population explosion which threatens the world supply of food, the economic and social

changes that put new pressures on family life, the costly educational needs of children, and the changing role of women. Pope Paul listed three questions for the Church in the light of these changes:

1. Do present moral norms for married life need to be changed?
2. Can the procreative finality of marriage apply to married life as a whole rather than to each individual act?
3. Can the regulation of births be left to human reason and will rather than to biological rhythms?

The Pope explained that consideration of such questions cannot be limited to biology, psychology, demography or sociology, but needs to begin with the overall vision of the human person. He presents a very beautiful picture of married love as human, total, faithful, exclusive and fruitful.

This is the ideal that Christian couples aspire to, and it is the context in which they must plan their families. Planning a family is sharing in God's work. The Vatican II document on *The Church in the Modern World* (par. 50) says that in this married people are co-operating with the love of God the Creator and are, in a sense, its interpreters. The text invites them to judge matters correctly in a spirit of obedient respect for God, reflecting together, considering their own well-being and the well-being of their children already born or yet to come, reading the signs of the times, assessing their own material and spiritual situation, all in the context of the good of the family, of society and of the Church. It insists that it is the married couple themselves who must in the last analysis make these judgments, and in doing so they must not simply follow their own fancy, but must be ruled by conscience. Fr Gustave Martelet, S.J., a French theologian reported to have been involved in the drafting of *Humanae Vitae,* said at the time of its publication that an encyclical is not a book of recipes, that many difficulties still remain and it is for every man and woman to resolve them in the secrecy of his or her heart. He emphasised that the encyclical cannot be a substitute for individual conscience. The question is: how should couples use their conscience responsibly in this aspect of their married life? Few people will begin their reflection with a study of the encyclical, but many of its insights will naturally be part of their thinking, even if they have problems with its central teaching prohibiting artificial contraception.

When people marry they would love to give free rein to the natural rhythm of spontaneous sexuality to express their love, without having to calculate against the risk of conception. But they know that, however much they would welcome a family as the fruit of their love, there are all kinds of pressures working against this ideal, and they are forced to regulate their family. There are couples who have no difficulties and can gladly accept whatever children God may send them, and thus enjoy the spontaneity of married love, allowing nature to take its course. In the simple context of former times this was quite common, although it was often a question of having no choice. However, for thousands of years people have sought to have some control over their fertility, and tried various forms of contraception. In the complexity and pressure of today's world there are many situations in which it would be irresponsible, and therefore immoral, just to 'let a family happen.' It is an awesome responsibility to bring a child into the world, so it ought to be the outcome of a responsible decision. It takes little effort to produce offspring, but to be a parent means being responsible for its upbringing, health and education. Planning a family means that the couple must first of all put their heads together to decide whether, in their circumstances, it would be wise for them to have children at all, and then to discuss how many and at what intervals. Given the seriousness of what is at stake, their decision must be based on objective criteria and not mere whim. Their discernment must be governed by the precepts already mentioned, that they *be attentive* to all the facts in the case, that they *use their intelligence* in trying to understand them, that they *reason about* what these facts mean, and that they *be responsible* in making their choice. As Christian believers, they will make their discernment in a context of faith, sensitive to the teaching of Jesus and confident of God's help when they pray for it. But there is no magic short-cut in this kind of help, because divine grace does not bypass the ordinary human means through which it works.

Initial reflection
To be attentive to all the facts of their situation means that they consider a host of factors. First, the physical, psychological, moral and religious state of both husband and wife, and the welfare of present and possible future children. There can be cases where the physical or psychological health of either partner is so impaired that the couple would be incapable of caring properly for children, or that the illness might be transmitted to their children. A wife whose two pregnancies brought on severe mental disturbance requiring a year or more in a psychiatric hospital each time could very responsibly decide that she should on no account risk another pregnancy, because of the damage it would bring not only to herself,

but to her present children (left without the care of a mother and at the mercy perhaps of an inadequate father), to her husband, and of course to her very marriage, which is the highest value of all to the couple caught in such a situation. A couple who already have two severely handicapped children and are just barely coping with their situation, but who have been warned that there is a high probability that another child could be handicapped, may decide that their marriage could well break under such a strain and they could not risk such a disaster for themselves and their present children. They would be acting responsibly in deciding against further children and then searching for the most effective protection available. It could happen that no contraceptive apart from sterilisation can provide the security they need.

A couple's material situation is also an important factor in discerning the number and spacing of children. Lack of housing and employment puts a severe strain on a relationship, and all the more if the relationship is already fragile. Economic problems are a major cause of marital breakdown. In some cases the general conditions of the times can be a determining factor in a couple's decision, for example racialism, persecution, famine, or war. During apartheid in South Africa some expatriate couples living there decided that while they could protect themselves from the racialist atmosphere surrounding them, they felt they could never protect their children, so they postponed having any until they left the country.

Only when the couple have decided, in the light of all these factors, and when possible and necessary with the help of advisers (doctor, social worker, spiritual adviser, family or friends) to plan their family, can the question of birth control arise, and it is only at this point that they need to consider possible methods. The various methods cannot be *morally evaluated* apart from the wider discussion of the couple's total situation. The primary value in the whole discernment process is the *good of the marriage as a whole*, namely the welfare of the couple as a couple. In a sense the welfare of the children is secondary because their well-being depends so much on the marriage relationship between the parents. As the primary value, the welfare of the marriage itself takes precedence over so-called 'nature' or the natural biological rhythms of reproduction, and it is traditional Catholic morality that in a conflict of values the secondary must be sacrificed in favour of the primary. The right to life of a starving person takes precedence over the right to private property of the person whose food he takes without permission and seems to 'steal.'

Essential factors in discernment

After the initial discussion of the couple's overall situation there are five factors that need to be examined before it is possible to reach a responsible decision. These are:

1. the state of the marriage;
2. motives;
3. methods;
4. consequences;
5. circumstances.

Only when all of these factors have been considered *together* can a decision be reached. If the decision is responsible, it will be morally good, if irresponsible it will be morally bad. Without this kind of discernment, taking account of all the factors involved, it is difficult to see how a responsible decision can be arrived at. Unfortunately, large numbers of Catholics see Church teaching on responsible parenthood simply and solely as condemning artificial contraception, which is labelled as intrinsically evil, never allowed.

Responsible parenthood, like responsible medicine, is *morally* concerned with motives and values, and only secondarily concerned with techniques or methods, namely: what is the best way to achieve the values we cherish (life, marriage, children) with a minimum of harm done? When values clash, as they do in all areas of life, we have to find a responsible compromise. There are situations in which it is not possible to ensure that all values will be equally promoted: survival of the marriage, the physical or emotional health of the partners, the welfare of the children both present and future, and respect for the natural rhythm of reproduction, and in these cases *the couple themselves* have to *decide together* what is the best way of preserving the values in question, in keeping with their importance and the degree to which they are threatened. There can be no pre-packaged, slot-machine solutions to such intimate and personal problems. Each of the following five factors needs to be carefully examined.

1. The state of the particular marriage. The marriage itself is the primary value to be protected and promoted, but marriages vary in their concrete reality, and it is their own individual marriage that is the concern of the couple, not some abstract notion of an ideal beyond their personal experience. A particular marriage can be close, warm, solid, healthy and enduring, or doubtful, fragile, threatened, on the verge of breakdown. A decision valid for one marriage could be disastrous for another, and to ignore this is to act irresponsibly. A close, dedicated and highly motivated couple might find that one of the natural methods of family planning suits them and even binds them closer together in their commitment, whereas the same method could wreck a fragile marriage because one or other partner could not bear the strain.

2. *The motives for avoiding or spacing children.* There can be a variety of motives. They can be selfish or unselfish, serious, light or even downright frivolous. It is not unknown that couples for whom the natural methods of family planning work easily and effectively use them without scruple for purely selfish motives, justifying their behaviour on the grounds that the method is 'allowed' by the Church, while condemning another couple whose circumstances require that they avoid conception at all costs, but for whom the natural methods simply do not work. All of the factors listed above under *initial reflection* could be motives or reasons for a couple to decide on some form of family planning. Responsible parenthood requires that they evaluate the seriousness of their reasons. Although Pope Pius XII in 1951 spoke of the Christian duty to procreate, he recognised that there could be serious motives (medical, eugenic, economic and social) to justify a couple in avoiding a family for a long time, even for the entire duration of the marriage (although he had only periodic continence in mind as a means). In practice, a serious motive means a proportionate reason.

3. *The methods.* Many methods are available and they need to be evaluated from the point of view of *effectiveness* and *safety*. It is necessary to know what they involve, how they work, and what probable or possible side-effects they have, not only immediate but also long-term. A couple for whom it is absolutely imperative that they avoid a family needs to find the most effective method of contraception possible, whereas a couple whose reason for avoiding children is less serious might responsibly choose a less effective method. In the latter case an unplanned pregnancy might be harmful for the couple, but not a tragedy that would seriously damage their marriage or the children they already have. Where a particular method has dangerous side-effects, the couple needs to check whether the risk is certain, probable or just a possibility, and then to weigh the risk from the method against the risk of pregnancy and the seriousness of the harm feared from the pregnancy in their situation. Artificial contraceptives have side-effects that can be a serious risk to health, but in some cases natural family planning can involve risks, for example the strain on an already fragile marriage. Human life has never

been without risk, and even commonly-used medicines can have unwanted side-effects. It is a question of weighing the risks against the benefits. Risk-taking is a normal part of everyday life. Moral responsibility requires that the risks be evaluated, and that they be justified only by a proportionate reason.

4. *The consequences, insofar as they can be foreseen:* of the methods, of the decision, for the couple and for present or future children. We are responsible not only for our decisions and actions, but for the consequences that flow from them to the extent that we foresee them. To plead ignorance of them does not lessen responsibility if we could and should have foreseen them. For example, it is not enough to say that natural family planning is more in keeping with nature, or that it is favoured by Church teaching. It must be asked: what will it do to this particular marriage? and: are both partners committed to it and ready to accept all that it involves?

5. *The circumstances of the couple,* for example, their age and their physical and emotional health, and the many other factors mentioned above under initial reflection. Some of these may be quite serious and enter into the determining motives for family planning, whereas others may be simply circumstances needing to be kept in mind in the discernment. A couple who are both at critical points in their career might decide to postpone a family. But if they put off their first baby until the wife is in her early forties they should know that having a first baby at that age can give rise to complications for both mother and child that could be serious. Besides, if they wait a considerable number of years they may grow accustomed to such a level of social life that it would be difficult to adjust to the restrictions that the arrival of a baby can bring, or they may feel more like grandparents when the child becomes a teenager and they will find it difficult to cope. These may not be determining factors in their decision, but they need to be taken into account for a balanced judgment, a responsible decision.

Church teaching

It may seem surprising that *Humanae Vitae* is not listed among the five essential factors that need to be considered in a moral discernment about birth regulation. This is not because Church teaching does not matter or is only of secondary importance, but rather because it is presumed that Christians who take this matter seriously and wish to make a responsible decision will be influenced by their faith at every step of their discernment. Their Christian faith will give them a particular sensitivity to, and appreciation of, the basic values of life, married love, family and children.

They will have experience of these values in their own lives and have seen them reflected in the life of the Christian community which is God's family. They can discover some beautiful insight-full passages in the encyclical about married love, but they will have known these already from their own experience of the faith, enriched by Catholic writings on the subject and by some of the documents of the Second Vatican Council. They know that Pope Paul's encyclical is an important, authoritative statement of Catholic teaching on marriage and they will respect it and do their best to integrate it into their decision-making. Some may feel that they have to obey it when it condemns artificial contraception. But most adults know that *obedience* is the response to an *order*, a *command*, not to teaching. The respectful response to teaching is docility, openness, the willingness to learn and to be convinced. To act in serious matters without understanding and conviction is irresponsible and can be immoral.

But large numbers of married Catholics find that the teaching of the encyclical on contraception does not make sense in the light of their experience, and that its reasoning fails to convince them. In all good conscience they confess that no amount of good will or mental gymnastics can force them to see it as God's will. If it is true, they believe that it ought to shine by its own light. Truth cannot simply be decreed, but only presented and explained. The encyclical is described as teaching, but no teaching takes place until somebody learns. Those who have had the opportunity to study the encyclical know that the assertion that artificial contraception is intrinsically evil, wrong of its very nature and therefore never allowable in any circumstance, is based on a particular theory of natural law. If natural law is valid for the whole human race, it seems strange that only a tiny minority of Catholics can see it. When Church leaders claim that the Pope receives a special help from the Holy Spirit to understand natural law more fully than others, it seems even more strange, indeed a great pity, even tragic, that the Holy Spirit cannot give the extra bit of help to the Holy Father that would enable him to convince others of this deeper meaning of natural law. A later section of this chapter will return to the encyclical.

Natural methods

Birth control methods can be described as either natural or artificial. *Natural family planning* is so called because it does not interfere physically with the reproductive system or the act of intercourse. It involves periodic abstinence from intercourse, during the fertile periods of the menstrual cycle. It is based on the fact that conception is possible only on certain days during the cycle. Avoiding intercourse during these days ensures that no conception will take place. Pinpointing ovulation, when the ovum is released from the ovary, is the key factor in determining the fertile period, but allowance has to be made for the fact that the ovum can only be fertilised during the first few hours after its release, and the further fact that the male sperm is capable of fertilising the ovum for up to three days after intercourse, although some studies show cases in which the sperm retains its power to fertilise for up five or seven days. If the fertile period in each cycle can be calculated, conception can be avoided by abstaining from intercourse.

The first method used to identify the fertile and infertile days was the *calendar method*, based on the fact that ovulation occurs twelve to sixteen days before the beginning of the next menstrual period. By keeping a record of the varying length of the individual menstrual cycles over a certain length of time, for example six to twelve months, it is possible to estimate the date of ovulation and calculate the beginning and end of the fertile period. Because of the variations in the cycle, the formula cannot provide a mathematical certainty, so an element of risk is present.

Another method, the *Basal Body Temperature method (BBT)*, is based on the fact that there is a noticeable rise in a woman's basal body temperature at the time of ovulation, which is maintained until the beginning of the next period. Allowing for the life-span of ovum and sperm, it is calculated that the time from the third consecutive day of the higher temperature until the onset of the next menstruation is infertile and therefore 'safe' for intercourse. It is claimed that if intercourse is restricted to this post-ovulatory phase of the cycle (about ten days), the risk of conception is about 1 per cent, which is equivalent to the success rate of many oral contraceptives and much higher than that of condom or diaphragm. But couples wishing to avail also of the pre-ovulatory phase, determined by the calendar method, would have an increased risk of pregnancy.

A further advance in natural methods came from the work of Drs John and Evelyn Billings, based on the changes that take place in the cervical mucus during the menstrual cycle, making it possible to recognise the infertile days in the first, pre-ovulatory, part of the cycle, as well as those in the second part. This is known as the *ovulation method*. Its advantage is that it enables couples to make use of both first and second infertile parts of the cycle, although use of the first part is less reliable.

The most recent development in the area of natural family planning is a high-technology variation on the rhythm method, providing computer-guided advice on when to abstain from sex. It involves a hand-held monitor in conjunction with disposable urine-test sticks. A green light on the monitor indicates safe sex for the following twenty-four hours, a red light signifies that it is unsafe, and on eight days of the month a yellow light signals the need for a urine test to measure the level of hormones associated with ovulation. Initial trials have shown very positive acceptance by women, and it seems that its reliability level is between that of condoms, which the World Health Organisation says is 88per cent, and that of some pills, 98 per cent.

It is difficult to get absolutely reliable figures for the effectiveness of the various methods of family planning, but Dr John Marshall, emeritus professor of neurology in the University of London, claims that the oral contraceptive is the most effective, reversible method of avoiding pregnancy, followed closely by the BBT method when intercourse is restricted to the second, or post-ovulatory, infertile phase of the cycle. The Ovulation method may be equally successful when only the second phase is used. The barrier methods of the condom and diaphragm come next in effectiveness, whereas the most risky methods are the BBT and Ovulation method when both the first (less reliable) and the second infertile phases of the cycle are used. Sterilisation and total abstinence seem to be the only infallible means to avoid a pregnancy; all others are less than totally reliable. In the case of natural family planning, a really successful ovulation indicator must be capable of indicating accurately the bounds of the fertile period, and to be of real service it must also be simple, cheap, painless, rapid, specific and reliable, and the phenomenon being measured must be recognisable in most women.

Artificial contraception
Artificial methods involve interfering with either the reproductive system or the reproductive act to prevent conception taking place. This may be done by:

1. Changing the *reproductive system*, either by surgical sterilisation (male or female), or drug sterilisation (anovulant pills which inhibit ovulation).
2. Interfering with the *reproductive act* by any of the following means: withdrawal by the husband before insemination; condom or sheath (used by husband to contain semen and prevent insemination); diaphragm or cap (used by the wife to close entrance to the womb); coil, spring or other intra-uterine device (IUD, generally thought to

prevent implantation of the fertilised ovum, in which case it is abortifacient); spermicidal creams, jellies, pastes, suppositories and
foaming tablets, aerosols (all intended to kill sperms or to prevent
them from reaching the ovum); douche (washing out after intercourse, practically useless, since a sperm may be in the cervix within
ninety seconds of insemination).
3. The *morning after pill*, which attacks the already fertilised ovum or pre-
vents its implantation in the womb. This is abortion rather than
contraception.

In the sexually liberated 1960s the various anovulant pills were hailed as
a miracle of science that would solve the birth control problem. But in
recent years more and more evidence shows that many of the pills on the
market have quite serious side-effects, especially when taken continu-
ously over a period of years. They are far from simple, and it is not easy
to discover the less harmful ones among the variety of types available. As
chemical agents, spermicides have the same problem. Few are free of
dangerous consequences. A mother in the US who sued the manufacturer of a spermicidal jelly with the claim that her use of it was responsible
for her child's birth defects, was awarded $4.7 million in damages. More
suits like this could mean that it would no longer be profitable for manufacturers to produce such chemicals. Some US companies produce
injectable contraceptives that prevent pregnancy for three months or up
to five years which are sold in many countries around the world, but are
not approved by the Food and Drug Administration. Many British members of parliament have asked the government to ban one of these,
Norplant, because of its dangerous side-effects.

But producers learn from their mistakes and research continues to
provide safer and more effective pills. Not all chemical contraceptives
are so dangerous as to render their use automatically irresponsible. In
1973 it was reported that 36 per cent of married women preferred the pill
to all other birth control methods, yet its use dropped by almost half in
the following years. A medical survey recently showed that many contraceptive pills do not increase the chance of breast cancer, even in
high-risk groups, but very many women are still wary, perhaps rightly
so.

An interesting development in the area of intra-uterine devices is that
in early years products were removed from the market because they
were inferior, but nowadays production of superior products has
dropped because of the high cost of insurance for the manufacturers. It is

claimed that the IUD has a failure rate of only 5 per cent in the first year
of use, in contrast to 19 per cent for the diaphragm, 17–24 per cent for
sponges, 18 per cent for spermicidal foams and jellies and 10 per cent for
condoms, but on the other hand, not only are infections from IUDS quite
numerous, but they have given rise to crippling lawsuits. One US company spent $1.5 million in legal fees to defend itself in four cases, which
they won, but another manufacturer spent $490 million on 9,450 lawsuits
and had 6,000 further legal claims. Whatever is said about the effectiveness of this form of contraceptive device, it seems to have quite serious
side-effects. Where IUDs are abortifacient, they cannot be considered as
lawful means of birth control in the context of responsible parenthood.

Sterilisation
It is reported that at present in the US the most popular form of birth control is sterilisation. It is claimed that one-third of sexually active women
are either sterilised or have partners who are. It does not seem to have
major side-effects, and for those who have serious reasons for sacrificing
their reproductive capacity it could be the most satisfactory solution. An
example of a not infrequent case is the mother of two with a blood disor-
der which made any pregnancy and birth a serious risk to her life. She
used natural family planning for years, but without much success,
resulting in two children and ten miscarriages. Added to the strain of
observing the method was the major fear for her health and future each
time she became pregnant. She had a loving, caring husband, but this
recurring fear, lasting for the duration of each pregnancy until it ended in
miscarriage, left both partners so tense that their marriage was seriously
affected. Doctors assured her that she would continue to conceive for
another twenty years but would never bear a live baby. Sterilisation
solved her problem and the couple have had a totally new experience of
marriage ever since. The wife, understandably, gets quite angry when
she hears some clerics criticise her decision, accusing her of mutilation
and of interfering with nature. Sterilisation removed her capacity to conceive, but the doctors told her that it was nature itself which deprived her
of the ability to produce a live child. She prefers realities to philosophical
abstractions.

Unpublicised consequences
Many people choose natural family planning in preference to artificial
contraceptive devices because it seems more natural, has less dangerous
side-effects and has a high rate of reliability when used faithfully. For

Catholics it also has the approval of the Church, thus relieving them of the risk of a guilty conscience in not following Church teaching. They know that it involves considerable sacrifice on their part, but some couples see this as a challenge to their love and find that it can deepen their commitment to each other. The experience of such couples has to be accepted and respected, but some supporters of natural family planning present that experience as the norm, suggesting that, with effort and good will, it could become the experience of every couple using the natural methods.

Very many couples and some pastors and marriage counsellors know another side of the reality, but unfortunately they seldom speak of it publicly. The question arises: do theologians and Church leaders realise just how serious the other side of the picture really is? The negative consequences of natural family planning are not simply the unfortunate result of human weakness or ignorance on the part of the occasional couple. They are of sufficient importance to warn us against absolutising any one method of family planning to the level of God's plan for all people, especially as God has said nothing about the matter. The question may be asked: can it be God's will that people have to suffer so much in such an intimate area of their lives in order to be loyal, not to the Church as the community of God's holy people, but to an item of teaching that has nothing to do with divine revelation, and is not convincing to the vast majority of Catholics, including some cardinals, bishops, priests and religious, and most of all, to those married Christians who alone have personal experience of the reality in question? To speak openly of the difficulties of the natural methods does not mean that they should not be used, that they are not reliable, or that they are in some way inferior. On the contrary, natural family planning has very positive values and can certainly be recommended, and in some ways it is better than artificial contraception. But for a responsible decision, people need to know all the facts of a situation in order to evaluate what is involved. Decisions about family planning are difficult enough for most couples, but they should not be made more complicated by hiding significant facts.

It would be easy to quote some case histories from personal experience, but they could be dismissed as general impressions from a few exceptional couples. Fortunately, we have the testimony of an impeccable witness, a dedicated Catholic of unquestioned integrity and love of the Church, who has done a major service to the Church in publishing a short book called *Love One Another, Psychological Aspects of Natural Family Planning*.[1] It is a fascinating book. The author, Dr John Marshall, is emeritus professor of neurology in the University of London, and was a member of the original commission of six people established in 1963 by Pope John XXIII to study the question of birth control. He has the added qualification of forty years of teaching natural family planning by correspondence and has had the written and oral confidences of over ten thousand couples who shared their experience with him. Summarising that vast amount of human experience, he says that for some, it was liberating and fruitful, but for others it was destructive of their relationship and the cause of much suffering and sorrow. Dr Marshall maintains that this unique archive of human experience should be made available to those who teach natural family planning and to those who practise it. But it should also be studied by Church leaders and all those who debate the subject, especially to those who speak too glibly about 'natural law.'

Survey

Dr Marshall reports on a survey carried out from the headquarters of the Catholic Marriage Advisory Centre in London in 1965–67 involving over five hundred couples following the BBT method. Statistics were compiled of the success/failure rate of the method, distinguishing between couples who used only the post-ovulatory infertile phase of the cycle (most reliable), and those who used both pre- and post-ovulatory infertile phases, and taking account of those who kept the rules strictly and those who did not. Among those who used only the second phase and kept the rules strictly there were only 1.2 accidental pregnancies per 100 women per year, and 4.2 for those who were less strict in keeping the rules. For those who used both phases, and therefore took a greater risk of conception, the numbers were 5 pregnancies per 100 women per year for those who kept the rules and 13.3 among those who were careless. In terms of effectiveness, the figure of 1.2 for those who were able to accept a longer period of abstinence and were faithful to the timetable is a significantly high success rate of the method.

This survey was followed up by a further investigation involving a questionnaire sent separately (to preserve anonymity) to the wives and husbands who had taken part in the field-trial. The response was an unusually high 82 per cent. When asked whether they experienced anxiety about a possible pregnancy when using the method, three-quarters of the women answered 'Yes,' but once the learning period was over just over 40 per cent of both men and women responded that they still worried. Asked about the difficulty of abstinence, over half the men said it was often difficult and a slightly higher percentage of women said they sometimes found it difficult. Only 1 per cent of men and 8 per cent of women replied that they never had difficulty with abstinence. When asked whether the method had any effect on their relationship, almost 70 per cent of both men and women said it had no effect, but a quarter of both men and women reported that it had a bad effect. A high proportion of both sexes said that they were more conscious of sex during the periods of abstinence. When asked if they engaged in forms of love-making short of intercourse during periods of abstinence, almost 90 per cent of both men and women said 'Yes,' and over 40 per cent admitted that this sometimes led to orgasm, even though orgasm was not sought, but even resisted.

A common criticism of natural family planning is that it removes spontaneity in love-making and intercourse, but more than half of the men and women in this survey said that this was not true in their experience. About a third felt that spontaneity was indeed impaired and they felt they could not express their love adequately during periods of abstinence. Over 60 per cent of men and women felt that their appreciation of intercourse was greater after abstinence. Overall the survey showed a very positive judgment of the BBT method, with 66 per cent of men and 75 per cent of women asserting that they found it satisfactory, whereas less than a quarter found it unsatisfactory. Three-quarters of both men and women in the group said that the method had helped their marriage, whereas less than one in ten found it a hindrance. This is indeed high praise for the method, which is often criticised unfairly. Many of the people who use it are enabled to regulate the size of their family in accordance with their needs, and in many cases its use improves the marriage relationship.

Facts behind the figures

The above statistics give a fairly positive picture of the *effectiveness* of the BBT method, but they do not speak of the price to be paid for this effectiveness. One has to read the letters behind the figures to get some grasp of the strain and heart-break caused by the high degree of abstinence required. While some couples express satisfaction with their experience of the method as a whole, a large number recount sad stories of disappointment, frustration and anger at not being able to comfort their partners as they would wish in moments of serious need. One couple found the method quite effective in spacing out their three children, but the efforts required over several decades left them emotionally crippled to the point where in the freedom of the post-menopause years they had become incapable of even the simplest physical expressions of affection. A particular hardship was experienced by those cases in which the husband's job required that he be away from home for a week or more at a time, but more than six months could pass before his home visits would coincide with his wife's 'safe' period. Is it not a serious misuse of language to describe this as 'natural' when the couple concerned felt it was totally unnatural?

This couple and others like them could well feel that although they were obeying the laws of the Church by using the safe period, they were being unfaithful to the vows they took before God on the day they were married. Fidelity to this so-called 'natural law' proclaimed by the Church prevented them from experiencing their marriage as the ongoing sacrament that it is meant to be, a powerful sacrament of affirmation, healing and growth. Some of the couples had such a negative experience of natural planning that they changed to the pill to save their marriage. One mother described how she felt a hypocrite going to the sacraments as a 'good Catholic' because she was using the natural methods, but felt guilty knowing how un-Christian her home life was with all the bickering and tension. She and her husband decided that the family came first, so they changed to the pill, and they are convinced that they are now following God's will in good conscience.

Authority of the facts

It is tempting to continue the list of cases, but the reader should study Dr Marshall's unique collection of these very special human experiences. One is saddened by the fact that all of this valuable experience seems to have had no influence whatsoever on the writing of *Humanae Vitae*. With so much emphasis on *authority* in the debate, it is incredible that the most important authority of all, the *authority of the facts*, was totally ignored, and almost thirty years later is still seldom recognised. In fact, the papal commission that preceded *Humanae Vitae* was provided with first-hand accounts of the experience of married people. One of the three married couples invited to be part of the commission, Patrick Crowley and his wife Patty, the lead couple responsible for the phenomenal growth of the Christian Family Movement in the US and throughout the world, prepared for their task by collecting three thousand letters from Catholic married couples from eighteen countries, describing their experience. They were from devout members of the Christian Family Movement, dedicated Catholics active in their parishes who met regularly to share their faith. Just recently Patty asked author Robert McClory to write her experience, the inside story of the papal commission (*Turning Point*).[2] It complements and reinforces Dr Marshall's book.

Patty says that she and her husband were shocked by what they learned from the experience of those they contacted. They could not believe the hardships people were going through to be faithful to Church teaching in the matter of birth control. She was even more shocked at the reactions of the few minority group theologians on the commission who seemed to have their minds made up and did not want to be confused by facts. Their glib response was that 'hard cases make bad laws.' A humorous note was the fact that the three married couples were obliged to celibacy while in Rome, since the husbands and other male members of the commission were housed in the Spanish college while the wives were lodged in a convent a mile away. The books of Marshall and McClory are essential reading for an understanding of the genesis and context of *Humanae Vitae*. They provide material seldom acknowledged by Church leaders and they show how Catholics fully committed to Catholic teaching and supportive of the Church came to change their convictions about its teaching on birth control.

Most of the theologians on the commission were deeply impressed by the dossier of information and felt that it was relevant to the business of the commission. But the traditionalists held to their narrow philosophical view that the meaning of human intercourse in the context of married love could be defined unmistakably, infallibly, without reference to the experience of committed married Catholics. A sad but humorous note was introduced during a debate by the impatient outburst of the Spanish theologian, Fr Zalba: 'What becomes of the millions we have sent to hell if this teaching is not valid?' Courteously Patty Crowley asked him: 'Father Zalba, do you really believe God has carried out all your orders?' But she was up against a Church convinced that it had all the answers, even before hearing the questions or looking at the facts. A perfect example of this attitude was the visit of Mgr George Kelly, a member of the expanded commission, well known for his marriage apostolate, who flew in to Rome to read a document on the evil of contraception, and returned to New York the following day without any dialogue with the commission that had been discussing the matter for months. He made no secret of the fact that he objected to people like the Crowleys, Dr Marshall and even experts in a variety of human sciences being members of the commission, since he claimed that birth control was a moral matter, to be decided solely by the teaching authority of the Church.

Laity ignored

When the Second Vatican Council discussed marriage, Pope Paul VI removed the question of birth control from the agenda and reserved it to himself, because, he explained, he wanted to hear the results of the special papal commission that had been set up in 1963 to study it. The original group of six were convinced that the Church would not change its traditional teaching, and they saw rhythm as the Catholic solution. The commission was expanded to fifteen members the following year and most of these believed that the pill could not be approved. In 1965 there were fifty-eight members, and for the final session in 1966 there were seventy-two. It included fifteen cardinals and bishops, as well as priests, lay men and women, including three married couples, people whose expertise covered a wide area of philosophy, theology, scripture, law, history, medicine, biology, psychology, sociology and economics. Many were involved in teaching natural family planning, and the majority at the start supported traditional Church teaching, but they changed their stand totally in the course of the discussions. In the 1965 sessions the commission came to understand how the Church had changed over the centuries in its approach to sex, marriage and procreation. The following year the theologians voted that *Casti Connubii* could be reformed, and everyone began to question the benefits of the rhythm method. In the end, the vast majority agreed that contraception was not intrinsically evil, and that the Council should remove the ban on contraception. Cardinal Doepfner, one of the most outspoken members, declared that *Casti Connubii* (1931) was not infallible, but was subject to doctrinal development, just as the Council accepted religious freedom in spite of the Church's very different record in the past.

The voting was practically unanimous. Even the four theologians who favoured holding on to the traditional position had to admit that they had no arguments to prove the majority wrong, except that to change the teaching would damage the authority of the Church, which cannot admit that it ever made mistakes. This seems to have been the fear that prevented Pope Paul VI from making any change in the teaching when he wrote *Humanae Vitae*. The media at the time spoke of majority and minority reports from the commission, but there was never any minority report. There was simply a private letter to the Pope, after the commission was disbanded, signed by the four priests who repudiated the official report of the commission; it was an unauthorised alternative report to the one presented officially to the Holy Father as the almost unanimous view of the cardinals, bishops, priests and laity who formed the commission. The traditionalists kept up private pressure on the Pope long after the commission had finished its work. One of these is reported to have boasted to friends that Pope Paul was open to change and was almost convinced by the report of the commission, but he would give in to the traditionalists eventually, and this seems to be what happened. In fact, the many draft texts used by the Pope to help him write *Humanae Vitae* were mostly the work of representatives of the minority opinion which repudiated the report of the papal commission. Members of the commission were disturbed at the rumours they heard of their report being ignored. Bishop Reuss begged the Pope to publish the documents of the commission, but this was refused. Cardinal Suenens warned the Pope that if the Vatican continued along the line it seemed to be taking, the Church would have not only a credibility gap, but a credibility chasm.

One can sympathise with Pope Paul, so deeply conscious of his responsibility for the unity of the Church and his duty to safeguard its teaching. He later admitted that the years leading up to his final decision in 1968 were the most agonising of his life, causing him great spiritual suffering. He said that he had written the encyclical with a feeling of love and pastoral sensitivity for married couples. Could he have foreseen the earthquake which *Humanae Vitae* provoked in the Church? It brought about perhaps one of the greatest crises of conscience that the Church has ever experienced. Although it was not an infallible pronouncement, Pope Paul asked that the teaching be accepted with respect. But no teaching takes place unless someone is taught. The question should be asked: what can the Church learn from the experience of this encyclical and its aftermath? Bishop Christopher Butler, one of the most respected participants in the Second Vatican Council, asserted that the fact that the encyclical was not 'received' by the Church could be seen as 'invalidating' its teaching.

Teaching rejected
In the conclusion of his encyclical, Pope Paul invited bishops to uphold this teaching of the Church, exhorted priests to give an example of obedience by preaching it, assured married couples that the grace of the sacrament would help them to follow it in spite of its difficulty, and he appealed to doctors and scientists to show that there can be no contradiction between God's law concerning human reproduction and the fostering of married love. The factual position in today's Church makes one wonder if all of these appeals fell on deaf ears. Many episcopal

conferences (surely a recognised part of the teaching Church) issued pastoral statements to help people understand the encyclical and they
considerably softened the declaration of paragraph 14 condemning all
artificial means of contraception. It is an open secret that many cardinals
and bishops today (like most of those on the papal commission) are not
convinced of the teaching on this point, but out of loyalty to the Church
or fear of offending the present Holy Father, will not admit this publicly.
Cardinal König, the retired archbishop of Vienna, is an exception. In a
debate with Cardinal Ratzinger in 1992 he dismissed the 'irritating distinction between artificial and natural contraception,' and declared that
on the question of birth control we have ended up with a bottleneck
mostly because of this distinction, almost as if the morally important
thing is the 'trick' of cheating nature.

A large majority of the world's foremost theologians no longer accept
that artificial contraception is intrinsically evil, but are forced to be cir-
cumspect about their views lest they lose their teaching posts. Shortly
after the encyclical was published, over 600 US theologians and other
academics, some of the most outstanding in the country, signed a document saying that 'spouses may responsibly decide according to their
conscience that artificial contraception in some circumstances is permis-
sible, and indeed even necessary, to preserve and foster the value and
sacredness of their marriage.' Soon afterwards a group of equally emi-
nent European theologians with world reputations, signed a similar
declaration. Had some not signed it, it is highly probable that they would
be bishops today. When in 1987 Pope John Paul II declared that the
Church's teaching on contraception is not open to free discussion among
theologians, there was a formal protest by 163 theologians from Germany, Austria, the Netherlands and Switzerland (*The Cologne
Declaration*), and this was endorsed by 130 French theologians, sixty
Spanish theologians, sixty-three Italian theologians and 431 members of
the Catholic Theological Society of America. In many countries up to 80
per cent of married Catholics do not accept the teaching. Confessors
report that while formerly contraception was an agonising concern in the
confessions of Catholics, it is seldom even mentioned as a scruple nowadays. This situation ought to be a cause for concern in a Church which
claims to be a sacrament of Christ, the Way, the Truth and the Life, a
Church committed to radiating joy and hope, confident in the belief that
perfect love casts out fear.

It has been remarked that the continued repetition in the strongest
terms of the condemnation of artificial contraception is reminiscent of

the marginal directive once found in a preacher's sermon notes: 'Argument weak here, shout like mad!' In spite of Pope Paul's appeal for more study and research to strengthen his teaching, the past three decades have not produced a single argument to move it a step forward or to make it more convincing. Indeed, the sad fact is that in all these years people seldom heard a worthwhile explanation of the Vatican II teaching on marriage and what responsible parenthood in the full sense really means. The fear and lack of openness surrounding the subject have not lessened over the years. The one-metre high pile of documentation from the papal commission that preceded *Humanae Vitae* has unfortunately never been published, so the facts assembled by all those experts and especially the rich contribution of so many dedicated married Catholics are omitted from discussions of the subject. It is not clear that Pope Paul would have had time to study it all in detail. At the 1980 Synod of Bishops on the subject of the family, Cardinal Basil Hume insisted that married couples, who have experience of marriage, are an authentic theological source to be listened to in any discussion on family life. He pointed out that their problem was not frailty or weakness of will, but the fact that they simply were not convinced that the use of artificial contraceptives is in all cases intrinsically disordered. He suggested that if the synod would listen to all the different points of view it would find a solution.

At the same synod Archbishop John Quinn of San Francisco declared that many couples of good will did not accept the intrinsic evil of each and every use of contraception, and he said that the same conviction is to be found among theologians and pastors whose learning, faith, discretion and dedication to the Church are beyond doubt. Sadly, these two prophetic voices, so much in tune with what the Church ought to be, either were not heard or were deliberately excluded, and there was no 'listening to all the different points of view.' In fact, the synod was so orchestrated that no real dialogue was possible. The traditionalists were still in control in the Vatican. The encyclical produced after the synod shows no sign of any influence from the laity, or any reference to their married experience. Indeed, some commentators claim that it could have been written in the same terms even if the synod had never taken place. The teaching Church will continue to lose credibility until it gives more convincing evidence that it is also a listening, learning Church. How can it be asserted that Church leaders are listening to the gospel and to the Holy Spirit if they cannot listen to their lay brothers and sisters who make up the vast majority of Church members and are uniquely qualified to speak of their experience as people who live the sacrament of matrimony?

Disillusion

According to Robert McClory's study, the members of the papal commission were not only surprised, but shattered that their three years of hard work seemed to count for nothing. It seems that the Vatican never even thanked them for it. McClory says that many of them have become more and more disillusioned since then, because instead of trying to develop the teaching of *Humanae Vitae* with supporting arguments, the Church seems to discourage and even suppress any real discussion of it. Apart from the difficulties people experience with the so-called natural methods of family planning, with their psychological, marital and aesthetic ill-effects, there are inconsistencies and contradictions in the encyclical itself. Pope Paul said that he could not accept the conclusions of the papal commission because it put forward criteria for resolving the birth control question that departed from the Church's teaching. But he never said what these were, nor have they ever been made public by the Church since then, so the question cannot be debated.

After condemning absolutely any action before, during or after intercourse which would prevent conception, the encyclical in the next paragraph says that therapeutic actions which produce the same effect are quite lawful provided this effect is not directly willed. In other words, it is lawful to take contraceptive pills as therapy, for example to regularise the female cycle. A Vatican spokesman said that, on this principle, religious sisters in danger of rape in a war situation could take contraceptive pills as preventive therapy. But contraceptive pills act according to nature in its chemical and physiological laws to inhibit ovulation in these cases just as they do when taken as contraceptives. If contraception is 'intrinsically evil' then there can be no exceptions. But if the good intention of therapy makes it less evil, then the good intention of saving a marriage, protecting the mother's health, or safeguarding the upbringing of children should also qualify as justifying reasons for the pill as a method of family planning. As explained in an earlier chapter, the phrase 'intrinsically evil' is rejected by most theologians today as misleading and unfounded. An action cannot be described as morally evil of its very nature, in all circumstances, without reference to its human meaning, therefore to the intention, context and consequences. Why should the reproductive system be more sacred than a person's life? Human life is sacred, but tradition has accepted that in some situations it may be sacrificed. Life is a near-absolute value, but this does not give rise to an absolute moral norm. The papal commission that spent three years studying the matter came to the conclusion that, with the exception of abortion, no method of birth control can be called intrinsically bad or good. Its moral value depends on how and why it is chosen as a means in the exercise of responsible parenthood.

What is natural?

Chapter 5 should warn against a too facile, indeed a mistaken, recourse to natural law to justify natural family planning and condemn artificial methods. To label something immoral, and intrinsically evil, because it is artificial, a frustration of a natural process, seems arbitrary when most of human activity in today's world involves artificial materials and techniques, and modern medicine is continually interfering with nature to improve the total nature and overall good of human persons. Moreover, we are more aware nowadays that many things which in the past were labelled 'natural' were simply chosen on the basis of the prevailing culture and then labelled as natural. Classical moralists preached that our behaviour should conform to 'what nature teaches all animals,' but in fact nature teaches nobody anything; it is an abstraction. For centuries it was taken for granted that certain sexual activities like male and female homosexual behaviour and masturbation were aberrations introduced by human free will, but not found in nature, among animals. We now know that all kinds of sexual behaviour are to be found among animals. Those who quote nature as God's will should be reminded that there is a species of chimpanzee which avoids all aggressive behaviour by having immediate recourse to sexual activity (both heterosexual and homosexual, male and female) whenever a conflict flares up, which results in one of the most peaceful examples of communal life in the animal kingdom. In what sense can 'nature' be a guide to morally good behaviour for humans?

A further misunderstanding was that all laws of nature follow a physical one-to-one, cause-and-effect pattern, whereas in human reproduction nature's pattern of coition and conception is a matter of statistical probabilities, so that the vast majority of acts of intercourse do not lead to conception. Interfering with these probabilities (or taking advantage of them), which is what the various natural methods do, is as artificial as taking the pill to alter nature. If it is wrong to set up a barrier against conception, what *moral* difference is there between a physical or chemical barrier (artificial) and a temporal or time barrier (natural methods)?

Most people would prefer to enjoy the spontaneity of love-making in their marriage, but the pressures of modern life make this almost impossible. Their concern with birth regulation is not necessarily the result of selfishness, but mostly because of economic necessity, and of more complex changes in society, like their desire for equality, their need for sexual fulfilment, and the emancipation of women. People who, through no fault of their own, but out of responsibility for their marriage and family, are forced to practise some form of birth control are understandably angry when *Humanae Vitae* assures them that, 'as all honest men know,' the use of artificial methods leads to infidelity and a decay of morals, and tempts husbands to treat their wives as mere sex objects. This is not the experience of responsible parents. They may well ask: if the Holy Spirit can be so wrong about the psychological effects of birth control, how can we trust that same Spirit on the more difficult subject of natural law?

The Holy Spirit

The *Humanae Vitae* experience caused an earthquake in the Church. It was a shattering experience for the dedicated members of the papal birth control commission to see all their hard work totally rejected. The married Catholics for whom it was an agonising problem of conscience were left with a heavier burden and an even more acute dilemma. It was a major blow to the many world-class theologians who had studied the subject for years and had become convinced that the traditional teaching had no convincing arguments. For many of these it was not just an intellectual setback but a test of their love of the Church, and some were so deeply affected that it had repercussions on their health. Time has softened the pain so that it is now possible to see that in spite of the suffering, it has benefited the Church. It has helped people to relativise some of their false absolutes and encouraged them to experience more deeply the meaning of personal conscience.

Those who defend the encyclical emphasise it as 'the teaching of the Church,' but teaching is not limited to words. The way in which the problem was treated and the document was written is also Church teaching, giving rise to the question: where was the Holy Spirit in all of this? It is difficult to accept that the Holy Spirit should ignore the world gathering of bishops in the Second Vatican Council, pay no attention to the special papal commission set up to study the question, allow the many volumes of testimony from committed married Catholics from all over the world to sink into oblivion, and work exclusively through a tiny intransigent group convinced that the Church should never change, a group which worked in almost total secrecy and who finally got their way by playing on the fears of Pope Paul VI. In spite of, or perhaps because of, agonising for years over the gap between 'Church teaching' and the demands of responsible parenthood, many Catholics are now experiencing a special presence of the Spirit in the joy and peace of a good conscience.

Our changing Church

Responsible parenthood was studied in this chapter as a concrete example of moral discernment, but it can also serve as an example of 'changing morality.' Sacred scripture has absolutely nothing to say about contraception, but the history of the Church shows that the topic was always a moral problem for its members. John T. Noonan's masterly study, *Contraception: A History of its Treatment by the Catholic Church*,[3] makes it clear that it is difficult to speak of a 'constant teaching of the Church' on the matter. Even when the teaching seemed to be the same, there were radical changes of emphases and a whole variety of reasons given for condemning different practices. Cultural conditioning and simple ignorance are clear in the more bizarre formulations of the teaching. The teaching was always a mixture. Aquinas could lyrically write that 'there is something miraculous in a man finding in one woman a pleasingness which he can never find in another,' and at the same time maintain that the sole reason why God created women was for childbearing, because in all other things a man finds a better help-mate for himself in another man than in a woman. He went on to condemn as immoral any position in intercourse other than the 'natural' one of the man on top. The Vatican II understanding of married love cannot be called the 'constant teaching of the Church,' since it was only officially accepted, against opposition, at the Council itself. Moreover, contraception as we know it nowadays was unknown in the past. In 1930 Pius XI in *Casti Connubii* condemned all forms of contraception without exception, whereas twenty years later Pius XII allowed the rhythm method for serious reasons, and in time this came to be proclaimed as God's will for all marriages.

Not only did the *teaching* change over centuries, but Catholic *experience* also changed considerably in the present century. Large numbers of married Catholics during the first fifty years lived in scrupulosity and fear, and many women abstained from Holy Communion for most of their reproductive years because they could not make a sincere purpose of amendment in confession knowing that they had no choice but to continue acting against Church teaching to save their marriage. Even when

Pope Paul VI in *Humanae Vitae* encouraged them not to lose heart but to come to confession frequently, they still held back as they felt that this would mean treating the sacrament as a mere guilt-shedding process without any genuine purpose of amendment. There may be some people who are still troubled in conscience, but today most couples simply decide on the contraceptive method that in their circumstances suits them best in their efforts to live good married lives, and in all good conscience they feel no need to confess it as a sin. This is a major change in the life of the Church and there are no indications that it can be reversed.

Those who believe in the Vatican II images of the Church as the people of God, a communion of brothers and sisters, all equal in the Lord, a pilgrim people seeking the Truth and trying to be faithful to the Way, find it hard to accept as God's will a teaching that is so much at variance with their daily experience and their God-given intelligence. They know that truth cannot be decreed, but only discovered, shared and explained, whether it be called divine truth or human truth. In the area of revealed truth, the Church, in the person of Pope or Council, can only define what is already the faith of the Church, of the believing community. That is why such definitions need time, to mature and to become clear. In the area of morals the Church should be a little more humble in claiming to know God's will. Its teaching might be all the more forceful and convincing if it were presented a little more tentatively and humbly, remembering the many terrible things that in the past were presented as 'the teaching of the Church.'

One of the better consequences of the crisis provoked by *Humanae Vitae* is that it has encouraged people to take more seriously the question of personal conscience. The really sad effect is that in the three decades since its publication so much time and energy have been wasted on the subject of contraceptive methods that the *good news* about human sexuality, Christian married love and family life is seldom heard. We can easily forget that God's love becomes incarnate in people who touch our lives with love, and that the sacrament of husbands and wives, parents and children is a place in which this is experienced in a totally unique way.

CHURCH TEACHING

Few Catholics would spontaneously associate the notion of change with the concept of Church teaching. The traditional images of the Church as Rock of Ages and Pillar of Truth have created a popular impression that the Church founded by Jesus was entrusted with a 'deposit of faith' which it has conserved through the centuries and consistently preached and taught. Emphasis on consistency and continuity has meant that many encyclicals of the popes in recent times have more footnotes to previous popes, and even to their own writings, than to sacred scripture. Even when dealing with relatively new topics, official documents frequently refer to the 'constant teaching of the Church.' In fact, however, not only have there been radical changes in the *content* of the Church's teaching, but the Church's *teaching function itself* has undergone considerable development. It is clear from previous chapters how much the content of Church teaching has varied down the centuries. The present chapter will examine the meaning of the Church's *teaching function*, commonly called its *magisterium*.

The Church began as the remembering community of the believers in Jesus. Even after the coming of the Holy Spirit they were not aware that they were a new 'church,' but thought of themselves as the renewed Israel. They continued to live as faithful Jews, but also met as Christian groups to celebrate their Eucharist. With the destruction of the Temple and the influx of large numbers of non-Jewish converts to The Way, they gradually realised that in them God was doing a new thing. They remembered the words of Jesus and gradually came to understand the deeper meaning of his teaching. They experienced the power of his Holy Spirit as they continued their search for God's will. Jesus promised that the Spirit would lead them into all truth (Jn 16:13). In fact, the early communities were concerned about truth. The Pastoral epistles speak of the transmission of sound doctrine, and Luke quotes Jesus telling the seventy disciples 'Whoever listens to you listens to me' (Lk. 10:16). But this was all quite simple compared to the situation in today's Church, with its emphasis on magisterium and infallibility.

The teaching function

The term 'infallibility' first came to be used of the pope's teaching only in the fourteenth century, but the exaggerated claims made for it in recent times have given rise to considerable confusion for Catholics. When the infallibility of the pope was defined by the First Vatican Council in 1870, it was in quite limited terms. The Council made clear that the pope is infallible only when he is clearly defining a doctrine on faith and morals, when he is speaking as head of the Church, and when his obvious intention is to bind the whole Church. But these three conditions were often forgotten by theologians. In a textbook of theology still being printed in 1962 and widely used in seminaries throughout the world, infallibility was described as covering not only the Holy Father's solemn extraordinary teaching, but also encyclical letters, any personal position a pope might take on matters of faith or morals, and even less important areas, such as liturgy, the canonisation of saints, and the approval of rules and constitutions of religious orders. This inflated notion of papal infallibility is totally rejected by theologians today and it is not supported by the theology of the Second Vatican Council. But unfortunately its influence is still a source of confusion and conflict in the Church.

The teaching function of the Church has had a complex history not easily summarised in a short space. But it is essential to know something of that history in order to avoid the over-simplifications that are at the root of so much conflict in today's Church. The most thorough theological and historical treatment of the topic in English is to be found in the two books of the world-renowned expert, Francis A. Sullivan, S.J. *Magisterium, Teaching Authority in the Catholic Church*[1] and *Creative Fidelity: Weighing and Interpreting Documents of the Magisterium.*[2] These are complemented by *The Church: Learning and Teaching* of Ladislas Örsy, S.J.[3] Too often in papal and episcopal statements reference is made to the 'constant teaching of the Church,' when in fact there was considerable variety in what was taught, and in many cases later teaching flatly contradicted what was proclaimed previously. When reference is made to the 'tradition of the Church' it can happen that the tradition being quoted is barely a century old (e.g. the exaggerated notion of infallibility mentioned above), while the thousand-year-old tradition that preceded it is conveniently forgotten.

To attribute everything that happened in the Church's development to the direct action of the Holy Spirit is to forget that God's holy people are ordinary, fallible and sinful human beings, part of changing human history. God trusted them with his word and his Spirit, but how they understood and responded to these wonderful gifts was coloured and shaped by their experience and culture through the centuries. Theologians distinguish between God's *positive will* and *permitting will*, between what God *wants* to happen and what God *allows* to happen. This needs to be kept in mind in order to avoid absolutising what may be nothing more than the cultural conditioning of a particular period in history. The Second Vatican Council brought some *reality therapy* to the Church by looking closely at the Church in today's world and asking *Is this what God really wants?* It is a question that should be addressed periodically if we are to be faithful to the gospel. Of course in responding to it we are helped by all that is best in our tradition.

The early Church had a simple structure: Peter, the apostles and the other believers. It was a communion of local churches which recognised the special primacy of Peter because of the authority conferred on him by Jesus. In the course of time the leaders became the pope and the bishops, successors to Peter and the apostles. Bishops were chosen by local communities and they met together collegially in local and regional councils to deal with matters of common concern, but they always looked to the bishop of Rome as a special guardian of apostolic tradition and they accorded him special reverence and authority. But it took several centuries before the pope was recognised as having a juridical primacy. The word of God was not entrusted primarily to pope or bishops, but to the whole people of God, and it is the whole Church that has responsibility for it. It is for the whole people of God (including pope and bishops) to accept and live that word, to share it and to grow into a deeper understanding of it. In this sense the whole Church is both a learning Church and a teaching Church. But through sacramental ordination the pope and bishops have a special responsibility to safeguard God's word, to preserve it from error and corruption. Their primary function as pastors and leaders was to be bridge-builders and peacemakers, responsible for the unity of their churches. But how they exercised this responsibility varied considerably through the centuries. Naturally, the simple administrative structures that were sufficient for the early Church would be inadequate for today's world Church, but quite often the changes were the result of papal personalities and the culture of the time as much as being required by the real needs of the Church.

The popes in history

Gregory the Great, at the end of the sixth century, was one of the most outstanding of all the popes. When he became Pope, Rome was in ruins and he had to cope with floods, famine, plague and barbarian invasions. In the breakdown of imperial power he took on many of the roles of a civil ruler. He was not only an excellent administrator, but also an exceptional teacher whose writings influenced the Church for centuries. He was responsible for the mission to England and had a remarkable understanding of cultural pluralism. He refused to be called the Universal Pope, but he was the first to use the title Servant of the Servants of God, and he told his fellow bishops: 'My honour is the united strength of my brothers.' Unfortunately, his successors did not all follow his heroic lead as pastor. From the eighth century onwards the pope became the temporal ruler of central Italy, and many of the popes led unbelievably scandalous lives.

In the eleventh century Gregory VII was on the papal throne and initiated a totally different style of leadership. He insisted that the pope can be judged by no one, that he alone can depose and reinstate bishops, that he has the power to depose emperors, and that he is the only one whose feet are to be kissed by princes. This attitude continued with later popes. A high point is to be found in the theology of St Bonaventure, who claimed that the pope alone has the power of jurisdiction, which is the fullness of power as head of the Church, and that all ruling power is derived from him. In this view the bishops are simply delegates of the pope. After 1300 the popes moved to Avignon to avoid the civil strife of central Italy, and they established an incredibly efficient bureaucratic administration that reached into the smallest details of local church life through a system of patronage that was later described as organised simony. Several Church councils failed to improve matters, thus paving the way for the Reformation. The Council of Trent in the sixteenth century brought some order out of the chaos of doctrine and discipline, although it did not directly deal with the nature of the Church or the relative authority of the pope, councils and bishops with regard to teaching.

The long centuries during which the popes had political power over large areas of Italy led to a confusion between temporal and spiritual authority. As mentioned in an earlier chapter, since Christian faith was considered an integral part of the social fabric of Christendom, any tampering with Christian doctrine was considered a serious threat to the common good, on a par with treason, and had to be punished. One result of this attitude was the shameful experience of the Inquisition. But the attitude continued in the subconscious of Church leaders and surfaced from time to time. Gregory XVI in the encyclical *Mirari Vos* in 1831 outlined his policy for the exercise of papal authority. Quoting St Paul: 'Shall I come to you with a stick, or with love in the spirit of gentleness?' (1 Cor. 4:21), he announced that he would use the stick (which would mean harshness and condemnations) because he felt that it was needed in order to deal with the dire situation facing him. He was particularly concerned with the Church's doctrinal life and his frequent and insistent interventions in this area extended not only to matters of faith and heresy, but also into questions of how the faith should be expressed, with special attention to the naming and condemning of errors. In this way the papacy took over what for most of the Church's history had been a function of theologians and theological universities. Whereas previously theological opinions and new insights could grow and develop, be criticised, refined and perfected in debate, allowing truth to be recognised through the gospel criteria of time and fruits, and needing only an occasional judgment by pope and bishops, it seemed that in the new climate truth could simply be decreed without argument. With the new policy, the papacy increased the number of its interventions with various kinds of documents from the pope or the curia. Papal encyclicals or circular letters were not unknown in the past, but they reached their present weight and frequency only in the last century. Pope Leo XIII wrote over fifty in twenty-four years. Pius XII also wrote over fifty, but he supplemented his teaching with almost one thousand addresses in fifteen years.

Pope John XXIII

When the Second Vatican Council met in 1962 the Roman curia expected it to continue in the line of heresy-hunting and condemnation. But Pope John XXIII took a totally different approach. He saw the positive aspects of the cultural change in the world as a challenge to the Church. He invited the Council to be faithful to the essentials of the Church's tradition, but to present the gospel in a new way, suited to the modern world. He distinguished between the 'substance' of the faith and the various ways in which it could be formulated. He particularly asked that Christian doctrine be formulated in a way that would be more in keeping with the pastoral role of the magisterium rather than with any particular theological tradition. His view of how to exercise authority was diametrically opposed to the harsh attitude of his predecessor of 130 years before. He said 'Today the bride of Christ prefers to apply the medicine of mercy rather than that of severity.' Dialogue, understanding and mercy would take the place of condemnation and punishment. It was a noble ideal, a firm personal conviction, and a clear echo of the gospel. Historians will judge to what extent it was practised in succeeding pontificates. While there have been some excellent documents from Pope John XXIII (especially on peace), from Pope Paul VI (on the social problem, and evangelisation in the modern world), from Pope John Paul II (on the mercy of God, on the Blessed Virgin, on the vocation of the laity, on the mission of the Church, on human work, on social justice, etc.), there have also been pronouncements from the Holy See which are more in line with Gregory XVI than with John XXIII.

While papal teaching can be an enrichment for the Church, it can also be argued that the multiplicity of encyclicals and the tendency since the nineteenth century to restrict the Church's *magisterium* or teaching function to bishops and indeed mostly to the pope, is not healthy for the Church. There is no question of minimising the responsibility and authority of the pope and the bishops to safeguard the truths of faith and to supervise their faithful transmission, but the present situation is unbalanced compared to earlier times. Moreover it does not reflect the full Vatican II picture of the Church. Speaking of revelation as a continuing process to be newly expressed for every age in prophetic witness, the Council says:

> it is the task of the whole people of God, particularly of its pastors and theologians, to listen to and distinguish the many voices of our times and to interpret them in the light of the divine Word, in order that the divine truth may be more deeply penetrated, better understood and more suitably presented. (*Church in the Modern World*, n. 44)

It is the whole body of Catholic believers who are to be involved in the process of listening, learning, discerning, interpreting and presenting the divine truth, although it is particularly the task of leaders and theologians. The subsidiary clause linking pastors and theologians has a special importance today, as a corrective to the recent tendency on the part of the Roman curia to censure and punish theologians who have been faithful to their centuries-old traditional task of creative reflection on the truths of faith in the context of changing cultures. Sadly, the message conveyed in recent years is that theologians are expected to be mere public relations agents protecting and promoting decreed truths.

There are many lay theologians today, both men and women, some of them outstanding. Unfortunately, the laity, who make up the bulk of Church membership, are seldom consulted by Church leaders, and there are few meaningful structures in place that would enable them to participate in the task. That the laity share in the teaching function of the Church is not a new idea of modern times, but a well-established tradition over centuries. Most of the great theologians of the second century and later were laymen with a reputation for scholarship. Church writers like Tertullian and Saints Justin, Basil, Gregory of Nazianzen, Jerome and Augustine had produced important theological works as laymen before they became priests and bishops. Moreover, theologians enjoyed a privileged role as teachers and defenders of the faith. Many of them became bishops as a result of their competence in theology. Nowadays bishops are often appointed for their administrative skills or other qualities more than for theological expertise.

The Magisterium

The word *magisterium* originally referred to a person who is 'greater' (*magis*) rather than 'less' (*minus*) in a particular field. St Thomas Aquinas, a university Master (*magister*) himself, saw the primary magisterium of bishops as *pastoral*, whereas the magisterium of theologians is *academic* or *doctrinal*. For centuries the two roles were complementary in the Church as bishops and theologians worked in harmony, and at times the same person could be both bishop and theologian, and later a canonised saint. Both exercised the magisterium, in their different ways. All through history theologians had an important place in Church councils, and Luther's theses were censured by the theological faculties of Mainz, Cologne, Louvain and Paris before they were condemned by the Pope. But since the Counter-Reformation the movement towards centralisation in Rome increased until in the eighteenth century a division was introduced in the Church between the 'teaching' Church, comprising pope and bishops (a tiny minority numerically), and the 'learning' Church, containing all other members. The Vatican II understanding of Church leaves little room for such a division, but the attitude behind it seems to be still firmly in control with many Church leaders. Pius XII was clearly of this mind when he personified the papacy as 'this sacred Magisterium.' He applied the text 'He that listens to you, listens to me' (Lk. 10:16) not only to solemn pronouncements, but to the 'ordinary magisterium' of the papacy. He was adamant that theologians should not be considered teachers of the magisterium. Vatican II, on the contrary, says that laity should receive theological formation and that hopefully some of them will dedicate themselves professionally to theology and contribute to its development. It goes on to say that, for this, 'the faithful, both clerical and lay, should be accorded a lawful freedom of enquiry, of thought, and of expression, tempered by humility and courage in areas in which they have acquired competence' (*Church in the Modern World*, n. 62). Sadly, this would seem to be another of the many 'forgotten truths' of Vatican II.

The understanding of the Church's magisterium or teaching function varied considerably in the course of its history, but few people are aware that an important development of thought occurred among the bishops at the Second Vatican Council during the course of its four years. The document on *The Church* declares that the faithful are to show 'religious submission' to the teaching of their bishops and in a special way to the authentic magisterium of the pope, even when he is not speaking *ex cathedra*, i.e. infallibly. The later document, on *The Church in the Modern World*, with equal authority, says that the Church does not always have a ready answer to particular questions, that the laity should not consider that their pastors always have the expertise to provide concrete and ready answers to every problem, even the most serious, or indeed that this is their mission. In other words, it was only towards the end of the Council that the bishops recognised that the hierarchy had no monopoly of the Holy Spirit, nor of the task of responding to the moral problems of the world in the light of the gospel. This was the task of the people of God as a whole. In the thirty years since the Council, Church leaders have repeatedly reminded the laity of the statement of the first document, which seems to encourage a passive obedience to authority, but they rarely if ever mention the equally important second statement, which stresses the responsibility and rights of all the faithful in virtue of their baptism. This kind of selective quotation of Vatican II is also a form of 'teaching,' a kind of body language indicating that popes and bishops are more at home with the authoritarian absolutism of Pius XII than with the overall thrust of Vatican II theology. The paternalistic teaching of the past which considered the faithful as uneducated children who needed to be protected from errors was no doubt influenced by the fact that in the last century 70 per cent of Italians and 72 per cent of Spaniards were still illiterate. The sophisticated faithful of today require a different approach in Church documents.

The vast majority of the laity know little of the complicated history of the Church's magisterium, and they have no way of knowing that the exaggerated notion of magisterium they were brought up on is hardly a century old. Lest they imagine that the papacy of Pius XII and since was a peak of perfection, they should know that developments in the history of the Church were not a uniform progress from imperfect to perfect, from truth to greater truth. Like all human history, it was an uneven movement of development and decline, a mixture of light and dark. Knowing the historical background to our present situation can put us on guard against the unfortunate tendency to absolutise certain elements of our tradition at the expense of others equally important. A knowledge of history can be a help in keeping a balance. In today's critical culture where so many of the faithful are highly educated and many of them trained in theology, exhortations to obedience and acceptance of 'teaching' handed down will not build up the faith of the people of God.

Terminology

A particular source of confusion is the complicated terminology used to describe different kinds and levels of magisterium: papal and episcopal, *ex cathedra*, ordinary and extraordinary, infallible and non-infallible, definitive, irreformable, authentic, official. Then there are dogmas, both defined and undefined, conciliar decrees, and papal documents like encyclicals and allocutions, not to mention documents from the various departments of the Roman curia or civil service. A certain expertise is needed to weigh and interpret all of these, and there can be disagreements between the experts on the precise meaning and binding force of a particular 'teaching.'

'Magisterium' comes from the Latin *magister*, a master, and signifies authority to teach. There is only one such authority in the Church, and that is the Holy Spirit, whom Jesus promised would lead us into all truth. The apostles commissioned others (presbyters or elders, bishops or overseers) to succeed them in preaching the gospel. The pope and the bishops are the successors of Peter and the apostles, with special pastoral responsibility for the communion of churches we call Church. But it is only since the last century that the word 'magisterium' has been applied exclusively to the teaching office of bishops and popes. This is unfortunate, although it is not likely that the usage will now be changed, especially since it is used with this meaning in Vatican II documents, and these also use it to mean not only the teaching function, but also the hierarchy itself, when it speaks of 'the living magisterium of the Church, whose authority is exercised in the name of Jesus Christ.' Some would suggest dropping the word *magisterium* altogether, since it can be so confusing. It can give the impression that the good news of the gospel was entrusted to the pope and the bishops and that they alone have the right to teach it. But in fact the majority of believers were taught their faith by parents, teachers, catechists and others, and our understanding of the faith would be impoverished without the teaching of gifted and saintly theologians who enriched the Church's doctrinal life all through its history. All of these are part of the Church's magisterium, or teaching office. None of them needed special permission to hand on or explain their faith to others. In fact, they have that right and duty from their baptism as members of the Church, and on that level all believers, from the pope to the least of the faithful, are equal.

'Sensus fidelium,' the faith-instinct of God's people

All those who teach in the Church, including popes and bishops, exercise their magisterium in different ways, but they should be in harmony. The body of Christ is seriously weakened when the harmony is broken and the balance upset. As St Paul warned: 'The eye cannot say to the hand, "I have no need of you," nor again the head to the feet, "I have no need of you." On the contrary, the members of the body that seem to be weaker are indispensable' (1 Cor. 12: 21–22). These words ought to warn the hierarchy against mere token consultation of the body of believers. The grace of state which bishops can count on from their ordination to the hierarchy does not work automatically as a personal possession. It is a grace that is *available* to them because of their office. But in order to *appropriate it personally* they need to take the necessary means: study, discussion, reflection, prayer and genuine listening to and learning from the body of believers. When they fail to make use of these means they risk missing out on the special protection of the Holy Spirit, and this will become apparent when their decision or teaching does not resonate with the faith of God's people and it will become a dead letter in the course of time. History provides numerous examples.

As mentioned in an earlier chapter, Aristotle argued that the surest way to discover what is truly right in morals is to consult a morally good person rather than any set of rules, because such a person develops a certain instinct of discernment through the habitual inclination to do good. St Thomas Aquinas developed this insight in terms of Christian believers, who share in the divine nature through baptism and are capable of sharing in God's wisdom. They have a certain affinity with the realities of faith. In this way, the body of believers have a certain collective instinct enabling them to recognise and accept divinely revealed truth and reject what is opposed to it. But there is no magic about it. They still need a process of discernment, using the scriptural criteria of time and fruits. They will not rush in with rash judgments and hasty condemnations, but follow the advice of Gamaliel: 'If this be of God, it will endure.' The second test is the word of Jesus: 'By their fruits you shall know them.'

God's word, the gospel, was entrusted to the whole people of God. It is their possession, and not the exclusive possession of the hierarchy. The First Vatican Council in defining *infallibility* declared that the pope has that infallibility with which God endowed the Church, and the Second Vatican Council explained that the *body of the faithful as a whole*, anointed as they are by the Holy Spirit, *cannot err in matters of belief*. This is the basic principle that should never be forgotten in any discussion of Church teaching. The pope and the bishops are not the source of Church teaching. However, they have a special responsibility as the *custodians* of God's word, to safeguard it and to oversee its growth and development. This gives them the right and the duty to *teach*, to *intervene*, to *discern*, to *judge* and to *declare* when a particular teaching is at variance with Catholic faith, but always with the understanding that the criterion of judgment is the faith of the whole Church, not the formulas of a particular narrow and possibly outdated theology. It is the faith of the people of God as a whole which enjoys the special protection of the Holy Spirit to guarantee that the Church will never fail in the truth. Popes and bishops have exercised this right and fulfilled this duty in various ways down through the centuries, and it is essential that they do, empowered as they are in virtue of their ordination as successors of the apostles and shepherds of the Church.

Magisterium of the hierarchy

It is important to keep in mind this wider context of magisterium before discussing in more detail the narrower, but nowadays more common, sense of *hierarchical magisterium*, which is the teaching function of pope and bishops. Catholic faith holds that the Holy Spirit who led Jesus to preach (Lk. 4:1) is an abiding presence in the Church and will never allow it to fail. Through the power of that Spirit, the Church will always be faithful to the gospel, and its faith will be preserved from corruption. In other words, the *Church* in matters of faith is *infallible*. Since the teachings of the popes and bishops are an expression of the Church's faith, these instruments of the Church's magisterium are specially protected from serious error in their formal teaching, in other words, they are infallible. But infallibility does not belong either to the hierarchy alone or to the body of the faithful alone, but is to be found in the harmony between them, and they are mutually dependent. Since the pope and bishops are themselves part of the faithful, there is not a complete distinction between the two groups. The hierarchy can only teach infallibly what is already the faith of the Church, and Vatican II goes a step further to explain that when this is truly done, the assent of the faithful will never be lacking because the same Holy Spirit keeps the whole Church in unity of faith. On the occasions in the past when a particular papal or conciliar teaching did not find an echo in the faith of the Church, or in other words was not 'received' by devout believers, it was eventually corrected, sometimes quite radically, by later popes and councils. Every infallible statement of pope or council presupposes the *sensus fidelium*, the faith-instinct of the Church, and its purpose is to build up the *consensus fidelium*, the agreement of the Church. The tragedy of *Humanae Vitae* is that it fails on both of these counts. On the other hand, as Cardinal Newman pointed out, the assent of the faithful is not totally dependent on the explicit teaching of the hierarchy. At times the faith of the believers may even be ahead of the hierarchical magisterium, as was the case for centuries with regard to the solemn definitions of papal infallibility in 1870, the Immaculate Conception in 1854 and the Assumption in 1950. The martyred archbishop Oscar Romero made a similar point when in 1978 he said 'We bishops and priests must not think we are the cream of Christianity. We are mere signs, as the church-bell is a sign. But there is a danger that when the faithful respond we, like the bell, remain outside.'

Infallibility

Although infallibility is commonly accepted as a charism of the Catholic Church in its teaching, in fact it took almost a thousand years for the faithful to reach explicit belief in the infallibility of ecumenical councils (after experiencing their good effects), and only in the last century was the infallibility of the pope generally accepted. Our faith at present is that the whole Church is infallible. So too is the college of bishops, with the pope. The *infallible magisterium* is exercised when an ecumenical council of the Church (pope and bishops) defines an article of faith, or the pope teaches *ex cathedra* (that is, specifically as head of the church, clearly defining a doctrine on faith and morals, with the evident intention of binding the whole Church). The pope is also infallible when he officially approves or endorses a doctrine of faith decided by a general council. These are solemn and rare occasions and are commonly called the *extraordinary magisterium*. In fact most of Church teaching as it is exercised at present, is non-infallible. The infallibility of the pope is not an habitual or permanent endowment, but a quality affecting his teaching when the three conditions laid down by the First Vatican Council are fulfilled.

With regard to the bishops, Vatican II tells us that apart from the formal decisions of a general council, the bishops have an *ordinary magisterium* which is *also infallible*. This is exercised when, acting collegially as a body, they declare themselves morally unanimous (including the pope) about a matter of faith or morals to be held definitively by the faithful. This is obvious when they are in a general council with the pope. The principle is clear, but it is not easy to establish in practice just when and how this takes place if they are not meeting in council. They must be acting collegially and have some real sharing and debate before making a judgment. A sociological survey or a counting of individual heads is not sufficient. History shows no example of how this might be done.

In his apostolic letter *Ordinatio Sacerdotalis* in 1994, Pope John Paul II declared that he had no authority to change the Church's tradition of ordaining only men to the priesthood. An official clarification of the teaching level of this statement explained that the Pope was not speaking infallibly, that the letter was an instance of his ordinary (non-infallible) magisterium. But it was also said that while the Pope was not exercising his own infallibility in this statement, he was quoting the ordinary (infallible) magisterium of the Church as the unbroken, universal teaching of the bishops, and for this reason the teaching is irreformable. Theologians know that this latter claim is an historical statement open to question and verification. It is by no means clear that the world 'episcopate' as such ever undertook a serious study of the question or made a formal pronouncement on it. People will continue to discuss the issue. The human mind has a natural thirst for truth and will only rest when convinced by truth. A teacher may help in the search, but no good teacher would command that seekers stop thinking and searching. Vatican II declared that 'the truth cannot impose itself except by virtue of its own truth as it makes its entrance into the mind at once quietly and with power.'

In this context it is important to point out the ambiguity of the word 'ordinary.' It might easily be taken in its colloquial meaning, namely, as Paul VI once used it, 'usual and frequent, in fact day-to-day,' as opposed to the exercise of magisterium described as 'extraordinary,' that is, rare and unusual. In fact, this is not the correct meaning of 'ordinary' as applied to the hierarchical magisterium. The First Vatican Council used the term 'ordinary' in its canonical or juridical sense, not in the colloquial sense. The magisterium is 'ordinary' in the sense that it belongs to office-holders by virtue of their office (*ex officio*), not by delegation from a higher authority. It is inherent in the office and restricted to the limits of the office. In this sense the magisterium of the pope and the bishops is 'ordinary'; they have this teaching authority because of the office they hold. Sometimes they exercise it in an extraordinary way, for example when in an ecumenical council they solemnly define a truth of faith, or the pope makes a similar definition on his own. In these cases the definition is infallible. But most of the teaching of pope and bishops, their usual, day-to-day exercise of their magisterium, is non-infallible, therefore fallible, subject to change, as is abundantly clear from the radical changes that have occurred in Church teaching through the centuries.

With regard to the content or subject-matter of infallible teaching, Catholic faith holds that this can only be revealed truth, as transmitted to the Church in sacred scripture, understood and believed by the body of the faithful. It is generally held, but not infallibly taught, that the infallible magisterium can define propositions which do not belong, strictly speaking, to the content of the faith, but are necessarily presupposed by it or necessary in order to defend it. It is claimed that the charism of infallibility can extend to elements of natural moral law, but given the developments in natural law theory, this is an unclear area. The First Vatican Council defined that the pope is infallible when teaching on matters of 'faith and morals,' but there was considerable confusion about the meaning of the word 'morals' both during the Council and long before it. At the Council of Trent the Latin word *mores* (plural of *mos*, custom) was understood to mean rather 'religious practices.' The Church has still not clarified the precise meaning of the word, so the extent of the Church's infallibility in morals is not certain. In fact, it has never made an infallible pronouncement in the area of morals.

Creeping infallibility

The misleading use of the word 'ordinary' in the colloquial sense instead of in the juridical sense used in canon law is partly to blame for the dangerous extension of the Church's infallibility to the non-infallible doctrinal teaching of the pope and his curia. This has been called 'creeping infallibility,' which means treating non-infallible doctrines as though they were on the same level as defined matters of faith, calling for the same response on the part of believers. Not only will this kind of confusion not promote mature and solid faith, but believers are scandalised when Church authorities use sanctions against theologians who protest at this dangerous confusion. When the pope teaches on important matters and addresses the whole Church, but not *ex cathedra*, his teaching deserves special respect or due reverence, but not the act of faith called for by a dogmatic definition. Creeping infallibility tends to inflate the papacy in an unbalanced way, so that individual bishops and national hierarchies have very little real authority in their own right and are treated as mere delegates of the pope. Their ordinary magisterium becomes little more than an echo of Rome, as Bishop B. C. Butler once described it after the Council, at which he was a valued speaker. This pyramidal structure of authority is not in keeping with the Vatican II picture of the Church as a communion of churches. The apostles were not area managers with authority delegated by Peter. It is true that the Church is not a modern democracy, but neither should it be a multinational company, with all power coming from the top.

The First Vatican Council declared, with regard to papal infallibility, that when a doctrine has been infallibly defined, it is considered to be *irreformable*, which means that it cannot later be changed. This does not mean that the precise words used are the best to express the doctrine and may never be altered, but rather that the truth contained in the words will never change. The words are simply more or less adequate expressions of the basic truth, and could be improved later. As irreformable, a defined truth of faith is *definitive* teaching.

Another source of confusion in discussions of the Church's teaching function is the use of the word *authentic* to describe the magisterium. Even in the Vatican II document on *The Church*, and in the 1983 code of canon law, it is used in different senses. According to the dictionary, something 'authentic' means something 'of authority, entitled to obedience or respect,' or on the other hand 'something really proceeding from its reputed source, something of undisputed origin, genuine.' In other words, it can mean something official, or something genuine. It makes little sense to describe the magisterium as genuine; what else could it be? The word required in English is 'official,' 'authoritative,' meaning that the teaching or the teachers are authoritative, that they have the appropriate authority, and in fact we believe that the bishops and the pope speak with the authority of Christ. Theologians and other non-hierarchical believers teach with the authority of their experience and expertise, and indeed also with the grace of their baptism, but the pope and the bishops teach with the authority of their office, as pastors of the Church, with the mandate to teach the gospel in the name of Jesus. To call a teaching authoritative, however, does not indicate whether or not it is infallible. Indeed if it is not infallible, the fact that it is official, or authoritative, does not make the doctrine true. Church history shows several cases of doctrines officially and authoritatively taught for centuries by popes and ecumenical councils which were eventually given up as false. In fact, the centuries-old teaching 'Outside the Church, no salvation,' is now seen as not only false, but close to heretical. The temporal power of the popes was defended for centuries as part of Catholic faith.

Keeping the balance

Before leaving this section on infallibility, it is important to note that only very few of the truths of Catholic faith have been infallibly defined by councils or popes. The great majority of them are accepted in faith as part of God's revelation, but they were never challenged or threatened, and simply never needed solemn definition. To define a truth infallibly does not add to its truth, and it can be argued that new definitions would not add to the health or strength of the Church. Indeed, since consultation of the faithful is more and more accepted as a necessary condition for a solemn definition, and since we are now more sensitive to the Christian truth to be found in the Orthodox Church and among our separated brethren in our sister churches, it is difficult to see how a worthwhile consultation could be carried out in a way that would include them. No other Christian Church agrees with the way the present successors of St Peter exercise the primacy. It is interesting that Pope John Paul II asked for suggestions on how it might be improved. Another question is whether our fellow (and sister) Christians would be excited at the prospect of a new infallible definition. Moreover, as already mentioned, there has never been an infallible definition in the area of morals, and most theologians would probably say that there could not be in the future. One can have clarity in moral theology on the level of *universal principles*, but, as St Thomas Aquinas reminds us, one cannot generalise with absolute norms in the *application of principles*, since this involves so many variables of motive and circumstances.

As an antidote to the danger of creeping infallibility, it needs to be remembered that the 1983 Code of Canon Law says that 'no doctrine is understood to have been dogmatically defined unless this is manifestly the case.' Hence the importance of carefully interpreting documents of the magisterium. If it can be shown that a pope or council has infallibly taught a certain truth in a particular document, the infallibility in no way extends to the whole document, but simply to the truth being taught. This need not lessen the importance of the rest of the text. The Second Vatican Council did not define a single dogma, but it taught with authority, and most of its teaching is a continuing source of life for the Church. One of its nuggets of wisdom is the reminder of the 'hierarchy of truths,' that the truths of faith are not all on the same level of importance. Some are more important and central than others. To lose sight of that is to have an unbalanced faith, and that is the real danger of creeping infallibility. When everything is underlined, nothing is underlined. This lack of balance can undermine the Church's credibility and weaken its witness to the gospel.

Encyclicals and curial documents

Church teaching is not limited to infallible pronouncements of popes or councils. Most of it for the past century has come through the circular letters or encyclicals of popes. For most of the Church's history the popes saw their teaching role as exhorting the faithful, strengthening their faith, as in the writings of Pope Gregory the Great, or deciding issues on which the Church was divided. But since Gregory XVI, early in the last century, the style of papal teaching has changed. Encyclicals became more and more frequent as teaching instruments, sometimes explaining fundamental points of faith, but much more often dealing with other matters, at times quite technical issues of theology. Pius XII, in order to extend his teaching, used carefully prepared allocutions to the many groups who requested a papal audience during their visit to Rome (doctors, midwives, scientists, athletes, bus-drivers, bee-keepers, etc.). No individual could produce so many thousand letters and addresses unaided, so more and more help was needed from his civil service departments, the various congregations making up the Curia of the Holy See. In the case of encyclicals, the pope himself takes responsibility for the final text, but no one knows who the ghost-writers are. There is a general impression that nowadays they are seldom world-class theologians with a body of published work and the experience of having their ideas corrected and refined in debate with their peers. They are obviously carefully chosen, usually from one theological tradition, nowadays a minority group in the Church. Besides papal encyclicals, the Holy See has issued countless decrees, instructions and declarations, through its various offices and commissions, most notably through the Congregation for the Doctrine of the Faith. Many of these have been affected by the creeping infallibility mentioned above. Unfortunately it is forgotten that not only is the pope not infallible when he is not teaching *ex cathedra*, but he cannot delegate any degree of infallibility to his helpers, no matter how important or exalted.

Although the Holy Father, like all the bishops, can count on the special help of the Holy Spirit in his office as pastor and teacher, this is a *grace of state* which is *available* to him. *To appropriate it personally* he needs to use the appropriate means, as mentioned above. When he is speaking outside the field of his personal knowledge or competence, the mere fact that he makes a statement in an encyclical does not make it true. When it is claimed that a declaration from one of the offices of the Holy See has been signed, and therefore approved, by the pope, one needs to distinguish between documents *specially* approved by him (when the pope makes the teaching or decision his own), and others which are given merely *routine* approval, as a formality (so that the core of the document does not have his full authority).

The amount of material contained in this category of Church teaching is enormous and cannot all have the same importance, hence the need to evaluate carefully the individual items. Francis Sullivan's book, *Creative Fidelity*, outlines the necessary criteria for this. The book itself is an excellent example of fidelity to the best of Catholic tradition combined with the creativity to make that tradition relevant in today's world. It is a welcome antidote against those reactionary Catholics who always take a fundamentalist reading of magisterial texts. However, a dangerous side-effect of this kind of exercise is that it gives so much importance to the extrinsic, adhesive label or sticker, like the 'use by' date nowadays attached to perishable goods. While not denying the usefulness, or the need, for this kind of weighing and interpreting, it might be more conducive to moral maturity if the faithful could first take the more direct approach to the content of such documents. This calls for three simple questions:

1. What does it say? (words, context, language);
2. What does it mean? (wider context, culture, historical background);
3. Is it true?

The third question involves docility to Church teaching, openness to reality and to one's own personal experience, with the help of the four imperatives listed in Chapter 5 above on conscience: be attentive, be intelligent, be reasonable, be responsible.

Response to teaching
This third question draws attention to a central element in our response to Church teaching. I can obey an *order* even when I do not agree with it, but it makes no sense to obey a *teaching*. In fact, to speak of obedience in

the context of teaching is a category mistake. When a truth is presented for my *acceptance*, it is a call to my judgment (where truth ultimately resides) to recognise the truth and accept it; it cannot be a command to my will to obey. Reason or judgment cannot obey, but simply understand and assent. In fact, no amount of good will can make up for my lack of conviction, and to accept something which I am convinced is not true is an affront to my conscience. Of course, if I am presented with a scientific truth in an area in which I have no competence, I can accept it on the guarantee of somebody who is knowledgeable and whom I trust, but then my acceptance is a matter of faith, of human faith in the expert in whom I put my trust.

But when there is question of Christian faith in divine revelation, in God's word, in infallibly defined teaching, much more is involved. It is not simply a matter of taking on trust the word of an expert who knows more or can see further than I do. Christian faith is more than mere intellectual assent to words or propositions. It is an act of worship and a profession of commitment and loyalty, not simply to a particular truth, but to the reality expressed by the truth. That reality is Jesus the Lord. My act of faith puts me in personal touch with God, not just with ideas about him. This is what is involved when the Church calls us to *assent to* divinely revealed truth and to infallible expressions of that truth. While the truths of faith are mysteries beyond human understanding, they can be rationally accepted in faith and the believer can show that it is not unreasonable to believe them.

But this kind of divine faith and intellectual *assent* cannot be extended to any lower level of teaching. If, after much study and reflection, I honestly and sincerely *cannot see* the truth of *Humanae Vitae*'s teaching on the evil of artificial contraception, it is simply impossible to *assent* to it on the grounds that Rome has spoken, the case is settled. I cannot be forced to see what I do not see. The human mind is not made like that. But the Congregation for the Doctrine of the Faith does not seem to accept this. When Bernard Häring, one of the world's foremost moral theologians, declared that he was not convinced by Paul VI's teaching on this point, he was subjected to a harrowing process lasting four years, during which he suffered two major outbreaks of cancer. Since he could not in conscience promise conformity to a teaching he was unable to accept, his superiors were ordered to impose a number of sanctions against him. If *Humanae Vitae* were simply Church law, a command addressed to married couples on how they should regulate their families, it would be a matter of obedience, but it is presented as a teaching or doctrine of the Church to be accepted and assented to by all the faithful. Unfortunately, and incredibly, the 1983 code of canon law sets out penal sanctions enforcing conformity in this area, so that dissent is now considered a crime to be punished, unless the guilty person makes a full retraction. The law requires 'submission of intellect and will.' Submission of will is an act of obedience and is perfectly understandable, but it is difficult to see what submission of intellect could possibly mean.

Religious docility

There was considerable discussion both during Vatican II and afterwards of the kind of response required for the non-infallible teaching of the Church. The Council spoke of ready and respectful allegiance of mind, of religious submission of intellect and will. *Obsequium* is the original Latin word and there seems to be no single word for this in English that is generally agreed. Bishop Butler, who was an outstanding member of Vatican II, rules out *assent* and suggests the term *due respect*, or *deference*. An equivalent term might be *reverence*, but the latest Flannery translation of the Council documents translates *obsequium* as *religious docility* of spirit, of will and intellect. This makes a lot more sense. Docility, respect, reverence and deference indicate the basic attitude owed to the Church's non-infallible teaching. It means a willingness and openness to be taught, to learn, a recognition that one can be biased and obstinate, and that these need to be overcome so that the Church's teaching gets a fair hearing, and an awareness that one can be wrong. This basic attitude does not mean that the teaching is treated lightly as just another piece of information; it is studied with the presumption that it is correct and true, until one is forced to a different conclusion. Of course these words, reverence, respect, etc., admit of different degrees depending on the kind of document one is responding to. The convoluted and erudite arguments used to defend the phrase *submission of intellect* as the best English translation seem unconvincing and misguided.

Intelligent lay people unaccustomed to theological niceties might well ask, if it is the case that submission of intellect is required for documents like *Humanae Vitae* today, is there an equal obligation to suspend their God-given intelligence and common sense to submit to the teaching of *Divini Illius Magistri* on co-education? Both are encyclicals, both deal with extremely important issues (birth and upbringing of children), and both were issued by the same top level of authority, the former by Paul VI in 1968, and the latter by Pius XI in 1931. The encyclical on education solemnly declares that 'co-education is erroneous and pernicious, and is often based on a naturalism which denies original sin . . . Nature itself, which makes the two sexes different in organism, inclinations and attitudes, provides no argument for mixing them promiscuously, much less educating them together.' The papal condemnations of co-education and artificial contraception both appeal to 'nature' as the basis of their argument. Is it the same nature? Since the two popes were addressing their teaching to the whole Church, the two letters should require the same response. Does the forty-year interval between them justify treating one as a museum piece and the other as a serious obligation in conscience, indeed in some cases an impossible burden? Is not this a further reminder that all doctrinal statements, including those of the Bible, are historically and culturally conditioned?

Loyal dissent?

It is obvious from previous chapters how much and how radically Church teaching has changed over the centuries. It should be equally obvious that this was not a peaceful process of development of doctrine always moving to greater clarity from implicit to explicit. There were major discontinuities, brought about by changes in the surrounding culture and by critical theologians who challenged the mere repetition of past formulas as Church teaching. This is normal in the life of the Church. But it is sad that the official teaching Church does not seem to acknowledge this. In the 1950s the Church's central authority silenced and sacked some of its best and most loyal theologians, Yves Congar, Henri de Lubac, Jean Daniélou and so many others. Because of their deep love of the Church, they suffered intensely from this rejection of their God-given talents. It is not clear that they ever received an official apology, although it was some consolation to see most of their theological insights used by the Second Vatican Council, to which they were invited as experts by various bishops, and during which they educated the bishops with theological conferences. Two of them were later rewarded with appointments as cardinals. In spite of this experience and the more open theology of the Vatican II documents, the Church's central administration still continues its policy of censuring and punishing those who disagree with official ordinary teaching. Canon law describes dissent as a crime.

Dissent has been a central topic in theological discussions in recent decades, particularly in the United States. It is an unfortunate, unhelpful word to describe what is a normal, natural phenomenon. A softer, more neutral word is 'disagreement.' As Ladislas Örsy has pointed out, a theologian who expresses his disagreement with the views of those in authority may well be making a valuable contribution to the development of Church doctrine, while assenting to every part of revealed truth. Although the help of the Holy Spirit is available to all members of the Church in their efforts to understand, believe, and live the gospel, the authorities do not have access to any separate, hidden source of information. In their teaching, popes and bishops rely on their Christian faith, on scripture and tradition, and they use their critical faculties in the normal procedures of scholarly research, discussion and argument to discern, formulate and preach Christian doctrine. Theologians use precisely the same critical faculties and rational procedures in their efforts to get a deeper understanding of the mysteries of faith and make them meaningful in contemporary culture. Given that all non-infallible teaching is fallible, liable to be incomplete, imperfect or even mistaken, those who discover such mistakes contribute to the health of the Church, of the whole body of believers, by making it known. This is a service to the Church. They do not need any permission to do so. As mentioned above, Vatican II is crystal clear on believers having full freedom of enquiry, of thought and of expression in matters in which they are competent.

In *Humanae Vitae* Pope Paul said that 'people today are particularly suited to perceive how this teaching is in harmony with human reasoning.' This is a statement of fact, and ought to be borne out by the facts. It is a fact that most members of the papal commission set up to study the question at first agreed with the traditional teaching that contraception is intrinsically evil. But in the course of their study they came to the conclusion that this could no longer be maintained, and they were convinced that the Church could and should change its teaching. Indeed, Fr John Ford, one of the tiny minority on the commission who took an intransigent stand on the immorality of contraception, admitted, in a paper presented to the commission, that 'we lack convincing arguments from natural law which are universally valid and convincing' and he said that 'theologians have not, up to now, produced arguments which are clear, convincing, universally valid and admitted by all' against contraception. In the encyclical, Pope Paul exhorted theologians to develop such convincing reasons, but not a single argument has been produced in the past thirty years. On the contrary, most of the faithful who are directly concerned no longer think it is an important moral issue. This is a fact in the life of the Church at the moment, and no amount of preaching or censuring of theologians is likely to alter it.

Aristotle's principle still stands: no teaching has taken place until some-body has been taught.

The Holy Spirit, the ultimate teacher

Believers who are not convinced by the reasoning used in the encyclical are invited to accept it because of the special assistance of the Holy Spirit available to the pope in his teaching office. This is an appeal to faith, but it is not the assent of divine faith with which we respond to infallible teaching on the mysteries of faith. But neither can it be blind faith, and it is a test of faith to believe that the same Holy Spirit who assists the magisterium to teach true and certain doctrine seems incapable of helping the faithful to be taught and to learn, in spite of their best efforts. Pope Paul called on priests to preach the encyclical with confidence, 'in the certainty that while the Holy Spirit of God is present to the *magisterium* as it proposes correct teaching, he is interiorly enlightening the hearts of the faithful and inviting them to give their assent.' This is the belief of the early Church in the Holy Spirit as the internal teacher of all believers. The Pope implies that the Holy Spirit will help people to be receptive to his teaching in this matter, but the past three decades have shown only negative results in this direction. It might even be argued that the non-reception of *Humanae Vitae* is inviting the Church to have a second look at the question. In the meantime, the faithful will continue to follow their conscience.

If responsible disagreement is a normal part of Church life, there should be no question of theologians versus the pope or bishops. They both serve the same Church. The American bishops established norms for lawful dissent. A responsible theologian will be conscious of the possibility that he is wrong and he will also be aware of his social responsibility in the Church. When St Paul speaks of our freedom to follow conscience he reminds us of occasions when we need to be sensitive to how this may affect 'weaker brethren.' Some pastors echo this concern for the simple, pious faithful, but the number of such simple people is diminishing in today's more developed and educated world. On the other hand, the many committed Catholics who feel that their critical intelligence is not being respected when they ask searching questions are growing in number and they require special pastoring by the Church.

Word and deed

Church leaders who complain that people are no longer loyal to the magisterium tend to blame secularism and the influence of the media, but they seldom think of the Church doing a proper evaluation of its teaching, in terms of content and methods. Undoubtedly there is some excellent teaching in the Church, from catechetics programmes to pastoral letters, from declarations of national hierarchies to papal encyclicals. But because of the multiplicity of encyclicals during the past fifty years, people tend to think of them as synonymous with Church teaching. It might be asked: what effect do they really have on the life of the Church? A neutral analyst might point out some of their weaknesses as means of communication. *Humanae Vitae* is unique in the publicity it received, but that is no guarantee that it was read in its entirety by large numbers of people. Has any survey ever been carried out on what percentage of believers even see encyclicals? Of those who actually see them, how many read them, how many study and discuss them with others? It is true that most of them are addressed to bishops, who are expected to spread their content further, but it is hardly a rash judgment to say that only a tiny fraction of 1 per cent of laity ever see them, and 5 per cent might be an optimistic figure for priests. Can it be presumed that a high percentage of bishops make a deep personal study of each one? How many bishops are in total agreement with all of them?

Another obstacle to their widespread diffusion is their literary style. In whatever language, it comes across as ponderous, and sometimes convoluted, reflecting an older world, a different culture, and sometimes a minority theological tradition. Some of them are condemnatory, laying down the law as if the readers were schoolchildren needing correction. At times there is no real teaching in terms of attracting and convincing the readers. Too often the compassionate and tender side of the Church does not come through, even though those words are used in the text. The central control of *administration* and the preservation of true *doctrine* can at times be intermingled and confused. Too often what comes through is a subconscious identification of the Church with the papacy, and an emphasis on the institutional dimension of the Church that obscures the other dimensions of mystery, communion, fellowship, pilgrim people of God, herald of the good news.

Body language, faith in action

A major element in the credibility of Church teaching is body language. Jesus taught by word and deed, but discussion of Church teaching can focus almost exclusively on words and documents. If the Church in practice were living up to the ideals it preaches, its most effective teaching would be the silent sermon of its example. Outsiders do not read our documents, but what they see in Church action can sometimes reinforce their prejudices, and some see the Church as an ideological power-structure under the direction of repressive authorities. Its political concerns can often blur its gospel image, for example when it sides with dictators and military regimes. Its record in Haiti was a scandal. Moreover, when clerical sex scandals reached world headlines, the automatic, instinctive response of Church leaders was one of damage control, to cover up and protect the Church's image. Only later was it realised that this reaction did even more damage to the Church's image. It took considerable time before compassion and justice for the innocent victims became a concern, which would seem to indicate that the gospel response of mercy is not a spontaneous reaction of the Church.

What puts many people off the Catholic Church is not its authority, but its authoritarianism, its way of exercising authority. It presents a most unattractive picture when it publicly humiliates or disparages saints, prophets and pastors loved by millions of believers, people like Bishop Helder Cámara, Cardinal Arns, Archbishop Romero, and it censures respected theologians like Rahner, Schillebeeckx, Häring, Boff and others. It can seem more interested in power than spiritual insight or pastoral concern. At times the Church's central authority is not only at variance with the normal procedures of justice and fairness now commonplace in the civilised world, but even contradicts its own official teaching. For example, when it condemns a theologian for his views, there is no real dialogue. He is called to Rome to be lectured, and the same authority carries out the investigation, produces the evidence and pronounces the condemnation, while the accused is not even told who his accusers are, and the whole procedure is kept secret, allegedly to protect the accused, but in fact so that the prosecutors are saved the embarrassment of being called to account. Already in 1215 the Fourth Lateran Council decreed that 'He who is the object of an inquiry should be present at the process, and should have the various headings of the inquiry explained to him, so as to allow him the possibility of defending himself; as well, he is to be informed not only of what the various witnesses have accused him, but also of the names of those witnesses.' The harrowing experiences of Frs Häring, Curran, Boff and so many others at the hands of the Congregation for the Doctrine of the Faith in recent times would have been condemned as unjust by the Church itself in the thirteenth century.

Just a few years ago, an archbishop from one of the Vatican congregations publicly declared that the Church had nothing to be ashamed of in the Inquisition, that it was quite justified. A sobering thought is that in a few years time so many of the documents from Roman congregations will be lying in archives as material for students seeking doctoral dissertations, whereas the writings of Rahner, Schillebeeckx, Häring, Küng, Gutierrez and Boff have already entered into the Church's bloodstream to enrich its spiritual, intellectual and pastoral life.

More positive image

Against this negative image of the institutional Church, of course, there is the gospel witness of so many of its members, bishops, priests, religious and laity, women and men, people in whom the gospel shone out clearly. They preached by their example, but many also spoke out courageously in favour of a better kind of Church. Archbishop Franz König of Vienna was an outspoken member of the Second Vatican Council. In 1968 he warned Pope Paul VI against taking the stand he did in *Humanae Vitae*, stressing that birth control was ultimately a decision of personal conscience. At an interview he gave on his ninetieth birthday in August 1996 he did not look over his shoulder in fear of being overheard by the Vatican when he openly shared his views on controversial issues. He stressed that the appointment of bishops was not a matter for Rome to decide alone. Although the Pope would have the final say, the local church had to be consulted. He said that the law of priestly celibacy in the Latin Church was not at all irrevocable. In the Byzantine-rite Church in communion with Rome celibacy for priests is voluntary, and he said there was no reason why mature married men could not become priests in the Latin rite. Moreover, he saw no theological objections to women's ordination, although there was a danger that it could divide the Church and damage ecumenical relations with the Orthodox.

Another courageous figure in this line is the former Archbishop of San Francisco, John R. Quinn, who requested that the pope convoke an ecumenical council at the beginning of the third millennium. He asked that there be a thoroughgoing reform of the Roman Curia and the synod of bishops so that the ancient, and Vatican II-endorsed, doctrine of collegiality might become a reality in the Church. This was in response to Pope John Paul II's invitation to pastors and theologians to help him find new ways of exercising his papal office of primacy. The Archbishop is known as a moderate, prayerful, reflective person deeply influenced by the writings of Cardinal Newman. He made his suggestions in a public lecture delivered in Oxford in June 1996. In calling for a reform of the papacy he quoted Cardinal Congar's historical research showing that moral reform is not enough, that personal holiness of itself will not bring about a change. To be effective it must involve structures. His lecture was praised by Archbishop Weakland of Milwaukee, but Cardinal O'Connor of New York saw no need for any reform, simply a clearer explanation of Church teaching.

Cardinal Bernardin of Chicago, the senior cardinal in the United States and former president of the national conference of bishops, was concerned about the deepening divisions within the American Church, the hardening of party lines on the left and right, a mood of suspicion and acrimony, and the inhibition of candid discussion. In a document entitled *Called to be Catholic*, along with a group of others, he invited Catholics to leave behind what brings discord, to discern a revitalised Catholic common ground, and he proposed a programme to bring this about. The project listed the urgent questions facing the Church today and presented the challenge in an inspiring way that could make for peace and reconciliation, and lead the Church to gospel witness in today's world. Four American cardinals strongly opposed the initiative and criticised his views, saying that dissent cannot be dialogued away, that all that was needed is to be found in the binding teaching of the magisterium. Once again, Church leaders were showing in their actions what they were denying in their words.

Prophetic action, sobering questions

In October 1996 Cardinal Bernardin opened the first meeting of the project, but a week later the pancreatic cancer diagnosed the previous year took its toll. He wrote a last letter to his fellow bishops a few days before his death, urging them to continue their pastoral efforts together. By the time of his death he was corresponding with six hundred fellow-cancer sufferers. When he died in November 1996, more than 100,000 people filed past his coffin in below-freezing temperatures to pay their respects. The example of his life of mediation and reconciliation did more for the image and the morale of the Catholic Church than many documents of the magisterium. During the funeral homily, when Bernardin's name was linked to Pope John XXIII's great work for unity, there was an electrifying spontaneous outburst of applause in the cathedral, but some of the cardinals sat stony-faced. Is there a divided

Church in the United States as well as in South America? If magisterium means teaching, and teaching is by word and deed, more attention needs to be given to the Church's record and present practice in this area. Has it always reflected the *joy and hope* which the Second Vatican Council speaks of in *The Church in the Modern World*? How does it prove itself *a light to the nations*, as the document on *The Church* implies when it speaks of the light of Christ being resplendent on the face of the Church as it proclaims the gospel to every creature?

Pope Paul VI, in his exhortation on *Evangelisation in the Modern World* (1975), made the point that people today listen more willingly to witnesses than to teachers, and when they do listen to teachers, it is precisely because they are witnesses. Actions speak more loudly than words. Repeating Vatican II, he stressed that in order to evangelise the world with credibility, the Church must itself be converted. An examination of conscience in this area might well begin with the sobering questions voiced by Jesuit theologian Richard A. McCormick:

> Why is it that Rome generally consults only those who support its pre-taken position? Why does Rome appoint as bishops only those who have never publicly questioned *Humanae Vitae*, the celibacy of priests and the ordination of women? Why does a bishop speak on the ordination of women only after retirement? Why are Vatican documents composed in secrecy? Why does the Holy See not at least review its formulations on certain questions that it knows were met with massive dissent and non-reception? And on and on. Such questions spring from the coercive atmosphere established by the Holy See in the past decade. They have to do with basic honesty on the part of the teaching office, and ultimately its credibility.[4]

He speaks movingly from the heart when he adds: 'In my earlier years I would have thought that love of the Church translates into a benign silence on such issues. Now silence appears to me as betrayal.'

10

NEW CHALLENGES

If morality is about the responsible use of freedom, every increase in human freedom brings a corresponding increase in responsibility. Moral decisions can be simple in a primitive society where options are limited, but in today's world of almost limitless options it is less easy to distinguish right from wrong. Although millions of human beings are still unfortunately restricted in their choices, with very few options open to them, the human race as a whole has never before had such power at its disposal. In terms of Catholic faith, this is a blessing, part of God's plan. The Second Vatican Council noted that:

> People have always striven to develop their human life through their own effort and ingenuity, and nowadays they extend their mastery over nearly all spheres of activity through science and technology . . . This monumental effort through the centuries to improve living conditions presents no problem to believers, in fact, in itself it corresponds to God's plan . . . The achievements of the human race are a sign of God's greatness and the fulfilment of his mysterious design . . . But the more the power of men and women increases, the greater is their responsibility, as individuals and as members of the community. (*The Church in the Modern World*, nn. 33, 34)

The Council draws attention to the challenge arising from the speed of change: 'The accelerated pace of history is such that one can scarcely keep abreast of it . . . and so we substitute a dynamic and more evolutionary concept of nature for a static one, and this results in an immense series of new problems, calling for a new endeavour of analysis and synthesis' (n. 5).

The highest level of Church teaching thus encourages us to welcome the recent advances of science and technology. But moral responsibility warns us that not everything that *can* be done, *may* be done, or indeed *should* be done. Discernment is needed for a moral evaluation of these advances, in order to decide *when* we should go no further, and *which* technologies should not be availed of because ultimately they are destructive of basic human values. Even the most spectacular achievements must be evaluated in terms of human welfare and the dignity of persons, as individuals and in their relationships to each other and to the environment. The complexity of today's world raises moral questions to which there are no immediate or easy answers. Moral responsibility applies not only to personal relations, but to technology, politics and economics, raising questions about justice between nations, the concentration and monopoly of power, exploitation of the poor, waste of natural resources, upsetting the balance of nature, the kind of world we bequeath to future generations, etc. There are vast areas of human activity which are now so complex that it is difficult to see how traditional rules of morality can be applied, but we cannot avoid the moral choices needed. Enormous progress has been made in medical technology in recent years, and it may be helpful to look at some of the developments in order to understand the new challenges that arise for morality. Sadly, bioethics is the area in which official Church teaching is at present suffering its greatest credibility problem, and its repetition of simplistic solutions from the past only increases the problem. An excellent survey of medico-moral issues is *Life and Morality,* by David Smith, M.S.C.[1]

Remedying nature's defects
The development of the anovulant pills and the various contraceptive devices raised moral questions which are still debated, but 1978 saw a new breakthrough in bio-technology, with the birth of Louise Brown, the world's first test-tube baby after IVF (*in vitro* fertilisation). Pope John Paul I said it was a wonderful achievement and he was happy for the otherwise childless parents. The bishops of England and Wales at first welcomed IVF, saying that they could see no reason for considering it morally objectionable. But they later changed their minds, because the procedure involved the intentional destruction of human embryos, and it separated procreation from human intercourse. The procedure was condemned by the Holy See as unethical in its 1987 document on bioethics, *Donum Vitae.* But many theologians today hold a more ___ view. Over fifteen thousand people now living owe their exis-___ nd the experience of recent years is that IVF is both safe and ___ ficient, with no risks to parents or to the baby. The success

rate is not far behind that of the natural process, up to 25 per cent per cycle of treatment. The procedure can be financially costly, and there is no absolute guarantee of success, but IVF seems a God-given solution to provide offspring for a couple who are infertile through a defect of nature. In an age when millions seek abortions every year, it is heartening to know that science and technology can now help parents who really want children. For critics it is an interference with nature, but it can also be seen as a medical procedure to remedy nature's defects, no more artificial than any other use of creative human intelligence to promote people's welfare.

Space does not allow a full discussion of the various technical procedures, but basically IVF means that the union of sperm and egg takes place in the laboratory (*in vitro*, in glass), hence the term 'test-tube' babies. Two days after fertilisation the conceptus develops to about eight cells and is then introduced to the uterus through a catheter. Ideally four embryos need to be introduced for one to implant. Other techniques are: GIFT, gamete intra-fallopian transfer, i.e. stimulants provoke the release of multiple eggs, which together with washed semen are inserted into the fallopian tube; TOT, tubal ovum transfer, in which the sperm is collected during the marital act of intercourse in a perforated condom, and then ovum and sperm are injected into the fallopian tube; LTOT, lower tubal ovum transfer, is somewhat similar. Since these three methods allow conception to occur within the body, after intercourse, instead of in a glass dish in the laboratory, they involve less artificial interference, they avoid embryo manipulation or selection, and thus meet Catholic criteria for lawfulness. They are safe techniques and many couples are happy to use them, but others prefer IVF.

Official Church teaching condemns any artificial interference unless it is simply to 'assist the natural process' of conception through marital intercourse, since the unitive and procreative dimensions must be present together in every act of intercourse. This rules out IVF. But the experience of couples who have recourse to IVF as a last resort to make their marriage fruitful is that this abstract approach makes no sense to them. Their ordinary, infertile intercourse has no procreative dimension whatever, but when IVF is successful, not only is the procreative dimension restored to their marriage, but the unitive dimension is also enhanced. They never think of their child as a mechanical product of technology, but as the fruit of their love. A substantial majority of world-renowned Catholic moral theologians agree with their view and see no moral objection to couples resorting to artificial means to achieve conception when intercourse fails, provided that sperm and ova come from husband and wife, that no more embryos are created than can be safely implanted in the wife's womb, and that there is no intention to abort if abnormality occurs. To approve of the normal IVF case like this, however, does not mean that all of the experimentation that went on before the technique was perfected was morally good, nor does it mean giving moral approval to the many serious abuses to which the procedure has since given rise.

The official teaching is based on a static concept of 'nature' that has little acceptance nowadays outside a particularly narrow neo-scholastic philosophy which seems to identify natural law with biology. When the objection is raised that IVF may damage the fertilised ovum and produce a deformed child, it must be remembered that in the case of the 'natural' procedure of intercourse, up to 60 to 70 per cent of conceptions are spontaneously, naturally aborted, and a considerable number of deformed children are born 'naturally.' Moreover, one in seven of all marriages are infertile, and many Catholic couples cannot see how their faith can oblige them to accept this passively as 'God's will.' One objection against IVF in the official Church teaching is that masturbation is used to provide the male sperm, but theologians nowadays distinguish between 'moral' and merely 'biological' masturbation; in other words, masturbation in this context is not the same as 'ipsation,' self-pleasure or self-abuse. Artificial insemination by the husband is still officially rejected as unnatural, following a statement of Pius XII, but it is seen by many nowadays as another beneficial medical technology to overcome the handicap of infertility.

Pandora's box
IVF technology is not limited to the 'simple case' outlined above. There are developments that raise far more complex issues. It is now possible to have sperm, ova and embryos supplied by donors; to have surrogate mothers (with donors supplying either sperm or ova, or indeed both); to have single women artificially impregnated, lesbian couples having children, frozen sperm for use even after the death of the one providing it, frozen embryos, embryos created for experimentation, the use of deliberately aborted foetuses to provide organ-transplants. Some children born without a full brain have been kept alive to provide organs for transplantation. Many doctors are willing to use tissue from a miscarried foetus to help patients suffering from Parkinson's or Alzheimer's disease. One woman claims to have deliberately become pregnant and

aborted her foetus to provide tissue for the treatment of her grandfather. In 1996 a grandmother carried and gave birth to the IVF baby of her daughter. In England 5,000 frozen embryos were destroyed in August 1996 because they had reached the five-year limit allowed by law for keeping them. Over three hundred Italian mothers offered to adopt some of the frozen embryos. Women using fertility drugs have had multiple pregnancies, and then had the problem of selectively aborting most of them. In the same month of August a father of septuplets described witnessing the selective abortion of six of them: 'I watched on the ultrasound as potassium was injected into their tiny beating hearts.' A few months later a Greek woman was reported as carrying eleven foetuses and discussing with her doctor whether two or four should be spared to ensure having a live baby.

Fertility treatment in Britain has increased the incidence of twins from one in 100 births to one in seventy-five. Some mothers claim they could not cope with twins and ask that one be destroyed before birth. It is said that Japanese scientists are close to developing an artificial womb that will nurture human life created in the laboratory with egg and sperm from two total strangers. This is the nightmare world that technology has opened up, but the abuses are all the more reason for serious evaluation of the way in which it is used. Technology in itself is morally neutral, but the new options now available have enormous moral implications, since they affect basic human values such as the meaning of marriage and family, parenthood, human sexual relationships, the sanctity of life. It would be irresponsible to say a blanket 'No' to all developments in the field of bio-technology, but there is a greater need than ever for vigilance and moral analysis to see that the miracles of science do not turn into nightmares that will change the meaning of human life.

As early as 1967, Karl Rahner, S.J., the greatest Catholic theologian of this century, wrote a courageous essay on the problem of genetic engineering which is still a challenge to traditional Catholic thinking. It was a major break with the long tradition of automatic negative reaction to the discoveries of biological science. He explained that natural law theory does not at all require a static, non-evolutionary view of human nature. He warned against a comfortable conservativism hiding behind misunderstood Christian ideals. He recommended 'cool-headedness' as the appropriate reaction to genetic manipulation. He recalled that humans have always modified their natural environment, using their God-given intelligence and skill. Human life has been altered down the centuries through diet, medicine and environment and Rahner asked why we should fear future developments in science and technology. He recommended that theologians and Church authorities admit that they cannot pass judgment on scientific matters until they know all that is involved. Theologians cannot speak absolutely about 'human nature' without taking into account the new knowledge available from biology and the other human sciences. Rahner was not proposing unfettered licence for genetics. On the contrary, each new procedure needs to be carefully evaluated in its context, with a clear understanding of what it involves, its motivation and its consequences, not merely for the individuals immediately concerned, especially the future offspring, but also for the wider human society. The question is not simply to decide whether or not to use genetic techniques, but to discriminate between those which enhance human welfare and personal dignity, and those which are detrimental to basic human values.

Immoral procedures
There are situations in which artificial insemination from the husband, IVF or tubal ovum transfer would be morally acceptable to help an infertile couple. But it is impossible to imagine cases in which third-party donors or surrogate mothers could ever be justified. In these procedures there is too much at stake in terms of the welfare of the offspring and the harm done to marital relationships and morally responsible parenthood. With centuries of experience, society has discovered that certain conditions are necessary for human flourishing, and has devised a system of laws forbidding incest, prostitution, the buying of brides, and the selling of babies or of bodily organs, in order to protect and promote the values necessary for a healthy society. In recent years we have become aware of the horrendous damage done to people through child abuse, with thousands carrying the psychological scars for the rest of their lives. How can one measure the harm done to the sense of identity and self-esteem of children who discover that they owe their existence to a commercial arrangement between their 'parents' and some unknown outsider? How can they seek redress for damage done to them without their consent? It is even worse if the surrogate mother who rented her womb decides that she wants to keep the child for herself and a court of law has to decide where the child belongs, or if the 'parents' change their mind and rescind the contract. When sperm or ova come from an outside donor, will the non-contributing partner be committed to the welfare of the child when difficulties arise? If only one parent is biologically related to the child, what psychological effect will the biological imbalance have on the non-

contributing partner, and on the relationship? What kind of world will it be when large numbers of people will be totally rootless, with no possibility of knowing who their parents were? Technically, a child could have five different 'parents,' counting nurturing, carrying and genetic parents. The central objection to any kind of third-party intrusion in the marital relationship is that it interferes with the exclusiveness that is an essential element in marriage, and this includes the genetic, gestational and rearing dimensions of parenthood. IVF for a loving couple is an act of intimacy helped by medical science, and no outsider (whether egg or sperm) should be allowed to invade that intimacy.

Frozen embryos

Embryo freezing is another technique associated with IVF. In 1983 an Australian mother miscarried during her first attempt at IVF, but had some embryos frozen and preserved for a later attempt, from which she successfully bore a child. In theory, a case could be made for this as an improvement of the IVF technique, but serious questions arise that would condemn it as morally unacceptable. In the simple case of IVF, the ovum and sperm are helped to unite in the present, here and now, as in intercourse. But freezing and storing embryos for some future possibility (later attempts at IVF, having a child after the death or departure of the husband) is a totally different matter. Since it is a question of a mere possibility in the future, there is no proportionate reason for creating embryos that are not clearly needed and would eventually have to be destroyed or allowed to die.

These are just some of the factors that need to be considered in order to decide the morality of these new procedures. It is true that single parents can be helped to cope with their children, or less than adequate persons may successfully adopt, but these are hard case exceptions, emergency solutions, not general norms for a healthy society. Recent research indicates that the increase of crime in first-world countries is linked more to the large proportion of one-parent families than to poverty and drugs. There is a consensus among sociologists that the traditional pattern of family life is still the most beneficial to children, and therefore to society as a whole. Children are not mere property, artefacts that can be produced for various reasons at personal whim. They are persons with human rights, with claims on others. That is why society makes laws about adoption, custody and child abuse. Moreover, it is not clear that every individual has an absolute right to a child, regardless of circumstances such as the ability to take responsibility for it, any more than people who claim a right to marriage can expect society to provide them with spouses. Parenthood is more about duties and responsibilities than rights.

Because scientific advances need experimentation, there is now an immense amount of laboratory research going on with early embryos. This is intended to provide new knowledge about fertility and fertilisation, and about birth defects. Pre-natal diagnosis of genetic disorders is now possible, leading to pre-natal therapy, including gene-changes. The experimentation involves the creation and freezing of large numbers of embryos as material for experiments. The civil law of many countries allows this, but many moralists, including the official teaching of the Church, reject it as immoral. The advance of scientific knowledge is a great benefit to human welfare, but not at any cost, and the cost is too high when it involves the deliberate creation and destruction of human embryos. Even to use 'spare' or surplus embryos not needed in IVF can be judged immoral because of the strong temptation for doctors to produce more than is required in order to benefit their research or try out new drugs. With so many drugs waiting to be tested, there would be enormous pressure to produce embryos on which to test them. It is because embryos are not simply disposable bits of tissue, but human life with the potential to become human persons, that they need to be treated with the utmost respect, the kind of respect that forbids their deliberate destruction.

Abortion

Because of the publicity surrounding the more sensational developments in bio-technology, it can easily be forgotten that abortion is the gravest and most shameful experience of the human race. The large numbers of victims and the savage nature of the genocide in Rwanda and in former Yugoslavia were a shock to the world, but they pale into insignificance compared with the annual abortion rate of forty to fifty millions worldwide. Over one and a half million abortions each year are carried out in the United States, and 95 per cent of Russian women had between eight and twenty abortions during their reproductive years. A survey in Poland some years ago claimed that one in every three urban women and 16 per cent of rural women had abortions. In the summer of 1996 a senior doctor remarked on BBC that, without abortion, there would be 200,000 more people each year to look after in Britain. The sheer callousness of his statement makes one wonder just how many professionals make serious judgments in a moral vacuum. Ordinary people are beginning to wonder if the pendulum has swung too far in the wrong direction. This is a new challenge for Church teaching.

One of the reasons for the Church's loss of credibility in the area of moral teaching in recent times has been the practice of lumping together in a single condemnation (often in a single paragraph) permissiveness, contraception, abortion and divorce. These are quite serious problems, but they need to be analysed separately, and it should be obvious that abortion is by far the most serious. Given the widespread rejection of *Humanae Vitae*, Church teaching should have clear, strong arguments to show why abortion is wrong. The case is not helped by careless use of language. It is incorrect to speak of human life as an absolute value, when the history of Catholic morality shows that it was only a near-absolute, since tradition justified killing in self-defence, capital punishment and just war. Likewise, it is not necessary to insist that the embryo is a person from the moment of conception. In fact, 'person' is a philosophical and not a scientific concept, so that it is impossible to prove scientifically whether or not the embryo is a person. In fact, traditional Church teaching has always refrained from defining the precise moment when the human person comes into being. A strong consensus among moralists would now claim that since twinning and recombining are possible for the zygote or pre-embryo within the first two weeks after fertilisation, one cannot speak of a unique human individual being present until the appearance of the 'primitive streak' at the end of the second week. (The fertilised ovum, or zygote, is called an embryo after two weeks, and a foetus after eight weeks). However, it is also a fact that the pre-embryo, if not interfered with, will develop into a human person (which cannot be said of sperm or ovum separately). It deserves special respect.

Human life a basic value

The abortion debate is about the value accorded to the new life arising from fertilisation. Some see this new life as simply maternal tissue, part of the woman's body, which the mother can dispose of at will. But the classical Christian tradition is that it is human life, with a near-absolute value, and that it deserves all the respect normally shown to human persons. Human life is a basic good, the foundation for all other human goods. It is such a basic value that it should never be sacrificed, unless in such extreme circumstances that taking it happens to be the lesser of two evils, as in self-defence, on the principle of proportionate reason. In a healthy society there should be an uncompromising commitment to protecting human life, particularly when it is most vulnerable. There is a solid consensus among moralists that this certainly applies to intra-uterine human life, at least from the appearance of the primitive streak, at the end of the second week after fertilisation. In the first two weeks, since the pre-embryo is in the process of becoming a human person, it deserves the same profound respect and protection. But given the uncertainty about its precise status, some moralists would say that the pre-embryo could be sacrificed in extreme cases of genetic abnormality, or of rape and the mother's inability to bear the child without grave damage to herself.

There is a challenge to Church teaching not only from the advances in bio-technology, but also from the moral vacuum in which life and death decisions are often made in today's world. That challenge is sharpened by the feeling of so many committed Catholics that official pronouncements often seem simplistic, unconvincing and out of touch with the realities of everyday life. People like Dr John Marshall have no hesitation in criticising the incoherence of the Church's official position, when on the one hand it denies the use of God-given artificial means to create new life for couples for whom intercourse is ineffective, while on the other, it insists on the continued use of artificial means to maintain someone in a persistent vegetative state which seems to be distressfully and unnecessarily prolonging death rather than saving life. Church teaching, which has such an excellent tradition of gospel proclamation and prophetic stands, does itself an immense disservice by its blind attachment to an archaic notion of 'natural,' and its inability to explain why some artificial procedures are displeasing to God while others are acceptable to him.

Abortion is an agonising and complicated problem involving many issues (value and protection of human life, freedom of choice for women, right to privacy, public policy and private conscience, etc.), and any simplistic approach is counterproductive. Cardinal Hume at the end of 1996 spoke of abortion and the responsibilities of legislators, but he rightly warned voters against choosing single-issue candidates for political office. Legislators should be elected for their commitment to the common good, not just to one issue. Abortion is a most serious issue, but it is not unconnected with other moral issues such as housing, employment, social security, education. The late Cardinal Bernardin spoke convincingly of the need for a consistent life ethic that would be as concerned about the quality and protection of life after birth as before. Some pro-life activists can damage their cause by unacknowledged anti-life attitudes. All sides in the debate should be challenged on a careless, or perhaps deliberately biased, use of language. Some pro-choice speakers are careful to avoid the phrase 'abortion on demand,' which is essentially their position, because they know that large numbers of people do not want that. Instead, they use the neutral-sounding euphemism 'termination of pregnancy.' It should be acknowledged that every person has a God-given right of choice, but this right is limited by corresponding duties, and most fundamentally by the basic right to life of other human beings. One can choose not to be pregnant, by avoiding intercourse or by taking contraceptive measures, but there is no right to conceive and then to destroy the new life conceived.

Search for a middle ground

Because so much of the abortion debate can descend to extremists shouting at each other, it is important to seek a middle ground where responsible dialogue becomes possible. An admirable set of suggestions towards this was proposed by Richard McCormick, S.J., probably the most authoritative, respected and balanced English-speaking moralist of the past three decades.[2] Briefly, he proposed that it be recognised that:

1. There is a presumption against the lawfulness of taking human life;
2. Abortion means killing;
3. In the rare case where the foetus is a direct threat to the life of the mother, it may, regrettably, be sacrificed to save the mother;
4. To claim that abortion is simply a matter of the mother's choice would mean that *any* abortion, at *any* time, for *any* reason, would be justified as long as the mother freely wants it. Do many people believe this?
5. Abortion for mere convenience is morally wrong; consideration of this invites the pro-choice lobby to reflect on why and how the life in the womb has claims on society;
6. Attention needs to be paid to the factors that lead to abortion: lack of education, of social support, of alternative solutions to abortion; it is a social problem, and not simply a problem of individual choice;
7. Abortion is always tragic, and can be dangerous, psychologically traumatic, divisive of families;
8. Women tempted to abort on the basis of free choice should be helped to discern whether their decision is truly free or unduly subject to pressure from others or from society at large. Viable alternatives need to be available to make a free choice possible. A poor or disturbed pregnant woman whose only choice is an abortion is hardly 'free' in her choice;
9. Abortion is not a private affair; it affects husbands, families, nurses, doctors, politicians and society;

10.   Unenforceable laws are bad laws, and an absolute prohibition is
       unenforceable. An absolute prohibition would leave no room for
       morally acceptable exceptions like saving the mother's life. On the
       other hand, to extend legal protection to the pre-embryo creates
       legal difficulties, since there is no evidence of pregnancy before
       implantation;
11.   Public policy on abortion needs some control;
12.   Rational argument should be backed up by practical witnessing to
       the conviction being argued for;
13.   Worldwide experience shows that making contraception more eas-
       ily available does not reduce the number of abortions;
14.   Permissive abortion laws remove all notion of 'sanctity of life' for
       the unborn;
15.   Hospitals where abortions are performed should have a policy to
       govern the procedures; leaving it to patient autonomy creates a
       moral vacuum, leading to ever more laxity;
16.   Genuine concern for the unborn should lead to a consistent ethic of
       life, to include concern for human life issues outside the womb.

What kind of life?

The permissive approach to abortion in recent years has spread beyond
birth and is now evident in the treatment of handicapped newborns.
While Catholic moralists totally condemn as unjustified the abortion of a
foetus suffering from Down's syndrome, since such children can live
happy lives for decades, civil legislation in many countries allows this.
There have been cases, however, where not merely a foetus, but newborn
babies with this handicap were deprived of feeding and ordinary care so
that they might die, as the mothers did not want them. It was not a question of 'allowing them to die,' since they were in no more danger of death
than other newborns. Such cases are a warning against the 'slippery
slope' danger, and they emphasise the need for vigilance and rigour in
the moral assessment of these developments.

The medical technology that raised new moral issues at the beginning
of life can also cause problems at its ending. In developed countries four
out of five people die in hospital, and with all the high technology now
available for prolonging physical life, a point is often reached where one
wonders whether the medical service is really saving life or just prolonging death. The 1980 Vatican declaration on euthanasia sums up the
traditional Catholic stand: when it is a question of the means used to preserve life, the type of treatment needs to be studied, its degree of

complexity, its risk, its cost, and all of these need to be compared with the result that can be expected, taking account of the physical and moral resources of the patient. In simple terms, life-sustaining treatments are not a moral obligation if they are a serious burden or of no avail. Traditional Catholic teaching is that there is no obligation to use extraordinary or disproportionate means to sustain life. Of course, what was once considered extraordinary can later become quite ordinary. But the judgment between the two should be made in reference to the patient in the concrete situation. The treatment considered ordinary by the medical staff using it frequently may be quite extraordinary for the patient since it involves considerable expense, invasive surgery or continuous painful treatment. Since death is a natural part of life, the right to life includes also the right to die with dignity, with peace of mind, in reasonable comfort, relating to family and friends.

The principle seems clear, but problems arise in its application. Because of the emphasis on the preservation of life, many severely brain-damaged patients, in a 'persistent vegetative state' (PVC), have been artificially kept alive for twenty or more years, at enormous pain to families caring for them. The British House of Lords, in the Tony Bland case, established the right of doctors to withdraw tube feeding from such patients without facing murder charges. On the other hand, the bishops of Pennsylvania declared that there is an obligation to continue supplying nutrition and hydration to unconscious patients, except when death is imminent or the patient is unable to assimilate what is supplied. The bishops state that to withdraw nutrition is not simply to let the patient die, but to kill by omission. A majority of Catholic moralists would see this as an exaggerated position, and in fact the bishops of Texas see it differently. For them, the PVS is the real cause of death when nutrition and hydration are not provided, and there is no moral obligation to prevent death in these circumstances because preserving mere physiological functions without any cognitive-affective potential is of no benefit to the dying patient. To preserve indefinitely a person's purely vegetative functions with no hope of improvement is to depart substantively from the traditional Catholic position. In fact, nurses caring for such patients often feel that the nursing home seems like a concentration camp uselessly torturing the elderly to keep their bodies alive while they are prevented from dying with dignity.

An additional element has entered the debate recently with the claim that many PVS patients may be incorrectly diagnosed and, with the proper treatment, may be helped to communicate. An English girl in

Leeds told her mother that she would never want to be kept alive artificially, and after she suffered brain-damage in an accident and was in a
coma for over a year the doctors wished to withdraw artificial feeding.
They were prevented when it became possible to communicate with the
girl, who pressed a button to indicate that she did not wish to die. But the
research in communicating with such patients, now advancing in Germany, is still at a very early stage, and many moralists are not convinced
that it justifies keeping PVS patients alive indefinitely with artificial
means at such traumatic cost to their families, with no clear benefit to
themselves.

Genetic engineering

Perhaps the biggest challenge to moral analysis and responsibility comes
from the 'genetics revolution.' Since 1988 an international research
organisation, involving top scientists in the USA, Japan and Europe, has
been involved in what is called the Human Genome Project, trying to
locate and identify the 100,000 or more genes that constitute our genetic
inheritance. It is hoped that a complete genetic map of the human person
will be available within the next decade, and with this information it will
be possible to locate defective genes, in order to replace or modify them.
In this way genetic defects could be cured or weeded out to eliminate
crippling diseases that until now have resisted medical treatment. The
benefits are obvious, and some results have been positive. Gene therapy
is still quite difficult, and for the foreseeable future it will be restricted to
extremely ill patients. But it is not too soon to consider its moral implications.

Such technology is morally good if it does not involve disproportionate risks for foetus or mother, and if it can lead to successful therapy. But
there is a danger that the techniques can go beyond simple therapy and
involve selective abortion to prevent the birth of children with certain
types of abnormality. It could also mean in the future adding genes to
promote height for small people, or hair for the bald, or a host of qualities
like intelligence, musical ability, or athletic build. This may sound like
science fiction, but many of the things we take for granted in daily life
were once classed as science fiction. Dr James Watson, the discoverer of
DNA, the molecular structure from which all life is built, told a London
newspaper in February 1997 that women should have the right to abort
for any reason, including Down's Syndrome, homosexuality, dyslexia, a
genetic lack of musical ability, or even being too short to play basketball.
He suggested that some day a child may sue its parents for being born,

accusing them of callously not checking for genetic effects. This is the moral vacuum in which life and death decisions are already being made.

Genetic screening can be helpful to discover defects that can be cured with gene therapy, but there are other aspects of screening which cause serious concern, whether it be pre-natal, post-natal or adult, namely questions of personal privacy, confidentiality, its use in job applications and in the purchase of health and life insurance. Because of such concerns, several countries have asked for government controls for the ethical, legal and social implications of the genome project. Lest protective legislation be limited to mere practical considerations, it is necessary to promote ongoing public debate about what the new technology can lead to. The need is urgent, because the tendency in technology is that what *can* be done *will* be done. The temptation to reduce questions of morality to ones of technique and efficiency needs to be resisted. A basic moral question is not only: what are we *doing?* but: what is the *doing* doing to us, what kind of people are we becoming? With the new technology certain things *can* be done, but we need to ask: *may they*, or *should they* be done? To what extent are we undermining basic human values, or indeed altering what it means to be human?

Cloning is another spectre of the future. In the animal world mice, rabbits, toads, sheep and cattle have already been successfully cloned, by dividing an embryo at an early stage and encouraging the resulting cells to divide on their own to produce perfect copies of the original, but the technique is not a commercial success. In 1996, however, scientists at the Roslin Institute in Edinburgh succeeded in cloning an exact copy of an adult sheep from a cell in its udder, which could lead to animal life endlessly re-created without the need for sperm. The cell was taken from the udder of an adult ewe and grown in the laboratory for six days. Its nucleus was then fused by electric spark with an unfertilised egg taken from another sheep, from which the nucleus containing DNA had been removed. The resulting embryo was transferred to the uterus of a third sheep acting as a surrogate mother which eventually gave birth to the lamb genetically identical to the ewe from which the udder-cell was taken.

There are considerable benefits from this breakthrough: the creation of animals that can produce lifesaving human blood products for the study of genetic disorders and to provide agents to fight disease. But there are fears that the technique will be extended to humans, and this raises frightening prospects for the future. One of the scientists involved in the new technique was asked by a woman if she could clone her father, who had just died, bringing him back as a baby and perhaps even carrying him in her own womb. His reply was that it could be possible much sooner than she thinks. Society should already be examining and controlling the future direction of genetics, since it raises fundamental questions about the meaning of human life. In 1993 Jerry Hall, in Washington, cloned a human embryo for the first time. The embryos he produced survived for six days and could have been implanted in a womb, but this was not done. The technique could shed light on how twins are formed naturally, and this might help infertile couples, but this degree of interference with the human reproductive process is out of all proportion to the possible benefit, and would be rejected as immoral. It is illegal in Britain, and other countries are likely to follow suit.

Stewards of the environment

One of the effects of gene research has been to make us more aware of the unity of all life, of our rootedness in nature and of our belonging to a wider whole. The physical world is not simply the stage for human history, but an essential part of our human story. Our life is continuous with the soil, the plants, the animals, the birds and the atmosphere. Our awareness of being part of this mysterious complex gives rise to feelings of awe and reverence, which are dimensions of religion and morality, and they alert us to our obligations with regard to ecology, raising new moral questions beyond the scope of traditional morality. We have become painfully aware of the damage we have done to our environment, most of it the result of materialism and uncritical consumerism, based on sophisticated modern technology. The irony is that the traditional notion of 'natural law,' which should have warned against this, in fact supported the idea of humanity 'dominating' the earth, and this, together with the quest for scientific knowledge, has reduced nature to a purely instrumental value to be exploited for human consumption. Science and technology have raised the standard of living and helped to reduce disease and famine, but these benefits to the human race are quite tiny compared to the harm inflicted on mother earth. Pesticides have poisonous side-effects, acid rain is a major problem in Europe and America, the important rain-forests of the Amazon are being devastated, with disastrous consequences for world climate, hundreds of species of animals are now extinct, and deserts are extending. Natural resources are being shamelessly squandered, and unfairly used. The resources needed to sustain the life-style of one person in the USA would support 200–300 Asians.

Concern about environmental issues has grown considerably in recent years, but it has to be admitted that this is an area in which the Church's conscience is very much underdeveloped. The challenge is to go beyond individual morality and to accept a cosmic responsibility. This means recognising the sacredness of the earth as our home and garden, entrusted to our faithful and creative stewardship. It means recognising that our planet has limited resources and that each generation has a responsibility for what it hands on to the next. It means recognising the global consequences of policies, decisions, and actions, which requires the development of an international ethic. No person or country is free to do what it likes, without reference to the wider environment. It also means that responsible parenthood is not simply a personal issue for individual couples, but a concern for world population.

Although the Church has a respectable body of social teaching, now gradually being recognised by outsiders, the area of ecological responsibility is almost virgin territory as far as official teaching is concerned. What is needed is not pious exhortation, but serious study and analysis of the problems, and a mobilisation of opinion to influence decision-makers. The ecocrisis has a moral dimension, which transcends purely political, economic and technological solutions. Religious bodies, with their theology of creation, have a special obligation because states and politicians are often more concerned with private interests than with the common good, and international corporations give the impression that their gestures in favour of ecology are responses to pressure from environmentalists rather than from moral conviction about respecting the earth. More is needed than *ad hoc* solutions to individual problems. We need a radical conversion, a new way of thinking about our universe and our part in it. We need a new theology of the earth. There is an excellent beginning of this in the writings of Seán McDonagh, Thomas Berry, Paul Collins and many others in recent years. The roots of such a theology are to be found in our biblical faith, in Benedictine and Franciscan spirituality, and in the best of our mystical tradition. The new theology should flow into our liturgy, with new symbols and rituals to keep us in touch with our roots. But the major challenge is to bridge the gap between theology and science, and on the practical level to work for the kind of justice that will deal with social sin and overcome the ever-widening gap between rich and poor which excludes almost half of the world's people from any sense of belonging and from any worthwhile share in the goods of the earth.

Challenged by change

The above summary of developments in technology affecting human life and the environment give some indication of the new challenges for Christian morality. They give rise to complex problems with no simple solutions. Basic traditional values may remain the same, but their application to new situations is not always easy. Because of the complexity of the problems it is not surprising that people come to different conclusions in their assessment, as did the bishops of Pennsylvania and of Texas with regard to artificial feeding of PVS patients. Some bishops will differ from Vatican declarations. 'Church teaching' can be clear on matters of faith and of basic human values, but it is normal that in the application of principles to concrete cases, especially complex ones, there will be differences of judgment.

Another challenge to Church teaching is the field of business ethics. Economics is an area which has developed enormously in recent times, and any business person can give scores of examples of the need to conceal the truth or indeed lie and cheat to make a profit or save the business. Most business decisions have a moral significance, for example the loss of hundreds of jobs, the economic destruction of a small town, not to mention practices like takeovers, insider trading, bribery and misleading advertising. Many people have the attitude that 'business is business,' like Machiavelli's 'politics is politics,' as though business and politics were separate worlds that can be built up apart from morality and religion. At times it might be asked if a business person can afford to have a conscience. However, the picture is not all bleak. Some American companies appoint non-executive directors with responsibility for ethical matters, and there are some excellent Christian writings on morality and business. The same is true of ethical issues in journalism and the media, and of morality and international affairs. But thinking Catholics cannot help wondering why 'official Church teaching' is endlessly condemning artificial contraception while ignoring these other, far more important, areas of human life.

The bigger challenge

The enormous developments in the areas just mentioned are a challenge to the Church when its members look for guidance in their efforts to relate God and Mammon, faith and science, technology, business, etc. The values and principles of personal, individual morality are not easily applied to the complex world of today. Fortunately, there are theologians and Catholic scientists and business people who are already grappling with the problems and trying to develop a meaningful, convincing morality for these new and complex areas, so the Church is already there. But there is a special challenge to Church leadership, with responsibility for 'official Church teaching' to understand, encourage and in a sense to accompany that work. The challenge will not be met successfully unless those leaders learn from history, so that past mistakes, that are still a problem for the Church's credibility, will not be repeated. Obviously, they cannot be repeated literally, but similar or worse ones will be made if the new problems are met with the old mentality. The problems of ecology call for a whole new attitude and way of thinking about our planet, a real conversion. But a wider and deeper conversion is called for if the Church officially is to meet the new challenges in all areas. What is needed is a new way of thinking, a new culture, a new way of understanding and living out in practice what it means to be Church. In other words, an ecclesiological conversion.

When Jesus cured the sick he stretched out his hands to them, symbolising the healing power that came from him to make them whole, but the same gesture symbolised his taking them to himself, reintroducing them into the community. The mission of the Church is to continue that ministry of including people, bringing them in from the margins, and empowering them with a new freedom. Unfortunately, so much of Church history shows us the clerical leadership excluding people, with excommunication and anathemas. The Church would be a far more credible witness to the gospel if it would reach out to those on the periphery, to the excluded, to bring them into the fellowship God wants for his family, if it could make room at the Eucharistic table for those married people in so-called irregular unions; if it could facilitate reconciliation through generous use of general absolution; if it could provide frequent Mass for the millions of Catholics throughout the world who are deprived of the Eucharist for months and years simply because of a law of clerical celibacy that could be modified with the stroke of a pen; if it could enrich its priestly ministry by recalling those dedicated pastors who are excluded at present simply because they discovered after ordination that they had no vocation to celibacy; if it would stop patronising women but accept their equality by recognising their ability to fulfil all ministries in the Church on an equal footing with men; if it would take seriously the basic principle of Vatican II that the Church is the whole people of God, with special appreciation of the baptismal dignity of each member, a reality that is far more important than any additional status like priestly or episcopal ordination.

An important step in our conversion is to get rid of the clerical mentality, to relativise the institutional model of the Church, to think more of moral authority and influence than of power and control. The clerical culture is still acceptable to some comfortable, middle-aged churchgoers, but it makes less and less sense to the younger (and much of the older) generation in today's world. In spite of the beautiful documents of Vatican II still waiting to be implemented, there is a culture gap between today's challenging, fast-changing world and what is often perceived as an institution from another age. Of course, to recognise this challenge is not to deny the many wonderful things that have been done and are being done in and through the Church at the present time. In some ways the Church is dying, but with the eyes of faith it is possible to see the many signs of new life, and to remember that this is not its first experience of death and resurrection.

A personal statement

The purpose of this book was not to score points off fellow theologians or to ruffle the feathers of some bishops (who have a difficult enough time at present), but rather the pastoral concern to help people to feel at home in a Church which respects their God-given intelligence as well as calling on their loyalty and piety. I feel deeply for the many Catholics who are angry at the Church and have no ready answer for their neighbours who ask why they don't leave it. If it is any consolation to them, I share my own feelings and tell them that there is much in the Church's history, past and present, that makes me angry and thoroughly ashamed of it. But I could never think of leaving it. Although I have friendly experiences of other churches and religions, for me the Church is the only one there is, it is home. At times it feels like a tattered tent in the midst of a desert, but it is infinitely better than the loneliness and meaninglessness of the desert outside. Had I been born a Hindu I would no doubt feel differently, but I haven't, and I thank God for all of my past, for life, love, family and friends, and especially for the great gift of Catholic faith and seventy gracious and grace-filled years of life in the Catholic Church.

I feel deeply for parents who have to 'explain' and 'defend' the Church to their children as the youngsters grow up in a vastly different world from what we knew in the past. The young can see so clearly the sinful side of the Church, but it saddens me that most of them have not had our good fortune of knowing the other side of the Church's life and history, the deeper reality that has always been there, is still there, and will always be there. I thank God for the wonderful centuries-long tradition of reason, beauty, goodness and holiness, spirituality, celebration and joy, poetry, painting and sculpture. I think of marvellous Christian communities all over the world battling for justice, working for peace, struggling to support each other in forgiveness and love.

In spite of the uglier aspects of its history, I am passionately in love with the Church which brings me so much of the endless compassion of Christ, the kind strong gentleness and refined sensitivity of Mary the Mother of Jesus, the consolation from God himself to help us through the many dark nights of the soul, and the strength of grace in the midst of weakness, the deep-down conviction of the mystical meaning of all reality, the deeper meaning of living and dying, the magic of enjoying the earth as the home God gives us out of love, and at the same time realising that we have here no lasting city. And through all of this, I believe that in every tiny detail of daily living (getting up, making the coffee, going to work, trying to make ends meet, coping with illness or a difficult neighbour, touching and holding each other), we are constantly in touch with the divine and the transcendent. I firmly believe that God's love becomes incarnate, takes flesh, in people who touch our lives with love, and I can never thank God enough for the many incarnations of his love that I have experienced. I agree wholeheartedly with Karl Rahner's prophetic insight that the Christian of the future will be a mystic or not a Christian at all. The mysticism he meant is not some esoteric, parapsychological phenomenon for a small number of eccentrics, but a genuine experience of the transcendent God in the depths of the ordinary and the everyday, an experience available to every member of God's human family.

There have been some critical comments in the previous chapters, but my intention was to 'speak the truth in love.' It is not the truth in itself, but only the truth as I see it, partial, imperfect, perhaps even twisted, but it is the only truth I know at the moment, and I pray that I remain open to see it corrected and perfected, as Jesus promised his disciples that the Holy Spirit would lead them gradually into all truth. When he appeared to his followers after his resurrection his greeting was: 'Peace.' But more than once he asked them: 'Why are you afraid?' There is far too much fear in the Church. We need to get rid of our fear, and one way of doing this is to feel that we are trusted. We need to trust each other more. After all, God trusts us: with his Son (in spite of what we did to him), with his word in scripture, with his sacraments, indeed with his Church (and what have we made of it?). An incredible mystery, if only we could believe it. Perhaps God is telling us that the only way to trust people is to trust them.

Notes

Chapter 3
1. Enda McDonagh, *Gift and Call*, Gill & Macmillan, 1975.

Chapter 4
1. Ninian Smart, *The Religious Experience of Mankind*, Scribner, New York, 1969.

Chapter 7
1. Daniel C. Maguire, *The Moral Choice*, Doubleday, New York, 1978.
2. Richard M. Gula, S.S., *What are they Saying about Moral Norms?* Paulist Press, New York, 1981.
3. Donal Harrington, *What is Morality?* Columba Press, Dublin, 1996.
4. Richard A. McCormick, S.J., *The Critical Calling*, Georgetown University Press, Washington, D.C., 1989, pp. 47–69.

Chapter 8
1. John Marshall, *Love One Another, Psychological Aspects of Natural Family Planning*, Sheed & Ward, London, 1996.
2. Robert McClory, *Turning Point*, Crossroad Publishing Company, New York, 1995.
3. John T. Noonan, *Contraception: A History of its Treatment by the Catholic Church*, Harvard University Press, 1965.

Chapter 9
1. Francis A. Sullivan, S.J., *Magisterium: Teaching Authority in the Catholic Church*, Paulist Press, New York, 1983.
2. Francis A. Sullivan, S.J., *Creative Fidelity: Weighing and Interpreting Documents of the Magisterium*, Gill & Macmillan, Dublin, 1996.
3. Ladislas Örsy, S.J., *The Church: Learning and Teaching*, Glazier, Wilmington, 1987.
4. Richard A. McCormick, S.J., *Corrective Vision*, Sheed and Ward, Kansas City, 1994, p. 53.

Chapter 10
1. David Smith, M.S.C., *Life and Morality*, Gill & Macmillan, Dublin, 1996.
2. Richard A. McCormick, S.J., *Corrective Vision*, Sheed and Ward, Kansas City, 1994, pp. 189–200.

INDEX